SAILING

IN A

SPOONFUL

OF WATER

Sailing in a

Spoonful of

Water ~

Joe Coomer

Picador USA

New York

Library of Congress Cataloging-in-Publication Data

Coomer, Joe.
    Sailing in a spoonful of water / Joe Coomer.
      p.   cm.
    ISBN 0-312-15646-4
    1. Coomer, Joe.   2. Sailors—United States—Biography.
    3. Wooden boats.   I. Title.
GV810.92.C66A3   1997
797.1'24'092—dc21
[B]   96-53645
                                           CIP

Design by Ellen R. Sasahara

First Edition: May 1997

10 9 8 7 6 5 4 3 2 1

This book is, once again, for my family

ACKNOWLEDGMENTS

~

THANKS, Ralph, for taking a friend's son-in-law, a Texan yet, on his first cruise along the Maine coast. Thanks, Rob, for finding *Yonder*. And I'd like to thank the crew of *La Vida* of Cape Elizabeth, whoever you are, for rescuing a stranded author off Cape Small. John G. Alden of Boston, Massachusetts, designed a boat that fit me perfectly, and did it twenty-five years before I was born. Harvey Gamage of South Bristol, Maine, built her so well that she lasted the additional thirty-three years it took me to save up the money to buy her. And then Cal Morgan, Jr., my endearing editor at St. Martin's Press, paid the exact sum *Yonder* cost for this book about her. (I suddenly wished I'd bought a more expensive boat.) Cal made the editing process a smooth reach to the islands. Great thanks to Audrey H. Mason, wife of Frederick Mason, Jr., and Laura Miller Mason, granddaughter of Frederick Mason, for the family photos and stories. Margaret Ryan took the photo of me writing in my journal. Don Roberts took many of the photos herein on a cruise during the summer of '96. My wife, Heather, took the remainder of the recent pictures. If it weren't for her, I might not love the ocean. The acknowledgments continue throughout the text, as almost everyone mentioned deserves my thanks. Here's a book without bad guys.

J.C.

NOTE TO THE READER

~

THIS BOOK will not include the quotation "There is *nothing*—absolutely nothing—half so much worth doing as simply messing about in boats" (Kenneth Grahame, *The Wind in the Willows*). It will not inform you how to build a boat in your stairwell for less than it should cost. This book shares no tips on Bahama cruising, varnish maintenance, or single-handed circumnavigation. I don't know how to avoid embarrassment while docking. No races will be won. No lee rails will wash. No dogma will bark. No wives will be yelled at while anchoring in crowded coves. I haven't survived a capsizing. My mother never considered using sailcloth for my diapers. And, more than likely, imprecise use of nautical terminology will result.

The Cup captains, the hurricane and shark survivors, have all had their windy say. I speak for the vast majority of humble cruisers, the daysailers, the coast huggers, the tiers of two knots, who pay their towing insurance like clockwork and believe in electronic navigation. I bought an old wooden boat and went to sea. I was surrounded by my family and friends. I was afraid. I used only those knots fit to be tied. It will require a great deal of water to clear me of this deed.

Joe Coomer
Boiling Rock
Eliot, Maine
May 1996

YONDER

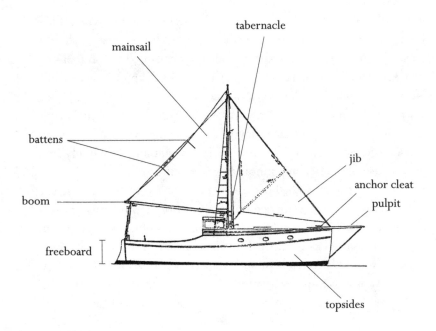

tabernacle

mainsail

battens

jib

boom

anchor cleat

pulpit

freeboard

topsides

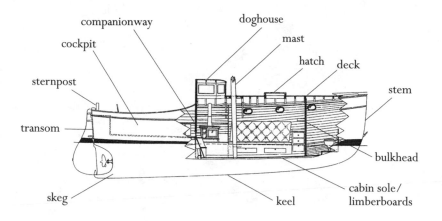

companionway

doghouse

cockpit

mast

sternpost

hatch   deck

transom

stem

bulkhead

skeg

cabin sole /
limberboards

keel

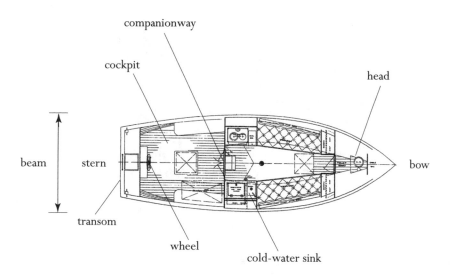

companionway

cockpit

head

beam   stern

bow

transom

wheel

cold-water sink

. . . wouldst thou drown thyself,
Put but a little water in a spoon.

William Shakespeare,
The Life and Death of King John

1

~

WE'RE ALL BORN in a gush of fluid and forever after seek a drier passage. So what is it that leads us back to the water, which often as not we refuse to enter? For me, beyond whatever prenatal remembrance, beyond the beauty of the sea, it's an urge to understand why I'm so restless. For years I came and walked the beach.

2

ON THE SHORTEST DAY of the year I went looking for the longest, looking for a languishing summer sun's descent over water on a snow-weary winter solstice hillside. Most mornings I wake unprepared, but there are days when minutes drop into place like seeds, and spare moments when I seem almost immortal, as much a part of the future as the present. Standing there in a clutch of spruce, beneath the dull red hull of an old motorsailer, my feet in six inches of snow and my cold hands dumped in my pockets like links of heavy chain, I inhabited one of these moments. It had nothing to do with religion or art, with memory or love. I was a liquid poured into a mold. I did fit. The closest water was a hundred feet below, in a hazard-strewn stream that might float a model of the boat above me. But I heard the water running and knew it ran the right way: to the sea. Everything was downhill from there.

I wasn't looking for a boat seriously. We were in Maine for Christmas, visiting my wife's family. I hadn't flown two thousand miles from Texas to comb the hills for old motorsailers. I'd come for presents. On this day I was indulging my father-in-law, Rob. Over the past few years my wife, Heather, and I found ourselves spending more and more of each summer in Eliot, Maine. Her grandmother's home sat on a bank of the Piscataqua River, a tidal estuary. A weathered driftwood dock staggered into the water. There were these possibilities. I'd mentioned that I'd like to have a boat someday. The summer before, Rob and I had looked at an old picnic boat on Badger's Island. She required too much repair, but through her I could see myself on the water. I'd look more the following summer, I thought. There was no hurry. But a couple months before Christmas, Rob called.

"Found your boat," he said, as if it were a watch I'd lost a week earlier.

"What?"

"Found your boat. Have you gotten your new *WoodenBoat* yet?"

"Yesterday," I said. "I've already gone through the classifieds, though." There's nothing so rich with prospects as a section of classifieds when I'm on a quest, nothing so worthless once it's been exhaustively perused, and nothing that can transform my emotions so thoroughly from hope to despair. Classifieds are like a home pregnancy test.

"The Cannell, Payne and Page ad," Rob insisted.

I found my freshly read issue and turned to the ad. There were eighteen boats on the page. "Which boat?" I asked.

"The Alden-Gamage boat down in the corner."

"It's got a mast," I said.

"Just a little one," Rob said. "It's really only a steadying sail."

I put my hand over the phone's mouthpiece and whispered to my wife, "Your dad's trying to get me to buy a sailboat."

"It's a raised-deck motorboat," Rob continued. "Alden designs are classics. Gamage was a fine yard, a Maine yard. It has the plumb bow you wanted, the ports. I've already sent for the particulars. I'll send them along. We can look at it when you come up for Christmas."

"Where is it?" I asked.

"Just across the river in Lee, New Hampshire."

When I put the phone down, Heather asked, "Well?"

"It's a sailboat." I showed her the tiny picture in the magazine. I wanted something on the order of an early Elco, a raised-deck cruiser from the twenties or thirties. I knew turning a key would be easier than raising a sail.

"I like the little house on the deck," she said.

"I want something we can go up the rivers in," I told her. "In a sailboat you have to turn around at the first bridge."

"Just go look at it," Heather said. "You'll make Daddy happy."

Ethan Cook stepped out from underneath his boat when we drove up, like someone who was comfortable in the shade of a hull. *Compromise,* twenty-eight feet from plumb bow to plumb transom, sitting on four rusty stands and blocked under the full keel, seemed colossal on that slope, like a bird on your nose. My in-laws and I walked around and underneath the boat, listening to Ethan. His boat was for sale, but only under duress: his business, art packaging and transport, needed a warehouse and truck more than it needed a boat. I suppose it's hard to get a Monet from the Metropolitan to the Kimbell in a motorsailer. He asked fifteen thousand dollars, which was why I was there. I was twenty thousand flush. If he'd been asking twenty-five thousand, I might not have crossed his creek.

The things I noticed, after the hugeness of the hull, were the hairy chin of the keel and the rust boils erupting from the dark green topsides. She was iron-fastened, both the old planks and a few newer ones replaced over the years. I asked Rob why they hadn't used stainless-steel or bronze screws on the new strakes. He told me you don't want to mix metals. The explanation was knotty with chemistry and physics, and I'm an English major. But I understood finally that mixing metals in salt water might rot out all the teeth in my head, so I just nodded to his authority. There was a single sixteen-inch four-bladed bronze propeller tucked behind an outboard rudder. Drape the propeller in a T-shirt, sit it on the corner of a bed, and it would be as sexy as my wife. The rudder, a great oak paddle, had a toehold ladder up its trailing edge. There were some dings in the brightwork of the mahogany transom, put there in a lexically proper manner by a dinghy during Hurricane Bob.

With the help of an aluminum ladder we all climbed aboard for a gam. (I have been waiting years for an occasion to use this *gam* word.) The more we listened to Ethan, the more we noted his pride in the boat, his reluctance to let her go. Beverly, Heather's stepmother, whispered sweet nothings about the mahogany into my ear. She was a terrible person to take along when trying to negotiate. What was worse: I liked Ethan as much as his boat. I tried not to show it.

The cockpit was like a living room, broad and comfortable, recently refurbished with new teak flooring (decking), new marine plywood sofas (lockers) and end tables (fuel tanks), and even a ma-

5

hogany coffee (chart) table. The bronze wheel, throttle, and gear controls looked like cherished antiques on a mantel. The blue tarpaulin over the boat cast a blue wash over the cockpit and our faces, as if the only light in the room were from a TV. The tarp was draped over the boom, a foot above my head. I liked this. Even while I was standing at the wheel, an unexpected jibe wouldn't send me to sea or remove half my skull.

Ethan opened each locker and showed us its secret: a pair of stainless-steel fuel tanks, a twelve-volt Norcold refrigerator, life vests, fire extinguisher, the steering gear and automatic pilot. Beneath a big hatch in the cockpit sole brooded a fifty-eight-horsepower four-cylinder Westerbeke diesel engine. Nine years old, red with patches of rust, it seemed more than ample. The engine shared the hold with a bank of batteries, a thirty-gallon copper water tank, and ten or fifteen pounds of rock salt. Ethan told us it rained before he covered the boat in the fall and he didn't want the fresh water standing in the bilge, so he'd turned it into salt water. Most of the frames were sistered, a new frame paired with an old, and there were new floor timbers.

We sneaked below through a bright mahogany bi-fold door, and I paused on the second step of the companionway, like a crystal suspended in my own showcase, and looked out through the five small windows of the doghouse, the blue tarp serving as ocean and sky. The automatic pilot controls, the loran, VHF radio, and depth finder were mounted here, a tight little foul-weather steerage.

Another step down and we were on the cabin sole. There was a cast-iron Lunenberg cookstove to port and a cold-water sink to starboard. The woodwork was painted white and trimmed in bright mahogany. Another step forward and we squeezed around the spruce mast. There was about five feet eight and a half inches of headroom. I'm five foot eight. Beverly and I sat on the bunk to starboard, Rob and Ethan to port. They were hunkered down under a hanging bunk, while Beverly and I had oblong portholes for halos. Mildewed charts were rolled and stuffed in a rack along the ceiling; foul-weather gear hung from bronze hooks. Forward, an oil lamp was mounted on each

6

side of the door to the head. I managed to stay seated for about twenty seconds and then started poking around. I opened every drawer, lifted each cushion, put my rude finger in the holes of the limber boards and pulled. There were two more oblong ports in the head, more storage there, and anchor line on a reel. Everything looked worn but sound. You wouldn't mind if a bluefish beat himself to death down there, but it was also spacious and comfortable. The lines were remarkably simple and elegant. It looked exactly the way a well-cared-for fifty-seven-year-old boat should. Many hands had been there. It had a past.

We climbed up on the raised deck and Rob showed me the tabernacle. I liked the sound of this word even before I knew what it signified on a boat: the mast hinged a couple feet above the deck and folded forward. This boat could duck and sneak under bridges, go where no sailboat had gone before.

Whenever I go to look at any antique boat, car, or Staffordshire dog, I always expect the worst. Usually, expecting the worst turns out to be the correct approach. But this boat seemed too good to be true. It needed some work, I thought, mostly cosmetic, in return for years of trouble-free, maintenance-only boating downeast. It was within my price range, and my wife would eventually forgive me. Rob and Beverly were supporters. I went inside Ethan's home, a house he built himself (a man after my own heart), and found that he was the father of courteous children. I even liked his dog.

3

~

MEMORY OF WATER: my aunt Melody slamming through the bathroom door, screaming, and then telling me forcefully that I could surely drown in a spoonful of water. However dramatic her entrance, I don't think she knew she was paraphrasing Shakespeare. I'd always rather enjoyed the word *spoonful* before that moment. My own mother had often assured me that a spoonful of almost anything—green beans, cough syrup, dog food—couldn't possibly hurt me. At the time of this more sinister revelation from my thirteen-year-old aunt, I was completely naked and immersed to my chin in many, many spoonfuls, having filled the bathtub to a level that, combined with my three-year-old mass, brought the water brimming to the rim. When I peed, the tub became incontinent too, little waves lapping over the porcelain beach.

4

THREE DAYS AFTER my original survey of the old motorsailer, I visited New Hampshire again. It was Christmas Eve. The Dover Hospital emergency room was brightly lit and cheery with Yuletide tunes. I'd borrowed my in-laws' truck to do some last-minute shopping. The van that struck me as I pulled out of a Kittery outlet mall totaled the truck and showered me with glass, but the only wounds I received were a bruised elbow and a refined awareness. This was the fourth time I'd been hit: by a drunk who rear-ended me when I was a teenager; by a Lake Worth, Texas, cop who ran a red light; by a trucker who crossed a double yellow attempting to pass; and now by this daydreaming urchin fisherman who'd also run a red light. I'd totaled four cars beneath me. I felt as if I'd held off all these attempts on my life with my tensed back and braced forearm. I'd rather be hit than hit someone else, but I was beginning to feel I'd done my share of target practice. I was only thirty-three years old. I'd been reminded enough of my mortality on the American highway, uttered my limit of guttural whines and roars, told myself with some confusion that I'd had a wreck once too often. The trouble was, beginning the next day, it would start all over again, the bull's-eye rehung. That evening I read the last entry in my journal, which ended with the word *dog*. I thought it would have been a satisfactory piece of literature to end with, my last written word, but I probably wouldn't be so lucky. I saw that each day's journal entry had to end with a word just as optimistic, dignified, and graceful as *dog*. This wouldn't be easy. I'd already used up most of my dog stories. Perhaps *boat* was also such a word.

A couple of days after Christmas, a couple of days before we flew back home to Texas, I took Heather to see the boat. She'd never been too keen on the idea of a larger vessel. A Chris-Craft speedboat more suited her personality. But she loved antiques as much as I did, and had an artist's sense of line. I hoped the boat would infect her at first sight, that she'd be drawn to its compass, be carried away, that her heart would float. Ethan, consummate salesman, had the oil lamps softly burning when we stepped aboard, and all the cushions were in place. Heather looked at me as if I'd called ahead and ordered these extras. I pointed out details in bronze and mahogany, the curve of the bulkheads between the galley and the bunks, the reliable diesel engine, the head with a door that could be closed (the head on a friend's boat was open for all to see). In Ethan's house we watched a video of the boat being launched and heading out to sea. I could tell that Heather liked Ethan's dog too, a big shepherd that required much petting. "Good dog," I said. On the way home I asked, "Well, what do you think?"

"I really liked their dog. Such pretty eyes," she said.

"No, no," I said, "what do you think of the boat?"

"It's a nice boat. I just don't think we need one."

" 'Need'? What about 'want'?"

"I don't want one."

"Why not?"

"I just don't." I despised her honesty.

"We're going to start spending most of each summer in Maine, right?" She nodded. I nodded too, as if the argument was won. "Well, I can't write novels all day long. I need something to do."

"Why can't you buy a little boat?"

"This *is* a little boat. I want a boat we can invite people out on, one our grandparents won't be afraid to ride in, one that people won't get seasick on. This boat has a comfortable beam. She won't roll as much as a little boat."

"It's a lot of money."

"Heather, we make a lot of money."

"Do what you want."

"You were the one who told me to go look at it."

"When?"

"You said it would make Daddy happy."

"You're not Daddy."

"Christ."

"I don't care. Do what you want."

"Christ."

"Joe, do what makes you happy."

I called Ethan's broker from my home in Texas and by the third of the new year, 1992, we'd settled on *Compromise*. We paid the asking price with the provisos that we would accept a professional survey and the boat would be newly painted and in the water when we took possession in late May. This would put off the maintenance challenge of a wooden boat for at least a season. I had now obtained the dubious distinction of boat owner and captain. My mate wasn't very happy with my promotion, but Rob and Beverly were thrilled. Small piece of advice: this is exactly the position, stationed between admiring in-laws and reluctant spouse, in which all husbands would do well not to place themselves. Rob and Beverly had owned old motor-sailers before, and tried to reassure Heather, but she just shrugged her shoulders. I tried to console myself with the thought that we weren't really putting ourselves under any kind of financial burden and that there was little enough time left on the planet to second-guess. I rubbed my sore elbow. If it's true that the light we see from the sun is already seven minutes old when it reaches the earth, then it's always possible that within the last six minutes and fifty-nine seconds the world as we know it has ended. This is my excuse for any action: hug or slap.

In Texas, five months away from seeing our boat again, prairies away from any ocean, there was little for me to do but arrange for a surveyor and contemplate names. I went through the three photos of *Compromise* I owned again and again, as if I could sail them.

My reveries were interrupted in the middle of February by a call from my father, who lives just up the hill. His mother, who lived in Indiana, had just died. Within hours my father, mother, brother, and sister and I were in a car mourning north. It was the first time since I was sixteen that we'd all been on the road together, a family on vacation. Phil and Sally and I left our wives and husbands and children at home rather than impose our burden on them. We stopped at one in the morning at the Ward Motel in Little Rock. Their drains didn't work as efficiently as their faucets and by the end of my shower I was shin-deep in soapy water. I was tired and weepy, so I just sat down in the water and felt how fine it was to be tired, fine to be on our way. The water was warm and ebbed ever so slowly. I thought my father was glad to have us along, to have us to think about, children to raise.

At the funeral, as I and the rest of my grandmother's grandsons carried her coffin to rest beside that of her husband, I had the selfish thought that I'd never be able to take her and Grandpa on a cruise in my old boat, that I was too late. I carried her to her grave, and carried home one of the old pressed-steel porch chairs that my grandparents used to sit in and watch the world go by. There was a rust stain in the middle of the seat where rainwater had often pooled. I knew at the time that I'd miss her most that summer, when Heather and I would be passing through on our way to Maine, miss driving down South Fifth Street and turning into her tight gravel driveway, the glass rattling in her aluminum storm door as I rapped on it. Her old house on its flat lot was surrounded by narrow moats that drained off many of my childhood summers. In mid-February, my grandparents both gone, the ditches were dry, shallower than I'd remembered.

Back in Texas I resumed my fevered search in old issues of *WoodenBoat* magazine. I couldn't find another raised-deck motorsailer to compare mine with. She couldn't be so singular, could she?

I'd hired Jonathan Klopman, out of Marblehead, Massachusetts, to do the survey, but he'd had trouble completing the job because the temperature had been below freezing for weeks on end. He thought the boat was generally sound but worried about the weeping iron fastenings. Finally, after what seemed an interminable wait (the weather was fine in Texas), there was a thaw in New England and Jonathan was able to probe some suspect wood and remove several fastenings. He sent a wonderfully inclusive package of information and photos to his starved patron. Two areas, on the stem and skeg, would eventually require attention, but he thought the iron fastenings, new and old, were holding up well. It appeared the entire boat had been refastened when the ribs were sistered ten years earlier. He recommended Paul Rollins of York, Maine, to repair a small split in the stem and some softness in the skeg. He suggested that when the present set of sails wore out, I might return the boat to its original sail plan by replacing the gaff mainsail with a Marconi rig. There were several other mechanical and safety precautions Jonathan thought I should take, which I planned to handle when I arrived in May.

I began to take the photos of the boat with me everywhere I went, showing them to people as if she were a girlfriend living in another country. I displayed them at my business, at the bank, at the supermarket. Everyone cooed appropriately. When they asked her name and I said, *"Compromise,"* I felt as if I'd stolen the boat. I'd never been satisfied with the name, although I could understand it. Years later, I learned that a former owner jokingly called her *Composite* due to the variety of materials in her construction. I didn't know at the time that in some sea circles it's bad luck to change a boat's name. When she was originally launched back in 1934 she'd been christened *Bay Queen.* Twenty years later another owner had

13

changed this to *Compromise*. The word left a dirty ring around my mouth. One evening I sat up in bed and asked Heather, "What about *Yonder?*"

"What?"

I got up, scratched myself, and went searching for a dictionary. *Yonder:* the word had Germanic roots and was traceable through Old and Middle English. It had lasted a long time. The *Oxford English Dictionary* described its use as "chiefly poetic," and its meaning as "over there." Most important, for both sets of my grandparents it was an everyday term. I thought about naming the boat *G.W.Yonder* for *Great Wide Yonder* or *W.O.Yonder* for *Way Over Yonder,* but I thought we'd just call her *Yonder* anyway, a boat by any other name. I've rarely been happy where I am; I've always yearned to be over there, somewhere else. I thought that when I was afloat, at sea, I'd always be over there, or at least on my way to it, unconcerned, satisfied. (I've since come across only one other boat name that makes me reconsider my choice. Lou Jacobs, in his recent book *Quest for the African Dinosaurs,* mentions a nineteenth-century side-paddle steamer whose nickname was *Chikapa. Chikapa* is a Yao word referring to the circular motion of dancing buttocks. My wife is a professional modern dancer.)

Heather's grandfather, known to both of us as Skipper, called when he learned we'd bought a boat. He spent most of World War II as the captain of a destroyer escort, and much of his retirement as captain of a Hatteras yacht. He was very pleased, and encouraged Heather to become a navigator. She told him, "I have always been good with maps."

Rob called and said he was sending along Maine registration papers ("We don't want her registered in New Hampshire, for God's sake") and that he was also hunting down some mooring chain and a buoy. He knew exactly where we'd put her in the river. "She'll swing fine there," he said.

I called Paul Rollins and set him to work on the two sections of suspect wood. He said he'd go take a look, that he could probably make the repairs there in Ethan's yard. Later, when I told him I'd just received the bill of sale, that I'd bought that boat, he said, "Well, you're a lucky man."

There is nothing more expensive and less satisfying than telephone boating, unless it's telephone sex. I was too far from the sea.

To curb my frustration I took up another interest, paleontology. I spent two days under the Lynch Bend Road bridge over Browder Creek digging up the remains of a one-hundred-and-five-million-year-old *Tenontosaurus,* a beast about the size of a contemporary horse. The site was four miles from my home. The *Tenontosaurus* was found by a county bridge inspector, the flooding creek having exposed a few bones. As a grunt, I helped remove about six feet of overburden and reroute the creek so scientists rather than the current could gnaw at the bones. The fossils rested in the sandstone like coins on the beach. It looked as if we had vertebrae, limb bones, a pelvis, but no tail or skull. It was possible the rest of the skeleton was a few feet away, under burden, or that the creek had carried the other bones away, to deeper, safer water, a better place to hide.

Several busloads of Springtown fourth-graders came to see the dinosaur as we dug. They peered over the bridge railing, kicked gravel onto our backs, and asked questions about the dinosaur's teeth. "How many?" they asked. "And how long?" I wanted to yell up to them there was no reason to be afraid: this troll has taken his last toll. "How old?" they asked. But it was hard to convey how long ago one hundred and five million years was.

What were we trying to understand? What did we look for under that county bridge while our own feet lingered in swift water? The paleontologists were beyond the immediate thought of death. I wanted to say, "Look, these are bones. We're the first living beings to mix with him since he died." But we did caress, took tender care, stroked his bones and stony tendons the way we would those of our long-dead childhood dog or our grandmother's coffin or our own broken elbow. To me, this dinosaur, warm- or cold-blooded, carnivore or herbivore, had died only a few months ago. A hundred and five million years was only the time it took us to find each other. And once we'd met, all that time was in the past.

"Why did he die here in Springtown?" a boy asked.

"Well," the scientists answered, "we've found several other dinosaurs nearby. This whole area used to be the shoreline of a shallow sea. When the dinosaurs died they sometimes fell or washed into the water; their bodies were covered with sediment and eventually the bones were fossilized."

I've been at sea for years, I thought, and never knew it.

5

A man that is born falls into a dream like a man who falls
into the sea. If he tries to climb out into the air as inexperienced people endeavour to do, he drowns. . . . The
way is to the destructive element submit yourself, and
with the exertions of your hands and feet in the water
make the deep, deep sea keep you up . . . in the destructive element immerse. . . .

Joseph Conrad,
Lord Jim

MY FATHER AND GRANDFATHER taught me how to swim in the
shallow, sediment-rich waters of Eagle Mountain Lake, northwest of
Fort Worth. I thought they were trying to drown me. I'd only known
them for four or five years and still wasn't sure they liked me. Walking down into that muddy water in front of my grandparents' home,
I saw myself as a fish thrown up on the bank. The fish couldn't live
in my realm and I wouldn't live in his. I began by paddling out from
my grandfather's tall, white, mole-and-dimple-dappled body and
orbiting him at a radius of three feet. Then as I weakened, gargling
silt, my bones beginning to fossilize, he'd reach out and bring me
home. As I became stronger, my father would cast me into deeper
water and then wade after me. Stronger yet, and they'd both duck
below the waterline, my grandfather pinching closed his garage-
door nostrils, and leave me alone on the surface, circling the ripples
where they'd been. I struggled along alone, a gasp from drowning

and a gulp from dehydration, and somewhat spastically came to the understanding that I'd become, of all things, a swimmer.

Within days I was underwater, groping along the bottom for my father's and grandfather's legs, recoiling when I touched a clamshell or a rock, sure that I'd bumped an alligator gar, a fish that actually thrived in that tepid darkness. And later I became a stump in the water too, an adult, my younger brother and sister paddling toward me, spurting spoonfuls of tan water and finally beaching themselves, climbing up my bony rib cage as up a palm tree.

Although the water was very warm, it felt cool in the one-hundred-degree heat of the day, and we children shivered and hugged ourselves as we stomped out of the shallows till Mom or Grandma threw us frayed towels. Afterward, our terry capes draped over our somehow victorious shoulders, we sat on the concrete embankment and waited for the waves to bring us treasure: shells, driftwood, the rotting hulk of a sixty-five-pound catfish struck by a boat's propeller, the wound gaping and white as our own vulnerable armpits.

6

WE WERE THREE DAYS on the road from Texas to Maine. For three days Heather and I argued over what or whom we'd visit first: the boat *Yonder* or the family. Rob and Beverly lived in North Berwick; the boat was moored twenty-five miles away in Eliot. But we'd pass within a half mile of the mooring on our way to North Berwick. Couldn't we just drive by? The bridge over the Piscataqua was as close to the water as I got. But after dinner, after hugs and slaps, with darkness descending, we drove down to Eliot and watched the night take *Yonder* in. It was the first time I'd seen her in her element, half above and half below water. She looked smaller and sleeker than I'd imagined. The mast was still folded forward like a closed jackknife, its tip reaching the bow pulpit. Her plumb bow gave *Yonder* a racing edge, made her a blade held to the current. The length of her waterline and

thus her speed couldn't be increased much by heeling, which elimi-
nated the need for that uncomfortable attitude. Rob and Heather and
I rowed out in a high tide. When I stepped over the high freeboard
into the cockpit, the boat moved under me, ever so slightly, as if she
were not only alive but tense. We tested lights and drawer pulls, depth
finder and radio, and after appreciating our good fortune, slipped the
key into the ignition, preheated the glow plugs, and turned the big
engine over. And over. It wouldn't start. This was disappointing.
Rob said he'd heard her running. "She sounds beautiful," he said. Over.
Over. Well. What could it be but a small problem, I theorized. Maybe
there was a secret.

We flipped out the lights, locked the companionway door, and
stepped back down into the rubber dinghy that had come with the
boat. On shore, I looked back, and there was just *Yonder*'s black silhouette against a dark blue background of water. The tide was ebbing,
running swiftly beneath the hull, coursing around lumber. That's all
it was. But I was anxious, almost envious of night and dark water.

The next morning Heather and I were opening lockers, lifting
cushions, looking for secrets in the bilge. We found items rusty,
slimy, infected, and worse and threw them all in a big green plastic
bag and suffocated them. The only signs of food we came upon were
a few limp gray peanuts under a bunk. They may have been there since
the christening. Keepers in this archaeological excavation included
three bronze screws, four pennies, and a dime, all of which had
found their way to the mouths of limbers, holes that allowed the bilge
to drain through the frames. Fourteen cents might have sunk the boat.
Disaster could be just as cheap as it was expensive. A tin propane
stove used for cockpit barbecues was flaking away with rust, so I
dropped it and a dubious spare battery into the dinghy for later shore
inspection. While Heather worked with a sponge and a bottle of Fan-
tastik, I tried to comprehend mechanisms, systems, routes of wiring.
I got the freshwater galley pump working: a languid stream with bits
of verdigris issued into the porcelain sink. Beneath the rim of the sink
was an ingenious button, a knee switch in case both hands were dirty

when you arrived. Why this switch isn't incorporated into every home in America is a mystery to me. The seawater valve or tap seemed to be clogged. I didn't have a wrench big enough to remove the seacock, or any idea what to do with all that ocean streaming in once I did. So I decided to leave this problem till later and went on to the head. There were three valves controlling the seawater here, but the bilge was so dark I couldn't tell if they were open or closed. I took it they'd been closed for the winter and so I opened them all, and broke free the pump arm. I heard some kind of siphoning action as I pumped, yet received no water. I turned each of the valves back to their original position and tried other arrangements, but no variation allowed me water. I decided to leave it till later. We had to pick up Heather's brother at the airport in Boston, so I was feverish with hurry. The engine still wouldn't start, cranked quick but wouldn't fire. This was depressing. Why wouldn't this engine make me feel secure? If I was going to deal with something as beautiful and unreliable as the ocean, I at least wanted to be able to leave when I desired, even if it was with a broken heart. By the time we rowed ashore that day, *Yonder* was brighter, if not more keen. She was constipated, dry-mouthed, and bedridden but was still somehow pleasant. Perhaps these small failures were a test, I thought.

Heather's brother, Tom, and Heather and I were back aboard the next morning. Tom pumped the head once and water squirted around the bowl, water and small chunks of river scum, but less scum with each flush. I loosened a hose clamp on the sink side of the saltwater pump, blew through the hose, and felt something give, like a soda straw sleeve. Reattached, pump switched on: salt water gushed into the sink. Water out, water in, a delicate balance. *Yonder* swung around on her mooring and seemed to sigh.

There was a whoop from Hutton's Landing and I stuck my head out of the companionway. Ethan was on shore holding a box of new life jackets and towing a barge of accumulated knowledge and assurances. He squirted a shot of WD-40 into the air intake and the diesel fired to life, as if it had only required this small pleasure, a little oil blown in its ear, to convince it to take us anywhere. We raised the mast to its full twenty-five feet and bent on the roller furling jib and the gaff mainsail.

"She will sail," Ethan said, as if the opposite was more easily proven. He showed me where and how to change the engine oil, bleed the fuel lines, pack the shaft box, engage the autopilot, lock the steering gear down, and so on and so on. He missed the boat already and talked of building one just like her, but bigger. I nodded, commiserating, but rowed him back to the beach double-time and stranded him on the continent. We shook hands on a fair trade.

At noon, Tom and Heather left for a Friday night party in Boston. I stayed behind to ready *Yonder* for her initial sail under new ownership and crew. Rob would be free Sunday and I wanted him along to show me the way. I rowed Heather ashore, walked down Pleasant Street to Village Pizza, and picked up a sandwich and a Pepsi and the very first migraine of my life. I was able to make my way back to *Yonder,* but for the next four hours I lay on the limber boards with a cushion over my head. I tried to figure out what had happened. Was it the boat? Was it the sea? Some reflection off the water, or an inner-ear imbalance caused by swells and waves? By late afternoon I could see straight again and my head began to forgive slight sensory perceptions. What I thought had been a knocking within my skull turned out to be my temporary tender, an aluminum skiff, scuffing *Yonder*'s hull. Wonderful, I thought, a new paint job and it's all downhill from here. I gave the tender more painter, a longer lead, but with the workings of the tide and a strong wind it inevitably worked its way back to *Yonder*'s cedar planks with the retort of a ball peen hammer. I went below, stuck my head in the Lunenberg stove, and wire-brushed out most of the scale and ashes. Then I swept the cabin sole and put everything back in its place.

Up on deck I checked all the lifelines for loose fittings, attached the anchor rode, or line, to the big forty-pound fisherman anchor, and repaired a loose ground wire on the port light. During this last job I lost my first tool overboard: a brand new Craftsman screwdriver rolled off the deck and plopped into the river. I actually looked over into the water hoping it might float. The water was blank and swift. Suddenly I realized I was in deep water, or the boat was in the water, something a little unnerving, a realization similar to the one I had when I was first shocked at an electrical outlet. Care, it seemed, was something you learned from time to time rather than all at once. It didn't accumulate. Lots of us get wounded and killed between more lenient lessons, and a full and successful course is only completed by a death whose cause is old age.

I packed my remaining tools toward evening, a ride came, but before leaving I stood at Hutton's Landing and talked with Nanny, Heather's eighty-nine-year-old grandmother.

"I'm so happy there's a boat in the cove again," she said, her voice quivering but positive.

"You'll keep an eye on her for me, then," I said.

"The first thing I do every morning and the last every night is look out at the river," she assured me.

We both turned to the river, ocean shaped as river, and looked out on *Yonder* with her raised mast.

"Beverly turns fifty tomorrow," Nanny said. A big party for my mother-in-law was planned. "There's going to be bagpipes and peach liqueur," she added.

"Sunday we'll take *Yonder* out for the first time," I said.

"You kids be careful," Nanny said, and I promised we would, knowing I had no right. I was a complete amateur.

Yonder heeled slightly with a gust of wind and swung with the change of tide. As dusk fell, I thought she did sail, even chained to the earth.

On Sunday morning we left the mooring for our inaugural sail. I had all the fears and tensions of being on a horse for the first time. There was something alien and ultimately unmanageable beneath me: wood, water, and current. Hank and Jan Taft's *A Cruising Guide to the Maine Coast* suggested, "It is not wise for anyone new to these waters to try to take a boat above Portsmouth on the Piscataqua River. . . . There are hazardous crosscurrents, and buoys sometimes are towed under." The Piscataqua is the "second-fastest-flowing river in the continental U.S." The diesel thrummed with confidence, though, and Rob seemed at ease, running me through checklists before we left the mooring: life preservers handy, fuel aplenty, an able hand to cast off, a warm engine, a charging alternator, a churning water pump. It was the moment of separation that was most poignant, the tearing of the umbilical, the mooring line melting into the sea.

Heather took pictures while I smiled uneasily, stood at the stern, and steered. The six knots of current took the bow and I turned the wheel perhaps an inch trying to correct.

"It's not a car," Rob said. "Turn that wheel." The spokes cracked my knuckles, but after a few moments we were heading upriver with the tide. A lobster boat passed slowly on our port. A huge AT&T cable ship and an even more monstrous gypsum freighter sat on the New Hampshire bank of the Piscataqua, engorging and disgorging themselves. We passed tiny Hot Dog Island (Frankfort), where Heather camped out as a child. At Dover Point, where Great and Little Bays emptied into the river, the water almost boiled. *Yonder,* as heavy and strongly built as she was, still jumped, darted, and spun like a Coke bottle slapped around at an intersection. Somehow I kept her bow pointed toward the center span of the General Sullivan Bridge. The bridge boards boasted forty-three feet of clearance, so we didn't even have to duck. Safely into New Hampshire, we raised the mainsail and let fly the little jib. The wind was sparse, but the sails gathered in everything within reach. I liked the shapes of the sails, their seams, battens, the curled leather eyes, and even the worn spots, little leaks in the universe. I cut the motor back to an idle; we caught something like a gust and watched the knot meter on the loran applaud the boat with five, then seven, then nine tenths of a knot more headway. I told Heather how much my father would enjoy this. We glided past an oysterman, many lobster buoys, and finally into Great Bay. There a world of water opened up before us, countless directions from which to choose. It was all too much for us and we turned around.

"Helm hard over," Rob ordered.

We stopped for fuel at Great Bay Marine. Rob guided me in: steer upwind or against the current, whichever is stronger, cut her hard with some power, reverse with power, forward, reverse, neutral, lines through the air, and *Yonder* was at the pumps. We took on $10.36 of diesel: wonderfully cheap entertainment.

Rain was coming, wind, and it was already cold. We headed downriver into the open mouth of the wind and the flood of the tide and saw the need for foul-weather gear and a serviceable awning for the helmsman. At the mooring, after waving to Nanny on the beach, Heather hauled in the mooring pennant and tethered us to solid ground. We took a little boat into shore. Rob slapped me on the back. As I rowed I realized that I'd found yet another way to leave home and return. I knew things had changed. Drops of water fell off my nose and I had in my grasp through the oars the full understanding of how much I did not know, and I was afraid.

7

~

MY FATHER VENTURED into depths of Eagle Mountain Lake we children never dared. Once, yards farther out from shore than I'd dreamed of reaching, he bumped into something solid on the lake floor. He dove, surfaced. "There's something," he said, and dove again. We stopped splashing and turned to the expanse of still, brown water where my father had been. He broke the surface, struggling with the something. My brother and sister and I, all still younger than eight, turned toward the beach, unsure. He was straining back, pulling on something beneath the water. "It's long," he said, breathing heavily. When he reached the shallows we could make out the snout, round and gray. When he'd dragged the hulk into a foot of water he sat down in the mud to catch his breath.

"Dad?" we offered, still hanging back.

"It must be full of silt," he explained, and then said, "Go get Grandpa."

We ran. Grandpa followed us at a trot, looked at my father and the gray snout protruding from the lake's surface like the tongue of a whale.

"It must be sixteen feet long," my father said.

Grandpa jumped from the seawall to the beach and strode into the water, but seemed unsure of where to place his hands. Together, he and my father dragged the bullet-riddled carcass up on the beach.

"Well, what in the world?" my grandfather puffed. We moved closer.

"It's half of a B-52's wing tank," my father said. "Found it right out there in the middle of the water." Dad had flown in B-52s in the Air Force.

"A B-52 bomber crashed in the lake?" I asked, hope thrilling my voice.

"No, no," he said. "Somebody probably bought it for salvage. Then they split it in half."

"But it's full of bullet holes," I pointed out. "It was shot down."

My father smiled. "Somebody used it for target practice."

The tank was about two feet wide and hollow, a perfect half round. The nose and tail were tapered and perfectly symmetrical. It had moved through high altitudes at five hundred miles per hour.

"What's it made of?" Grandpa asked.

"Aluminum," Dad said. He began to scoop out several inches of silt that had collected in the bottom. More bullet holes were exposed.

"This is the bottom half of the tank," Dad said.

With the silt removed, the tank was much lighter and we were able to drag it up over the seawall, where it rested on the perfect sea of my grandmother's St. Augustine grass. My father walked around and around the fuel tank. My mother came out of the house and stood by his side, her hands on her hips.

"It was sunk in the lake," I told her. "It's from a B-52 bomber. Somebody shot it full of holes."

She looked at my father and said, "Why didn't you leave it in the lake?"

Dad bent down and touched it once again.

As a child my father crossed a river every day to go to school. He made this passage with his brothers and sisters in a flat-bottomed skiff his father built. "Dad built the best boats and sleds in all that country," my father often says. "That country" was Breathitt County in eastern Kentucky, rural Appalachia. The river crossed was the Middle Fork, a slow-moving, muddy-banked, catfish-thick tributary of the Kentucky River, which itself eventually flowed into the Ohio, which joined the Mississippi, which ran all the way to the sea.

Dad often traveled with his father to the mill to buy boat lumber. They bought poplar. The boats had two strakes on each side; horizontal boards beveled at about fifteen degrees made up the bottom; a thwart at the bow and stern and one in the middle. The boats were about sixteen feet long.

One of my grandfather's boats

"He'd nail all this up," Dad said, "then he'd sink it in the river for a couple of days so it would swell. He built boats for everybody. There was nothing he couldn't build."

My FATHER BROUGHT the wing tank home and gave it half the garage and most of his weekends. He used the tank as a mold and structural member, coating it with fiberglass. He added a plywood keel for stability and a square hole in the stern, which he described as a dory box. An outboard motor could be hung on the box and dropped through the hull for propulsion. He'd seen these boxes in dories while stationed in Newfoundland. I suggested that a boat with a square hole in the middle of it would sink. It was obvious. He tried to explain. He covered the foredeck for storage and painted the hull white. I continued to look down through the square box and imagined a fountain of brown water spilling up and into the boat.

Dad couldn't afford an outboard motor, so the first lake trials were conducted with a paddle. He pushed the narrow hull back out into the shallows of Eagle Mountain Lake, stepped aboard, and the boat rolled. He stepped aboard again, wetter, with more respect. The boat rolled. The keel wasn't heavy enough. He pulled the boat back to the beach and added a makeshift outrigger. Now the boat incorporated features from Polynesia as well as Newfoundland. But the outrigger did provide some stability, a way to remain dry. I took my first ride in my father's boat and spent much of the voyage looking down into the square patch of water at the bottom of the dory box, uncomprehending. I suppose the outrigger made the wing tank difficult to steer and propel with a paddle, because Dad soon added a short mast and a sail made of the split bamboo curtain from our big living room picture window. I don't remember sailing any farther into the lake than we had previously walked.

Later, I don't know if it was the same summer or the next, or years later, my cousin Bobby and some of his friends took the wing tank into deeper waters, and seizing the opportunity, the boat rolled, and having no flotation, returned to its resting place on the bottom of Eagle Mountain Lake. I see it there now, part junk, part bomber, part dory, part canoe, but mostly Middle Fork skiff, sailing back and forth through the big picture window of my childhood, warm brown water embracing the hull, bubbling up freely at last through the flooded dory box.

8

"A man who is not afraid of the sea will soon be drownded," he said, "for he will be going out on a day he shouldn't. But we do be afraid of the sea, and we do only be drownded now and again."

John Millington Synge,
The Aran Islands

THE WHOLE SUMMER WITH *Yonder* was before me. I conducted our business in Texas over the phone and through the mail, and finished a novel in Maine with a pencil at odd hours of the morning and evening.

I chose a sparkling Maine day in early June, air at seventy-five degrees and water at fifty-three, to make my first cruise without Rob's assistance. But somehow managed to put it off till late in the afternoon. That morning, Jan (a German exchange student living with Rob and Beverly) and Cutter (Heather's younger brother) and I spent a heroic hour changing *Yonder*'s mooring buoy from a black, sinister, crud-encrusted barrel to a slick orange Romper Room ball. The weight of the mooring chain was so great that we could pull no more than two or three links, the size of soup cans, over the rail of the skiff. I wanted to give up several times, but after much instruction in cursing from Jan and Cutter I managed to carry on and we exchanged buoys. *Yonder* didn't float away.

The tidal current was incredibly strong, beyond all my expectations. It worked to separate what humans would gather. If you didn't make a decision, it would decide for you. The river had a capillary action at the flow, the land drawing water up the vein of this branching valley. I'd never suspected the moon before, suspected it so powerful. Has anyone studied the trunks of trees, telephone poles, tall buildings, to see if they're affected by this pull? Do they drift one way, then another, every six hours? Am I leaning downriver as I write, my own thoughts changing direction four times a day?

I jumped in my boat at slack tide, and for twenty minutes wandered from the cockpit to the head aimlessly. I polished the stove, acquainted myself with the crude canvas cockpit awning, cleaned the bilge under the engine. When I touched the alternator belt, checking for the correct play, it moved from one side of the compartment to the other. Perhaps this was the cause of the intermittent high-pitched squeal we'd heard on the way to Great Bay earlier. I tightened the belt and checked the engine for anything else that might be loose.

Heather arrived after lunch with large sacks from department stores. We filled the pantry, both shelves, with new plastic dishes and utensils, made up the bunks with new forest-green sheets and blankets, stocked the Norcold with Pepsis, and put fresh towels in the head locker. This all seemed to satisfy her greatly. Now she was ready to go to sea.

I drank a Pepsi.

Jan and Cutter rowed out and had a Pepsi.

The fourth time Jan asked if he could cast off, I reluctantly murmured, "Okay, but give me a few minutes." I checked the oil and water levels. I checked every seacock on the boat. I switched on the depth finder and reaffirmed that the water temperature was still fifty-three degrees. Rob had explained that I wouldn't last an hour in this water if I fell overboard. I turned the marine radio to Channel 16, monitored by the Coast Guard, just to be prepared. There were no foul-weather warnings. Still, I scanned the blue horizon. I started the engine, looked out over the transom at the exhaust. Water pumped out in a gurgling, reassuring stream. Plenty of oil pressure. I told the boys to let us loose. My mouth felt as if it were full of eggshells and I was trying to hold them in my mouth without letting them touch my tongue. I reversed a bit to clear the mooring and then took the diesel up to 1500 rpm and the boat out into the main current. If the engine should stop, I'm a dead man, I thought. I couldn't have sailed a plate, much less *Yonder*. If the engine should stop, I couldn't just coast to the beach. The beach was a rocky set of molars that turned lumber to lobster bedding. But I was as brazen as they come, at least in front of my wife and two teenage boys.

We motored upriver, past the AT&T ship taking on cable, past a big lobster boat docking at the cooperative, past the group of old men in lawn chairs at Dead Duck Landing. They waved as *Yonder* passed, and I lifted my arm feebly in return. I tried to hold to the double yellow line leading down the center of the river. Speedboats churned by on both sides. They waved too. We took in their waves and wakes alike, a nod of brow and bow. *Yonder,* with all her weight (the surveyor estimated eighteen thousand pounds) brushed aside these little waves with hardly a shrug. We turned around at the bridge before entering Great Bay, caught the ebb, and doubled our speed. Hugging the New Hampshire shore for a better view, we inspected the pier off the gypsum plant and the remains of two unfinished Liberty ships left to rot on the beach at the end of World War I. They were little more than long piles of collapsed timbers, iron spikes jutting out at the sky awkwardly, what *Yonder* would look like were I to fail. At the tightest joint in the river, where the tide bunches up and springs forward, we squeezed between a navy tug pulling a barge up-river and the local power plant. There was once white water here. A shelf of stone a few feet below water at low tide, known as Boiling Rock, made tanker navigation hazardous, so some time back the Corps of Engineers blew it up. I tried to imagine small boats rowing against this tide. It couldn't be done. Only in taking advantage of slack pools and eddies could a passage be made. We crossed over to the Maine side of the river to look at the old homes. A woman, completely unknown to me, came out on her porch and waved a dishrag. Then I realized she was waving at *Yonder*. I don't deny it, a sudden effervescent swell of pride in ownership swept over me. Momentarily I recalled that I didn't design or build, hadn't even maintained this boat under me, and my posture resumed its usual flaccid but comfortable state. We crept under the I-95 bridge and its unlucky, landlocked drivers. At Long Bridge a section of railroad bed had been rolled aside for small-boat passage. *Yonder's* VHF antennae cleared by six feet. In the heart of Portsmouth, after showing the outdoor patrons of several restaurants our graceful sheer and mahogany stern, we turned for home. There was one more bridge, Memorial, to pass under before reaching the open sea, but this required that the central span lift for us. I thought I'd come far enough that day.

On the way home a bow wave off a big tour boat caught *Yonder* on the port quarter and sent a salt spray, our first, over Heather on deck and the rest of us in the cockpit. Heather screamed, the boys ducked, and I smiled. It tasted fine. I licked it from my upper lip like a gift.

At the mooring it took two tries to snag ourselves on the chain. I shut everything down, overcome with relief that I hadn't sunk the boat. But then I realized I had countless opportunities ahead of me.

MY FIRST DAY at sea as a captain: Heather, Cutter, and I ventured beyond Memorial Bridge, whose name I hoped was not prophetic.

33

The ocean smelled like a watermelon. Seeds stuck to the roof of my mouth.

I'd made my first connection with another human being through the wonder of radio that morning, requesting thirty feet of height from Memorial and giving my position and boat name. When the man's voice broke back in static, addressing me as Captain and telling us he'd go up after a few cars cleared, I felt as if I'd just talked to someone on the moon rather than the guy up there in the little box on the bridge. Memorial soon raised her skirts for us, the central span rising vertically on steel cables, and we poked between her ample granite calves. The bridge master left his box and looked down on us, his arms spread like a cormorant drying his wings. He seemed to think we were too short, not important enough, to cause him to get up, but this was our visit and I thought it only polite. He kneeled down and swept his hand along the level of the road bed and then swept his palm at our mast, blessing it. I pointed at his broken and moss-covered clearance boards and then dried my own wings. Finally, he rose in exasperation and walked back to his little house. I'm sure he thought our mast was so low we could have squeezed under but I knew this wasn't so. Ethan had warned me about Memorial. "It looks like you can make it, but you'll snap your antennas," he'd said. More enjoyable than this was our return four hours later, when the bridge master dutifully stopped traffic again and let us pass, and Heather, now in a bikini top, gave him a single blast on the air horn and her glittering smile in thanks.

There was a nuclear submarine under repair at the Portsmouth Navy Yard, a stone-silent Victorian prison at the end of Seavey's Island, a pair of Coast Guard cutters at the harbor entrance, and suddenly we were at sea. Lighthouses, Whaleback and Fort Constitution, were to port and starboard, the twin pillars of this gate to the city. We were on the ocean in a boat. Three huge tankers, like bloated carp, were anchored off the coast, waiting for the turn of the tide to head upriver. Gulls swept alongside, unaware that I was an amateur and could have veered at any moment. There were blue skies above us, but beyond the Isles of Shoals a gray haze lingered. I was afraid of it, and turned east along the coast, keeping my back to the bar wall. We hoisted the mainsail and let out the jib; I cut the motor. Our speed dropped from six knots to two, but it felt the same because we sensed it differently. With the engine you sensed speed through the deck and your feet; with the sails it was gauged by the hair of your skin. Holding the sheet in my hand with the wind filling the sail was something like holding my dog by the collar when she's seen a rabbit. The sheet was as tense as the muscles under her skin.

Heather and Cutter relaxed and read after their short work with the halyards. She was relieved that raising the sails was such an easy job. I hadn't relaxed since I first thought of buying the boat, even though everything seemed simple enough. I thought my fears were a good thing. I thought I should be afraid of the ocean, with me, my wife, and my young brother-in-law on an old boat at its very edge. I was beginning to have small moments of confidence, pleasures of beauty and insight, moments when I recognized that in this particular instance I was capable. But then there was the next moment: what did the depth finder read; there's a boat closing; the engine sounds . . . what . . . different; lobster buoys to avoid; that definite gray horizon; cold water. Yet I liked the open sea, only a single coast to contend with. On the river, in its currents and narrows and traffic, I always felt uneasy. The ocean itself seemed to give me room to digress.

THE SHORE I EMBARKED from and returned to, Hutton's Landing, was the gravel crescent of beach in front of Nanny's colonial house. I tied my dinghy to a tree with a painter as long as the barren foreshore, which depended on the state of the tide. The painter might be two feet long or fifty. Next to this small beach was a dirt and stone embankment, what was left of an old coal wharf. The stubble of the original pilings can still be traced a hundred feet out into the water, and beneath a rich bed of mussels the mud oozes coal black. The shorter dock that now existed was built by Rob and some of Heather's cousins of collected driftwood, secondhand telephone

Hutton's Landing

poles, a scavenged cradle, and plywood panels from a dismantled hockey rink. It was sturdy but didn't advertise the fact. Boaters occasionally stopped and snapped pictures of this example of Maine technology. The tide licked at its farthest pilings at low; then, at high, nine feet later, the water sometimes swallowed the plywood decking. Mussels and periwinkles lived among the timbers and rocks at all times, birds at the ebb, and fish at the flood.

If the dock was ever going to be anything but picturesque, it needed a float. Then, when there was enough water, boats could be brought alongside to load and unload passengers and supplies. *Yonder* had a high freeboard and boarding required an effort similar to mounting a horse. A dinghy that bobbed and shimmied was your only stirrup. With a draft of three and a half feet, *Yonder* could be safely brought to a float anytime between the two half tides, a six-hour window of opportunity when I wouldn't have to lug guests, groceries, and dogs the fifty yards out to the mooring and then pitch and shove them over the coaming. At times it was actually necessary to place one's flat palm on the stern of a wavering boarding party lest they fall back into the dinghy, upsetting ship's stores and captain.

All that was required was a float. Rob had already built a gang-way from salvaged lumber. I spent an hour and a thousand dollars at the local lumberyard, salvaging enough money from my wallet to buy lumber and Styrofoam to build a twelve-foot-by-twenty-four-foot float: waiting platform, dinghy tether, river overlook, halfway house between sea and land. We built the supporting structure and locked in the Styrofoam logs on a Saturday morning, and then, at high tide, levered the work over the stone embankment and into the water. I rode this leaky raft out to the end of the dock, pulled by Rob and Cutter with a line at each corner. I stepped from joist to joist urging them along, then missed and plunged through the ribs to my hips. Cold water. It's amazing how wet you can get before you even realize you're falling. Once she was securely tied to the dock, we began the decking process and finally finished off the float by anchoring her to a pair of pilings with iron hoops. (Notice how the float became female when she entered the water. This was completely unconscious on my part.) In this way the float would slide up and down the pilings as the tide rose and fell, always remaining at sea level.

We all stood on the new lumber, undulated with it six inches above the waves. Then I ran back up the dock and over to my dinghy tied to the maple hitching post. When I pushed off the gravel beach I thought, No more low-tide, slosh-through-the-muck, muddy-up-the-boat beginnings. I rowed around to the float; Rob caught my painter and tied me off. Standing next to him, I offered, "Float like this, you could almost take her to sea." It was a fine place to get and lose your sea legs. We looked out at the boats and the river. Funny how it did seem as if this were almost enough. I put my hands in my pockets, widened my stance, and slowly, safely, surfed.

SOLO. I SLIPPED *Yonder* from her mooring with a slippery heart and began to curl out into the river, when I committed a possible error. I ran over my own mooring. It wasn't the new buoy I'd just attached but the pennant and Styrofoam float that held a short lead line. The crunch of the prop through Styrofoam and fiberglass stick was almost nauseating. I paused, my sneakers hovering an inch off the teak sole, and waited for the shriek of a seizure, but it didn't arrive. I kept powering upriver, and little pieces of white Styrofoam snapped to the surface astern like popcorn. It would make for an interesting return. Usually I'd idle up to the pennant, run forward, fall to the deck and grab the flag, haul up the heavy lead line, and drop the eye over a big cleat. I didn't know how much of this equipment was left. I hoped there would be enough line remaining to pull up over the raised deck, five feet off the water. If this was the case, perhaps I'd have time to get a turn on the cleat with the mangled line before the tide swept the boat away from the mooring.

I considered these and other alternatives while motoring upriver to the gypsum ship. She was off-loading, and a fine white powder, apartment-wallboard thin, floated across the river. When I could smell the gypsum I turned, hard over to see how tight *Yonder* could. The ebbing tide punched her nose, then kicked her in the stern, so we ran away.

It felt strange to be on the boat alone for the first time. I had two previous experiences to compare it with: my first solo in a car, when I felt confident of my abilities and free at last of advice that arrived at the same moment I'd thought of it, and my first date, when I experienced a complete and traumatic alienation from all things familiar. This first cruise on *Yonder* in no way resembled the automobile solo. On my first date I found I'd somehow lost the ability to use a fork, and actually dropped it, still encumbered with food, to the floor on three separate occasions. On *Yonder* my fingers repeatedly sought solace from my face, probing the eyes, nostrils, and open mouth for any scrap of knowledge. In a tragically transfixed loop I scanned first the oil pressure gauge, then the water temperature gauge, and finally the rpm indicator, only to return quickly to the oil pressure, sure that it had dropped in the last two seconds. Randomly, marked by an eye tic, the thought would enter my mind to look at the water ahead of the boat. I was like an American pedestrian in London for the first time, unsure of the direction from which the taxis would attack as I crossed the street.

The tide and the engine urged me along. As I approached the Schiller power plant a cloud of a different color drifted across the river toward Maine. Small black puffs coughed from the plant stacks, malignant smoke signals. This tightest squeeze in the river was a perfect choice for an ambush. If the engine failed here, the boat would be either ground into the remnants of Boiling Rock on the Maine coast or cast into the steel pilings of the plant wharfage. I went over the emergency anchoring procedure: let go the wheel; leap from cockpit to raised deck, remembering to duck under the stainless-steel shrouds; release the big fisherman from its chocks alongside the swordfish pulpit; and free the anchor line from its cleat. With luck the anchor would plunge the sixty-five feet to the river's bed and find good holding ground. Then I could try to restart the engine or, if there was sufficient wind, raise the sails or get on the radio and scream for help. There was ten feet of chain on the anchor, and three hundred feet of five-eighths line. Would this be enough, and could it bear the strain of snapping a nine-ton boat to attention in a six-knot current? Such were the fevered workings of my mind. *Yonder* had survived almost sixty years and I didn't want to be the owner who lost her. And although I'd read Chapman's *Piloting, Seamanship and Small Boat Handling* through, and badgered Rob for responses to every imaginable disaster, I still felt my lack of experience keenly.

Her Majesty's Ship *Cornwall* was in port, docked between Long Bridge and Memorial. I moved back and forth along her hull like an ancient pilot fish. Sailors, male and female, sunbathed on deck. A helicopter perched on the stern and a big gun on the bow. She was long, low, gray, and bristling with ominous appendages. In this, our very latest age, our species still devoted both its oldest resources and its latest technology to adapt war to the water, while I made timid efforts to understand the action of the ocean on an old wooden fishing hull. I was risking my life at sea, but the rest of the world had long ago advanced to the ability to risk everyone else's. After passing beneath Memorial Bridge I noticed there were now two nuclear subs in for repair at the Navy Yard.

At Henderson's Point the *Thomas Laighton,* the double-decked

Isles of Shoals tour and ferry boat, charged by, making for the open bridge. I waved at the many tourists aboard like a friendly old salt, but returned both hands to the wheel to receive the bow wave. The water churned with the movement of the many boats in the harbor, wake against tide against wind. The river at dusk and dawn, without a boat's wake to mar its surface, was deceptively smooth. Now its surface simply reflected the constant turbulence below.

I made for 2KR, the buoy just beyond Whaleback Light, our home buoy. I wanted to check my loran against 2KR's charted longitude and latitude. The loran's position differed by about a third of a second. I thought this could have been due to some movement of the buoy, or my reluctance to get too close. Rob had warned me that buoys, like Sirens, were known to lure boats in for a kiss. Later, after calling my loran's manufacturer, I learned the gadget's positions were only relative. "The rocks aren't relative," I said. I couldn't trust it to bounce me off a coordinate on the chart, only to return me to a coordinate I'd already visited. At first this seemed like a catch-22, but then I realized it was only fair. I just needed to make my first explorations in good visibility.

A bit farther out to sea, in open water, I turned the boat over to the Benmar autopilot. A good autopilot can hold a course and allow the helmsman some steering rest, a trip to the head. Strangely enough, my autopilot performed acrobatics, steering circles and tight figure eights. But with the instructions in hand I was soon on my way in a straight line. The Benmar just needed to be told which way was north every time it was switched on, in the same way that I need to be reminded to return the toilet seat to its proper resting position every time I go. I stood in the companionway with the autopilot remote, out of the wind and spray, and with a gentle nudge of a button dodged lobster buoys and returned to course. I looked back at the empty cockpit and watched the course corrections transmitted to the abandoned wheel. *Yonder* seemed a ghost ship steered by a specter who held a tight hand to the wheel, moving it only an inch this way, an inch that. Spray passed right through him.

The wind began to coerce the waves to whitecaps and so I made for Little Harbor. Wentworth Marina nestled there, beneath the mansard towers of the Victorian hotel Wentworth by the Sea. Massive plastic yachts snubbed each other here. I wandered in and out of the docks, gawking at gold and platinum name boards. I had no envy because I shied at the thought of just backing one of these massive milk jugs out of its slip. I couldn't get away from a mooring safely, much less from a web of piers and insurance policies. Squirming back out of the harbor, I rounded Fort Constitution Light and crossed the river's mouth to a small cove where Dion's Yacht Yard made its home. There were more wooden boats here than plastic, so *Yonder* seemed at home too, despite the dreaded accumulation of lobster buoys, every one of them a noose for her prop. With each turn I looked back to see if the buoy I'd come near was still on the surface. And for the hundredth time on this simple voyage, I checked to make sure the dinghy was still following obligingly. I might need it for an escape.

I caught Memorial with a half dozen other sailboats wending their way home for the day. At Hutton's Landing I turned *Yonder* into the running tide, cut to neutral when I was two boat lengths away from the mooring, and rushed forward with the boathook. The eye of the lead line floated a foot deep in the current and I reached down, caught it, and dropped it over the cleat. A tattered bit of quarter-inch line that had held the Styrofoam float and pennant to the mooring still clung to the eye like a loose cataract stitch. I'd been lucky. And it had been a first-pass success.

I shut everything down and then checked the lead line on the mooring one more time to make sure there were no abrasions or cuts. The boat popped and groaned, settling back into its nest.

The Piscataqua runs southeast and northwest here, a section of the river known as Long Reach. The sun sets down the river's length, bloodying the water for moments, making it thicker and more poignant, as if the loss of the day were a vital loss, this river the last cringing leak toward night, the last look back. The water, as I stood on deck, slid to pink and dyed black.

As I rowed into the float, filled with relief, satisfaction, and some pride, a pair of great blue herons settled on the beach. They wheeled into dusk, cackling with the length of the long day and its descent, and lit in two inches of water. Their wings folded like a carpenter's old ruler, and then they struck pensive poses, as if someone or something were stepping on dry leaves behind them.

9

~

. . . water spilt on the ground, which cannot be gathered
up again . . .

> 2 Samuel 14:14

WHEN WE WERE nine years old, my next-door neighbor and grade
school companion drowned in a muddy creek a few blocks from
home. I didn't see his mother in her front yard again for months.

10

MY MOTHER AND her mother have never been fond of the water. At the lake they'd rarely gone in over their kneecaps, preferred to sit in lawn chairs, ever vigilant, tempting us with slices of watermelon if we'd only come away from the water. As I rowed them out to *Yonder,* leaving Dad and Grandpa on the float, they peered down into the river, as if there were something there they recognized.

My parents and grandparents drove from Fort Worth to Hutton's Landing in three days and dropped out of the open car doors like partially deflated beach balls. The tide was too far out to bring *Yonder* in to the float, so I rowed them out two by two. They wanted a short ride before lunch, and then we'd spend the afternoon preparing for a three-day cruise downeast. My grandfather, tall, lanky, eighty-five years old, reminded me of the great herons in the way his limbs extended and collapsed as we levered him over the cap rail and into the cockpit. I didn't worry because Grandma, once she'd grasped his foot, wouldn't allow him to fall overboard. Of course, this didn't allow Grandpa the actual use of that foot when boarding. I gave a short tour, warned them to duck as they entered and exited the companionway, and explained how to use the head. Down below, I felt like a guide in a historic house with a group too large to fit in the dining room. "Could you push forward, please, everyone. Let everybody in. Here we have, on loan to us from the Bligh family, a porthole original to the boat. Notice the intricate casting detail on the hinge." My father had me explain the electronics and open the engine hatch. Grandma wanted to know if I had plenty of life jackets, so I showed her where they were stowed in one of the cockpit lockers, then sat her on the locker immediately above them. I started the engine and let Dad cast off, dropping my new mooring staff and pennant overboard. He was eager for something to do. Grandma watched Dad step slowly along the deck through the rigging. She held her hands out into the air to help him, planning each step and handhold. Dad went from pulpit rail to lifeline to shrouds, stepping over anchor, hatch, and stovepipe. He dropped down onto the locker lid from the raised deck with a thud and rubbed his hands together with glee.

"All right," he said.

And Mom countered, "Sit down."

The boat waddled a bit as I applied power. We took a short ride upriver and back. I just wanted to reassure them, show how simple things were. The cockpit was roomy and stable. I pointed out things on shore. Dad couldn't sit down, and Grandma wouldn't allow Grandpa to stand up. Just before we arrived at the mooring there was a pop from beneath my feet. I put the boat in neutral and we coasted down on the pennant. The alternator belt had snapped. Perfect timing, I thought. But I had a spare, and so Dad and I replaced it before we went ashore. I was lucky this had happened so close to home. The belt also powered the water pumps. I tried to understand why it had snapped and thought perhaps I'd tightened it too much earlier.

Mom and Grandma returned from the grocery store with a trunkload of food, eighty-six dollars' worth, enough provisions to last two weeks. I'm sure they were thinking about the possibility of becoming castaways.

"This is not the *Minnow*," I said, "and I'm not Gilligan." Oddly enough, the thought that I'd often yearned for Mary Ann as an adolescent suddenly occurred to me. "We'll go right along the coast," I told them. "If the weather looks bad, we'll duck into a harbor."

I tried to display confidence, as if it were something I could hang on the end of my nose. Yet I'd never been more than a few miles outside Portsmouth Harbor. I'd only anchored once, a practice run at the mooring. As I'd changed the broken alternator belt, my father looking over my shoulder, the engine suddenly seemed rusty, grime-ridden, unreliable. The water in the bilge had an oily sheen.

I pored over the chart book that night, marking possible anchorages. Rob had recommended Jewell Island in Casco Bay. It would take eight hours at six knots to reach what he called Cocktail Cove, a popular haven for cruising yachts and daysailers out of Portland. I'd wanted everyone to come up and see me, see the boat, but now I regretted the invitations I'd made. I wasn't experienced enough yet. My confidence eked out a thin living between my socks and the soles of my feet. We left at dawn.

The tide was high that morning, so I was able to make my first real docking at the float. I motored straight in and an eddy pushed me gently alongside. Grandma and Grandpa stepped aboard in a way befitting their dignity. Dad and I hurled the luggage and provisions below, and I quickly backed away from the float, sure that every moment there was grace. *Yonder*, with her single screw and outboard rudder, with her great weight and wide beam, turned like a limousine. I was always afraid of clipping curbs, knocking over lampposts. Many of the boating guides I'd read devoted a great deal of ink and paper to explaining how to avoid embarrassment while docking. This in turn made me very anxious. Chapter One of all seamanship manuals should be an author's best effort to humiliate his students to the extent that a mishap while docking will be deemed as inconsequential as adding water to the sea. As it was, I felt that if I should scrape a strake while docking—or, heaven forbid, have to make a second pass—it would be somewhat like standing among a convention of first-year nuns while exhibiting my syphilitic member. In this frame of mind I headed downriver and threaded my way through the boats at the Portsmouth Yacht Club, aiming for the current-racked fuel dock. I moved in slowly, preserving my ability to feign sightseeing if I thought it looked too difficult. The ebbing tide ran parallel to the dock. Of course there was no one there to catch my lines. It looked deserted. Perhaps they were closed on Tuesdays. Closer still, I saw the many fenders protecting the fuel float. Ah then, they were expecting me. I applied power and scooted in, reversed, turned the wheel hard over, and applied power again. Miraculously, a young boy and girl appeared at this instant with smiles and hands capable of grasping. They pulled us a bit farther down the float and tied off the boat. I began to breathe again. I was no ordinary mortal, I thought.

"Pretty boat," the dock girl said.

"Diesel or gas?" the dock boy asked. One of these two people knew how to earn a tip.

"Diesel," I said, and "I'll be putting this on my credit card."

"Very good," he answered, then ordered: "I'll need everyone off the boat."

I was stunned. Had I broken some obscure rule of yacht club etiquette? My father noted my concern.

"Why?" he asked.

"It's our insurance. Everyone has to be off the boat but the captain, and everyone needs to wear some sort of foot covering."

"You mean shoes?" I asked. Boy, I thought, this was a modest club, offended by both bare feet and the word *shoes*. He nodded and handed me the diesel nozzle.

I removed the cushions and locker covers from the dual tanks. They held a total of thirty gallons and I pumped in twenty-eight. I'd been putting this off as long as possible. Dad paid for the fuel and a bag of ice. The ice was for the extra cooler Mom bought when we discovered the refrigerator on the boat couldn't accommodate two weeks' supply of milk, bacon, eggs, and lunch meat for five people.

At last we headed for open water. At the mouth of the river we encountered the first relentless swell of a day full of them. They came from the south, three feet high and twenty seconds apart. There was almost no wind. "Greasy," my father said. Everyone seemed to be all right till Grandma was struck as if by a gust of wind and turned, almost in time, to empty herself starboard. I made eye contact with my father and nodded at Mom. She was sick, too. He'd have to clean up Grandma's swell. My father's face went through a series of expressions at this turn of events. His son had just told him to clean up his mother-in-law's vomit. He seemed to both defend and fight all the revolutions of the twentieth century, sexual, political, and cultural, in the space of three seconds. Mom followed her mother's example soon and emptied herself over the port side. *Yonder* had now been christened left and right. Dad and Grandpa seemed to fare well. Grandpa climbed up on deck, much to Grandma's consternation and disapproval, and had a sit-down on the doghouse. Dad made sandwiches for the men, and when asked, Grandpa said, yes, he wanted everything on his sandwich, with lots of mayonnaise. Grandma shook her head.

"I don't know why I got sick," she said. "It just came over me. I'm all right now."

"Do you want a sandwich?" Dad asked.

"No."

"Linda?"

"Not now," Mom whispered.

"Isn't this beautiful," Grandpa said, reaching down for his coffee and sandwich.

"You're going to fall, Tom," Grandma warned.

"Bosh. Horsefly."

Dad and I smiled.

The coast slipped by and I tried to match points on the chart with points of land. It was deceptive, and for the first couple of hours I was frantic, plotting, dead reckoning, watching the compass, referring back to the chart and then to the loran. But I soon realized that on such a clear day as this was, I had an hour or two to compound mistakes before I'd run into a lighthouse or headland, and I began to relax a bit.

Often I stood on the locker that covered the quadrant and steered with my foot, holding onto the boom with one arm, so I could see more clearly ahead. While I was negotiating a buoy field off Nubble Light in this manner, a fin, torn and black and very large, rose off the port bow only twenty feet away.

"A fish!" I yelled, and pointed with my free arm. The fish suddenly seemed to notice us and turned down the length of the boat; we all, leaning over, saw the broad white belly and slow Mona Lisa grin of a shark. He must have been ten feet long. I took my pointing

arm back and held onto the boom with both hands. To our amaze-
ment this incident provoked my father into baiting his fishing pole
so he could troll. He held his index finger to the taut monofilament
as if he were waiting for an eight-inch trout to strike.

With the women still pale we abandoned the idea of Jewell Island and turned in to Wood Island Harbor. The sea broke over ledges
at the entrance, and it took us some time to find the red and green
entrance buoys. They seemed so close together on the chart. The harbor was a choked mass of lobster buoys, barrage balloons protecting London during the Battle of Britain. My father was appalled that
the government would allow such congestion.

"I think they're pretty," Mom said. "Just go between them."

I motored in slowly, turned at the right angles plotted in my cruising guide, and anchored just on top of one of their little anchor in-
signias. The tide was dropping but we still had fifteen feet of water.
The thousands of lobster buoys were reflected in the sky by thousands of birds. Many of them chose a rock, Stage Island, at the mouth
of the harbor to sit on and shriek a sort of outraged dismay at their
lot. I wanted to shriek, too. I was worried that the anchor wouldn't
hold, that when the tide turned the rode would sweep up an armful
of traps and warp and eventually knot *Yonder* to this spot on the
ocean till our tectonic plate shifted. I set the anchor alarm on the
loran, matched points of land to my recollections of them from three
minutes earlier. Several times I stepped up on the raised deck and
tweaked the anchor rode like a harp string. Chapman suggested a
seven-to-one scope, seven feet of anchor line for every foot of depth,
or about a hundred and five feet for this spot. I had let out seventy
and even that much seemed absurd. I thought, if a hurricane comes,
I'll let out another ten feet. As it was, my harp string hung limply
down into the calm water of the harbor.

Dad had his fishing line in the water soon, Mom made coffee, and
since it was still early, I left them all in the cockpit and went below
for a nap. I figured my parents were as good an anchor alarm as I'd
ever have. Besides, I'd strained my eyes to exhaustion, and my fingertips were raw from fidgeting with the wheel. I slept hard for an

hour and woke with a start, sure that I'd heard the squeak of granite against cedar. I charged up the companionway and startled all my elders, who were enjoying a windswept dusk. Small clouds knotted into monkey's fists scuttled across the western horizon. Between them a rag-linen sky shone.

"Everything's fine, Joe," my dad said. "We haven't moved an inch."

My hands, which had been splayed in some instinctive spasm of self-defense, slowly collapsed. I sat with my family and watched the gulls fight over a bit of rock, watched the receding tide reveal ever more rock and slowly pacify the birds. We could hear the disjointed screams of children on a beach far away, and turned brightly toward them as if our own names were being called. We didn't want to miss anything: supper, a spoon's reflection, some secret. The sunset was a dog dragging his old pink blanket home to a dark corner of night. Later, the light on Wood Island swung around to us on a mindful beat. I watched it shoot over like a falling star or a UFO. And always the lap of the water against the wood hull, the tattered edges of an uneasy embrace.

Dad made himself a bologna sandwich and then put a piece of rind on his hook so he could share his meal with the fish. I warmed a can of Dinty Moore for Grandpa, Mom, and myself. Grandma wouldn't have any, although she "wasn't at all sick." Mom didn't eat much either. Even though the boat was now at rest, she and Grandma still rose and fell on the day's swells. Their weariness was in their eyes and the way they held their coffee cups to their lips for an extra moment. My parents and grandparents drink coffee the way I sigh, with inevitability and satisfaction. Grandpa talked about the beauty of our surroundings as he finished off the Dinty Moore left in the can and everyone else's bowls. The boat was still unfamiliar to him, but he didn't seem to mind bumping his elbows, knees, and head, responding invariably to each bruise with the expletive "Well." Every time we heard the distinct thud of his skull against mahogany or spruce, Grandma reproved him by uttering his name ever more sharply. He replied with a second, smaller "Well." I washed our bowls and spoons, even though Grandma could hardly stand the

sight of my hands in the sink. I explained smartly that at sea, to con-
serve, we washed the dishes in salt water and only rinsed with fresh.
This to a woman who owned and successfully operated cafés through
the Depression and the rationing of World War II.

"Fish on!" my father yelled.

The four of us rose out of the bowels of *Yonder* to his call. He
brought from the depths some fierce, alien creature. Its mouth hung
from its belly. It clearly wasn't a perch or bass or even a catfish. There
were no discernible fins.

"What in the world?" Grandpa asked.

"I'm going to let it go," Dad suggested.

"Let it go," I said.

Later we learned this was a skate. Dad caught another a half-hour
later. He examined this one more closely, decided it was a bottom
feeder, and reluctantly let it go too. "Not much fight in them," he said.
"I wonder where all the fish are." He slept on one of the cockpit lockers that night, his fishing pole draped over the rail. He wanted to be
awakened in the middle of the night by a fish, something I'd always
hoped to avoid.

I took the single upper berth, Mom the lower, and Grandma and
Grandpa slept on the pull-out double berth to starboard. The design
of the pull-out berth was ingenious, allowing ample room for two,
but it also partially closed off the entrance to the head. This was unfortunate. Grandpa was on medication that made it mandatory that
he have access to a toilet every two hours. At ten P.M., his first call,
he decided not to try for the eight-inch gap leading to the head. It
was dark, he wasn't wearing his glasses, the boat rocked slightly. We
heard the familiar sound of his forehead against wood. "Well." He
made for open air, the cockpit.

As he climbed over Grandma, stepping on her hair, she woke and
yelled, "Tom, where are you going?"

He whispered harshly back, "To pee!"

"You'll fall overboard."

"Bosh," he said, and slammed into the mast, tripped up the two
steps of the companionway, and tore through the invisible mosquito

screening. Grandma followed him on her hands and knees. In a few moments they tumbled below again, a cacophony of grunts, bone against board, and expostulations of the single word "Well." I kept hitting my own head against the ceiling an inch from my brow. This wrecked train of events was reenacted every two hours till four-thirty A.M., when Dad yelled through the companionway, "Everybody up. It's dawn." As the coffee warmed, my father kept commenting on how great the sleeping was here. I tried to console myself with the memories of my grandparents' concern for one another. Grandma had followed Grandpa to the rail on every occasion, and held firmly to the elastic of his pajama bottoms while he relieved himself. (Perhaps this was what had happened to the fish.) I was impressed with their ability to return so quickly and peacefully to sleep after each excursion: they snored with abandon. I couldn't understand how they could sleep so peacefully with their ears so close to their nostrils. I'd slept, I calculated, for much of an entire hour, but such is the difference between passengers and crew.

I roamed the cockpit half a dozen times that night myself, making sure that the anchor wasn't dragging, that there wasn't a foot of water over the sole, that a trawler or ocean liner wasn't bearing down on us. I'd watched other boats come into the harbor the previous evening, and to a one they took up moorings. We were the only boat on a hook. While other nautical writers might boast of saving mooring fees by anchoring out, I only worried that I was committing some monumental blunder. I imagined all the old salts of Biddeford Pool, as they combed through *Yonder*'s wreckage on the rocks, commenting, "Everyone knows there isn't good holding ground in that spot. What gold-plated fool would drop an anchor there?" Me.

Over breakfast we listened to the weather broadcast, which called for a clear today but a foul, rainy tomorrow. We decided it would be best to return home and avoid the mess.

I put Dad at the helm and went forward to raise the anchor. The rode was cold and wet, but I was surprised at how easily eight or nine tons could be pulled through the water. When the boat was immediately above old muddy tongue, a concerted tug broke us free. The galvanized fisherman cleared the surface with nothing more than a smear of silt to show it had ever known the earth. I soon found that forty pounds underwater was a bit less than forty pounds swinging in the open air from a bow pulpit, while my father dodged lobster buoys exiting the harbor. I tottered on the narrow pulpit and finally managed to bodily tackle the anchor and wrestle it to the deck, falling on it to make sure it didn't get up again.

We discovered there actually was a clear channel, of sorts, out of the buoy-infested harbor. It was even marked with buoys the exact size, shape, and color of lobster buoys. The lobster buoys floating in the middle of the marked channel were only camouflage.

Clear of the harbor we cruised west on the reciprocal course back to Portsmouth. Grandpa resumed his lookout post on top of the doghouse, and once he'd been handed his cup of coffee wouldn't be budged. Two hours along he turned to me and said, "Now, when we start back tomorrow I want you to move in closer to shore so I can see better."

I smiled. "Grandpa, the ocean's on the other side of the boat. We've been heading home all morning."

He looked once again to the coast and then out to sea. He took a sip of coffee. "I guess somebody else ought to take over the navigating," he said, and laughed and laughed, sure that he was the wittiest man on the ocean.

Grandma shook her head. "Why don't you come down off of there. You're going to fall in the water."

"I'm not going to fall."

"If the wind comes up, we'll raise the sail and that will get him down," I told her.

But the wind never arrived. The seas weren't quite as greasy as the day before, and I learned a little trick about turning the bow to the waves that didn't upset my mother's stomach so, but we never got a chance to sail. We motored along, and I inched in toward the coast so Grandpa might see the houses and beaches. Everyone seemed satisfied.

Halfway home we crossed paths with one *Silver Shalis,* a building laid over on its side and coated with fiberglass, whose wake looked like a series of depth-charge explosions. And although I veered away as far as I could, her bow wave still lifted us halfway out of the sea. We dropped back down in a sheet of spray and mist. I rather liked it.

After a day and a half at sea we stopped pointing things out to each other, simply passed around the field glasses and the bag of chips. I've never been much of a talker. Other people seem to do it so much better than I do. But I seem to speak even less around my family. It's not because we have nothing to say but that we allow each other the comfortableness of our silences. We love each other so much that language and speech don't seem necessary. But finally, my grandmother couldn't bear it any longer. She had to say something.

We'd missed the bridge by five minutes. Memorial opened on the hour and half-hour during the summer. We waited in the turmoil of Portsmouth's inner harbor. A trawler passed, rocking us, and my mother honored the navy on that side with another heave. She and Grandma spent the next day in their hotel rooms, pale as insect larvae. Next time, they resolved, they'd come prepared with seasick patches.

After they'd gone home to Texas, I rowed back out to *Yonder.* My mother had left boxes and boxes of food on board. Of the eighty-six dollars in groceries, we'd eaten perhaps three dollars' worth. Dad had left his jacket so he could someday come after it. In the drainer was my grandfather's coffee cup. They'd all been on my boat. What my grandmother asked of me, when we were surrounded by water, unable to hold her silence: "Joe Alan, promise me you won't ever go out alone."

11

~

OUR FAMILY'S FIRST factory-built boat was a 1961 Adventurer, a twenty-seven-foot plastic cabin cruiser built by a short-lived company in Austin, Texas. Dad bought the boat used in 1969 from a recent widow who was so happy to be rid of it, she let him take up the payments. We owned this unnamed boat over what I remember as a long, chapped Texas winter. Strangely enough, after twenty-five years, the things that come back to me from that season are the mishaps. Perhaps it might be best not to read Mr. Chapman too closely: if I should become an errorless pilot, I may grow old with nothing to remember. It's the disasters that commit themselves to a bronze memory; the triumphs are written in water. Disasters make a life recognizable. My mental image of the *Titanic* has always been that of stacks slipping beneath the waves, rudder and props pointing to the night sky and fame. Only her sinking allowed her to survive in our collective consciousness.

It seems I remember my father leaning into the hatches over the twin Ford V-8s on many occasions, but he says now it was only some corroded battery terminals that now and then gave him trouble. He says the engines never caused problems, other than those at the gas pump. The fuel tanks opened their fillers like the mouths of bass.

Barreling across Eagle Mountain Lake in the cruiser, a guest asked Dad what he was towing.

"Nothing!" he guessed. But behind him, in a burst of spray, as if he were towing a sneeze, were twenty feet of line, a cleat, and a corner of the fuel dock he'd just left. Another factor in the high cost of fuel.

It took an hour of pounding to reach Grandma's house on the far end of the lake. My brother and sister and I, gathered in a tangled clump on the v-berth cushions, screamed every time the weight of the bow overcame the drive of the engines and we became airborne, weightless in the forepeak. Then we'd meet the rising cushions in a crush of limbs and potato chips. It was relentless, and we always arrived joyously bruised.

The lot next door to Grandma's was overgrown with briars and weeds, but it did have an old rusty dock built of oil-well pipe. We'd never seen anyone on it. We tied the cruiser there one afternoon and walked ashore rather than waded. Sitting in lawn chairs on the St. Augustine lawn, sipping iced tea and staring at the water, we were taken completely by surprise. A balding man in khaki stepped from the brush next door, his arms scratched and bleeding, his mind boiling and his mouth running with sores. He stood on the edge of his lot, pointed at our boat, and started cursing. At first I thought our boat must be sinking, but soon realized he was outraged at the ropes tied to his dock. We hadn't asked permission. My father walked right past him on his way to the boat. Grandpa met the man at the property line and said, "I'm sorry. No one's been on this lot for years. We didn't know there was someone to ask." The man didn't hear him. He climbed up in Grandpa's nostrils and swore at him from there.

Dad had already moved the boat and Grandpa was still getting chewed out. Then the frightening thing happened. My grandmother moved across her lawn like a copperhead, rose up between the two men, and struck.

She pushed aside Grandpa, whose only weapon in a cuss fight was the aforementioned "Well." Grandma let loose her formidable arsenal of Fort Worth stockyards venom and café spit. There were always stories that she'd run drunks out into the street, paid off cops to overlook her slot machines, and kept loaded revolvers hidden all over her café. But I'd only known her as the head cook at my junior high cafeteria. I never worried about forgetting my lunch money. The man in khaki was so overwhelmed, he slunk back into the briars, never to be heard from again. Grandma's parting strike was to label him a "durn heathen." And so we know him to this day, know his cousins and dogs and grandchildren, his cosigners and coworkers, whether we meet them at work or play or at a boat dock. It's comforting to know them by name.

In between the marina and Grandma's we explored uninhabited coves, former arroyos that became narrow and sometimes shallow estuaries when the reservoir was initially flooded. We believed fish hid in them. Dad worked the cruiser as far up into the bights as possible and dropped anchor. The muddy banks on either side were so close that a fisherman standing on one of them could have cast over our boat and dropped his plug on the far shore. We caught drum and catfish, bass and perch, and an occasional turtle by mistake. On one memorable morning a school of stripers trapped us in a cove and we had to catch our way out, making a breach with spinners and spoons. Usually only the weather was biting; we stuck our poles out through zippered canvas that enclosed the cockpit, and warmed our hineys on a Coleman heater.

In a slough we discovered a vine-shrouded derelict, a homemade steel boat that had been abandoned to the mud and spiders. Rust-ridden and rag-fouled, she was so heavy, so trapped, she didn't even sway when we boarded her. I swiped a broken lantern that hung in the pilothouse. Phil jumped up and down on her decks to make her ring. I've always been enamored of the lost, the abandoned, the forgotten. I want to believe there's still some hope.

We were up another creek so far that tree branches met over the cruiser and scraped her topsides. The prop fouled. In midwinter, in a freezing drizzle, Dad went over the side into the shallow, muddy water and dived under the boat with his pocketknife. The relevant movie reference would be Humphrey Bogart in *The African Queen*. Dad dived again and once more returned with a tangled skein of trotline, black muck, and rusted hooks. During the moments he was underwater my mother crossed her arms and shook her head slowly as if no boating pleasure could be worth these moments.

We found cold fish at the warm outflow of the power plant on the lake and anchored there often, taking our limit. At last, the fish took something back. Dad tugged on the anchor rode but brought up only a bitter end. Not to be robbed, he raced back to the marina, built a grappling hook and returned. Even as a child I was amazed when on the third or fourth troll Dad caught his anchor. No fish ever pleased him as well, because he'd never lost a fish before catching it.

That spring, anticipating our first summer swimming off the cruiser, Dad was transferred to California and had to sell the boat. A prospective buyer appeared and was taken on a trial run. In the middle of the lake the boat died and wouldn't be started.

"It's those damned batteries," my dad apologized.

"Batteries," the buyer scoffed. "Hell, I own a battery store. I'll slap some new ones in."

Mom and Dad had accumulated three hundred dollars in equity on the boat loan over the winter. As we left Fort Worth for San Francisco, they gave my brother and sister and me one hundred each in return for the loss of the cruiser and the lake and our grandparents. Twenty-two years later I bought my first boat. I was the same age Dad was when he bought the cruiser. I like to think that included in my payment for *Yonder* was a creased and worn twenty-two-year-old C-note. If the Treasury should ever reclaim and wash it, they'll find in their filters a spoonful of lake sediment, a fiber of a frayed towel, a few fish scales, and a weary drop of water that saw me through.

12

I'VE DONE MOST OF my boating on dry land, under roof, where it's more comfortable. For every hour I've spent at sea, I've spent ten cruising the pages of a chart book or the aisles of a chandlery. I enter antique shops and bookstores heeled over, my ear awash. I sometimes think I bought my boat to justify my nautical shopping habit. There: I've confessed before I can be accused, and feel the better for it. I'm a member of Nautically Anonymous. I can't stop buying, looking at, or talking about boat stuff. N.A. meetings, which can be reached only by ladder and are held under canvas, are known as boat stand gams. We lean on tillers and bulkheads miles from any form of salt water, confessing our preferences in bottom paint. My obsession is worse in the winter, when I'm farthest from my boat, but it continues throughout the summer as well. I drive to distant chandlers, whether I need anything or not, between actual cruises, in the same way that I eat a bowl of cereal between meals. There's nothing anyone can say to me. I admit everything and deny all.

It begins simply. The places you go, you've always gone to— bookstores, antique shops—but once inside you specialize, you see nautical applications for toasters and jelly jars. Gone are the old interests in novels, biographies, mysteries. There's a new mystery: how does one monopolize the marine section in a crowded bookstore in a democratic nation? Spreading your self and a dozen open books out on the floor works. Other patrons turn down the aisle, see the obstruction, and seek a safer passage. Once hegemony has been established, I can then take my time reading all the books that haven't made my local library. Every book in the section draws my interest. I page through eleven knot guides, remembering I've once again forgotten my short piece of rope. Paper-kayak construction: is there any aspect I shouldn't know? Wreck of the *Titanic,* the journals of Columbus, the life of Joshua Slocumb's wife while he was at sea. The only thing that bothers me about the marine section is the preponderance of books dedicated to doom. There are countless tell-alls of sinkings and dismastings, lifetimes aboard life rafts, of raw-fish eating and urine drinking. Their message: only a fool would step on something that floats, because floating's natural inclination is sinking. I read Farley Mowat's *The Boat Who Wouldn't Float* and cried into my downeaster. There should have been a warning label affixed to the cover: "This book shouldn't be read by new owners of wooden boats."

In Harding's used- and rare-book store in Wells, Maine, I found a novel entitled *Yonder.* It wasn't about boats, but how could I pass it up? Here also was a yachtsman's yearbook for 1934, the very year my boat was built. My boat wasn't listed, but how could I pass it up? I've searched every used-book store from Texas to Maine to complete my back-issue collection of *WoodenBoat* magazine. I find an issue here, one there, but I'm not having great success. All the original subscribers are members of N.A. as well, and won't part with their prizes.

Even after the bookshops close, I fill the lonely hours between nine and nine by perusing my stock of marine catalogs: folding page corners, circling good buys on handheld radios and whipping dip. Perhaps I'll draw up a comparison chart on bronze screw prices or make friendly faces at the little photos of the catalog's employees.

At antique shops, while my wife looks at pottery or vintage clothing, I'm searching for telltale signs of bronze or galvanized hardware, something the antique dealer has sneaked out of the boat shed. On several occasions, on a bottom shelf, in an opaque Zip-Lock sandwich bag, I've found treasure: the verdigris remains, the battered cleats, pulleys, line guides, and step-plates, the surviving bones of a wooden boat. Perhaps none of this hardware has an application on

Yonder, yet I buy it anyway, just to keep it from any other obsessive. And reasonably, I might need it someday. At my home are windows full of port, starboard, and anchor lights, a room devoted to old charts, a deck hung with ancient cork life rings. Have I mentioned the artwork? Any bulkhead of our house can sail, harpoon whales, fire a salvo, or cast a welcoming beacon on a dark and stormy night.

Inevitably, at any estate auction along the seacoast, there's a wooden box hauled from the barn that's thick with oarlocks, broken boat hooks, and galvanized bolts. There's a bundle of single oars mixed in with old skis and fishing rods. If I buy enough single oars, there will come a day when the singles start to match, pairs will be born, my life won't row in an endless circle. I've collected several objects that I don't have a definition for but which I'm sure are nautical. They make fine whatsit conversations at meetings, and although I've received many offers of cash, I won't sell: the unknown is more valuable than the known. At an auction just up the road a huge brass ship's compass came across the block. I'm not sure why my heart leaps at every compass I find, but perhaps it's the idea that each one of them led somebody somewhere. I like anything that indicates direction: weather vanes, signposts, big neon arrows pointing to a swimming pool. I like it when my mind comes up with a notion of when and where to go.

And don't overlook yard sales. Only one in twenty will produce, but what's a Saturday to me? I bought two one-gallon ice cream buckets of slightly used bronze screws at a tag sale for one dollar, one verdigris Washington. *Ha!* At another sale I found a huge bronze hinge from the door of an old tugboat. There's only the one, but still.

Even when forced to attend the shopping mall, I've managed to dig out worthwhile artifacts. At the gift shop I ordered a brass oval engraved with the boat's name, designer, builder, and date of construction. It's now screwed to *Yonder's* mast belowdeck. There are opportunities everywhere. I took a life ring to our local sign painter and had "*Yonder*" grace its circle. Kevin Freeman of Cape Neddick also carved and gold-leafed *Yonder's* escutcheon board, applying a rich turning to the foil of "Eliot, ME." The sun flashes off our transom. He's since carved number boards and painted another ring for Hutton's Landing. Whenever Kevin sees me coming he puts on his sailor's cap and readies for sea; his brushes move in his hands like fids.

All of these places have their purpose, satisfy the scuppers of my obsession. But my first and last resort has always been the chandlers. I've been in the best of them from Galveston to Miami to Searsport, but my favorite, the store where I most often get my fix, is my local chandlery, Jackson's of Kittery, Maine. It's everything a chandlery should be: crowded, overstocked, conducive to browsing, carrying the ordinary and the elusive. And if they don't have it, by God they'll order it. I walk through the aisles in the same way I first walked through the bewildering array of vitamins and herbs in a nutrition shop, vaguely aware that if I knew what to look for, something on these shelves might save me. I pause and scratch my forehead over my eye till one of the clerks asks if anything's wrong. "How do I make this electrical whatsit fit the next size down plumbing whatsit so it doesn't leak, blow the fuse, and sink my boat?" I ask. Most of the time they'll have an answer. When they don't, other customers try to help. In regard to boating I'll entertain anyone who has an opinion. Even if I consider them a daily fool in their confrontations with life, it's just possible they might know something about a boat.

I bring my antique finds to Jackson's for retrofitting. At a shop in New Bern, North Carolina, I found a bronze-bound masthead light. Trying to find a bulb to fit the ancient socket, the crew at Jackson's suggested putting a new light inside the antique cage and glass. We found one from Italy that fit perfectly and came with spare bulbs. It's now *Yonder*'s closest and most comforting star. At an antique mall in Arundel, Maine, I took a chance and bought a brass grain or flour scoop that once rested on a country store's scales. The scoop had a four-inch round funnel at one end, enabling it to slip into a sack and empty its contents without spillage. With the help of some packing from Jackson's the scoop serves as an unusual and excellent vent over *Yonder*'s galley. Time and again I've gone into my home port chandlery as clueless as my anchor, and exited with a glue or screw or paint that once applied to *Yonder's* hull will actually save my life.

So the sea, I've found, is as close as my neighbor's yard sale, as close as my own library. Water isn't always required. An obsessive is always under sail. Did you know that Thomas Edison instructed his first telephone operator to answer each call with the salutation "Ahoy"?

13

And the Spirit of God moved upon the face of the waters.

Genesis

WHEN I WAS ten years old my family moved to San Francisco from
Fort Worth, and I swam into something I'd never seen before: an
ocean. It seemed a fairly formidable barrier, about as far as you'd want
to go. The sea was cold, induced vomiting, and unlike lake water, rose
up in white anger with a broad fist. Here, water made noise. I thought
it must be easy to immigrate to California from the western Pacific
islands because all the water was already coming this way. It occurred
to me that I might best back off. On the beaches south of San Francisco the ocean had spat out trees as big as our house, driftwood too
large to take home, the roots and branches stripped bare and
bleached. For most of the coastline the land had to meet the sea with
rocky cliffs to hold it at bay. The very sun was quenched here, skidding from the sky into a limpid shroud of bloody waters. I walked
along the beach with my little brother and sister and my parents in
the same way I'd walk along the rim of the Grand Canyon, wanting
to fly but knowing it wasn't worth the risk. We came upon a small
clear stream, sinuous through the sand, and watched the fresh water
forget itself in the salt. It somehow seemed terrible, all that sweet
direction and drive lost in the maelstrom. Everything but the ocean
seemed insignificant, and the ocean was a violent chaos. Perhaps

God had created this vast world with its incredible diversity and minute intricacies so that I could find someplace to hide. I was a child.

> *Mother may I go and bathe?*
> *Yes, my darling daughter.*
> *Hang your clothes on yonder tree,*
> *But don't go near the water.*
> —Anonymous

14

～

MY BROTHER AND SISTER flew to Maine in midsummer under the guise of a vacation, but I suspected my parents sent them to make sure I wasn't drowning. I took them on a short run up to Great Bay Marine for fuel, and while they spoke kindly of the boat, I could tell their interest was elsewhere. Sally groggily asked, "Are there any fish in this river?" My mother had jammed a seasickness patch behind her ear before she got on the airplane.

I told them about the half-dozen stripers I'd caught at *Yonder's* mooring. The schools of stripers would swim by announcing themselves with great applause and I'd cast out into the tail clapping with a plug.

"How big were they?" Phil asked.

"About two feet long—" I began.

"Oh, God," Sally yelped, swallowing her grogginess.

"—but I threw them back," I finished.

"Why?" she shrieked.

"They were too small. They have to be thirty-six inches long before you're allowed to keep them."

"Who says?" Phil asked.

"The state," I said. "I don't know. Game laws."

"Rules," he spat.

"I know." I shrugged. There shouldn't be anything between a human and his fish.

"How many poles have you got?"

"Just the one Dad bought when he was here."

"We need to get to a tackle-and-bait shop, right now," they concurred.

I took them to the Kittery Trading Post, sportsman's druggist, and we bought more gear, enough hooks and line and weights to get the tackle industry through another season. We traded hard cash for things to throw in the water.

"We're going to catch a big fish," Sally squirmed.

My sister was twenty-seven, and although she never cared anything about fishing as a child, she's since married a fisherman and was learning the love. The idea of landing a single striper that could eat an entire limit of lake stripers in one gulp had her in its fishy jaws.

"Bobby"—her husband—"is going to be so jealous," she said gleefully, washing her hands with invisible soap, in imperceptible water. There in the Kittery Trading Post, between the salmon eggs and Zebco reels, I watched my baby sister christen herself, become a true fisherman: she had learned to gloat about her catch before she'd caught it. I smiled at her with big teeth.

At a Badger's Island bait shop we told the woman behind the counter we'd never fished here before and needed to be baited.

"What are you fishing for?" she asked.

"A really big fish." Sally beamed.

I pushed her aside. "You tell us," I suggested.

"Most people around here are looking for stripers and blues. You'll want some sandworms and eels."

We looked at her with fish eyes. Phillip finally said, "What?"

She held up a take-out soup container, opened the lid. Worms with legs were inside. Sally grimaced.

"They've got pinchers," I said. "And they've eaten all your soup."

The bait lady tilted her head. "It doesn't hurt when they bite." She smiled.

"What else have you got?" Phil asked.

She hooked her finger, and we followed as if she'd snagged us by the earlobes. We were soon standing over a foaming bait tank, aerated but dark. She dipped a net into the bubbles and snapped it back up sharply. Sally yipped. Phil and I stepped back, drew our guns. A mass of knotted black eels writhed in the bottom of the net. She said the eels were each about twelve inches long, so she must have measured a dead one once.

"They've got jaws," I said.

"Yeah," she said.

"How do you fish with them?" Phil asked.

"On the bottom," she said. "Good at night."

I sucked the thing I was going to say back in my mouth like drool.

"I mean," Phil said, "*how* do you fish with them?"

"Oh, you use a glove or a rag to pick them up. They're pretty slippery. Then you thread the hook through their upper and lower jaws."

Sally turned away.

"What else have you got?" Phil asked.

"Mackerel. It's frozen. You cut it up in chunks."

"Which bait is best?" I asked, knowing.

"Eels," she said.

"Okay," Phil said. "We'll take some of everything." He wanted the big fish, too.

The clerk put a half dozen eels in a plastic bag filled with water since we hadn't brought a bucket. Phil placed it, the sandworms, and the mackerel on the floorboard of the car between his feet. "Hope this bag doesn't bust," he said listlessly. Sally pulled her legs up into the seat with the rest of her body.

We cast for stripers that evening, spread out on *Yonder's* deck while she sat at her mooring in the river. We had no luck.

"Where are they?" Sally huffed, as if the fish were late for a meal she'd made.

"They've always come by in big schools before," I said. "When they come there's no missing them."

Even though I was telling the truth, it was hard for me to make eye contact with her. Since I was host, it was my fault the fish hadn't come. For once it made me feel sorry for all those preachers who spent a lifetime promising God was just here and that he'd be back real soon.

68

"It's getting pretty dark," I said. "Why don't we switch tactics?"

Sally and I watched as Phil, the only one of us who dared to eat cat food as a child, made preparations to hook one of the eels. He pulled the bait bucket out of the water, opened its lid. We all stood over the bucket, looking down at the squirming eels as if it were possible for a human to fall into the four-inch circular opening.

"Okay, I'm going to grab one," Phil suggested.

"Okay," I accepted. "They look like baby moray eels."

Phil reached into the bucket with an old rag wrapped around his hand. He moved his hand around. He looked up at us. "I can't——" he started, then he jerked back. An eel took flight, seemed to be born from the snatching rag. It skidded off the cockpit locker to the teak sole, a paroxysm intent on finding a home in *Yonder*'s bilge. Sally and I kept lifting our feet and legs up into the air but they kept falling back down to the sole. Phil chased the eel across the teak on his knees, blanketing the squirm with the rag many times but losing it when he tried to grasp it. Blocking off the scuppers and companionway, we let the slither run out of the eel. When it started to gasp, Phil used both hands to gather it up as if it were a stream of mercury.

"This is sick," Sally said.

The hook punched through both mandibles with a crack.

"There," Phil said. It was the word of a conqueror. It was too horrible. "Now I'll bait the other rod," he said.

"Is there nothing to stop you from catching a fish?" I asked.

"These eels cost a buck apiece," he said. "I'm fishing with them."

"Try the thing the bait lady suggested this time," I said. She'd said if we were ever lucky enough to get a good grip on an eel to use that opportunity to slap his head against the hull of the boat. This would stun him long enough to thrust the hook through his lips. The second eel flipped from the bucket, slid back down Phil's arm, coiled around the bail, and hung there.

"I'll grab his neck and you unwind his tail," I suggested.

"His neck?" Phil said.

"It's got to be somewhere just behind his eyes."

I took a second rag, approached the eel from behind, I think, and then lunged for him as if he were a pig. Phil unwrapped the tail, and on the count of three I let go as he snapped the eel whiplike into the face of the locker.

"Jesus, Jesus, Jesus!" Sally yelled.

The eel lay motionless on the deck. "That did it," Phil said, and, picking him up, popped the hook through the jaws. The eel came back to life then, coiling around the fishing line.

We dropped both lines overboard, and through the next couple of hours brought the eels back up into the glare of a flashlight to see if they were still doing their job. At midnight we gave up, tied the poles to *Yonder's* sternposts, and went below. As we lay in our bunks, listening to Phil snore, Sally talked disappointedly of the big fish, of its place in her life, of the deep hole in her heart. I was wedged once again into the upper berth. I'd removed my eyeglasses because they kept banging into the ceiling when I inhaled. Fifteen minutes after we'd gone to bed, I heard Sally talking again. Something like, "Wassermatter?" I mumbled about the mooring line banging into the boat. Then more loudly, she said, "What's that?" And answering herself, "It's the fish. It's the fishing poles. God, God, God!"

I slapped my head against the boat ceiling. Stunned, I fell the four feet from my bunk to the sole instinctively clinching my jaw. This woke Phil.

"What's happening?" he asked.

"Fish on!" I yelled, and charged up the companionway behind Sally. One of the rods was banging its life out against the mahogany coaming. The lights from the power plants across the river lit up the boat and the houses on the Maine side. Sally grabbed the reel while I untangled the short cord that kept it from being dragged overboard. Then, just as suddenly as it had begun, the rod stopped jerking. Sally reeled in the broken, bitter end of the monofilament.

"Oh, he got off," she wailed, and stamped her foot. She was in an ankle-length white cotton nightgown that seemed to glow, well, religiously, with the light from the power plants. "I can't believe it," she added disgustedly. "We gave up too soon. We didn't deserve the big fish."

I stood on the deck in my bare feet, wearing only a pair of jeans, the six-inch tie-down cord hanging limply at my side.

"Shoot," I said weakly.

My little sister can frown a dog's tongue back into its mouth.

"I'm sorry, Sally," I said.

"It's not your fault. Why are you apologizing?" she said, and sat down on the locker seat heavily. "I can't believe it. I bet he was big, so big."

Phil staggered up the companionway in his underwear. Sally opened her mouth to say something but froze, her hands held in midair, as the second rod began to flail against the boat. I lunged for the monofilament instead of the pole and jerked back.

"What, what, what?" Sally cried.

"Fish on!" I yelled again. I untied the rod with my free hand and reeled in, but after a couple of turns the reel wouldn't turn. "Maybe I just snagged the bottom," I said. I tried pulling on the pole, but the rod just bent toward the river. "I sure thought it was a strike, but I think I'm hung on the bottom." I cranked another inch and a half of line in and then the line began to move, move against the current. I braced the butt of the rod against my pelvis and turned to Sally. I smiled slowly. "Big, big, fish on."

"No, no it's not," she said, and her face took on an expression I hadn't seen in twenty years, when I last teased her about the existence of Santa Claus.

"He's here."

Her hands came up to her chin, covered her mouth for a moment, but the pressure became too much. The explosion ripped her fingers from her lips. She screamed, "Don't let him get away!" The scream echoed off the shoreline. She screamed the words again and again: "Don't let him get away!"

I reeled in another two or three inches of line. The rod tip began to dip toward the black surface of the water. "He's going under the boat," I said. The rod tip entered the water. I was pulled to the rail.

"Hold on!" Sally barked. The rod bent along the curve of the hull. My gut was hanging on the rail; only the rod grip and reel weren't in the water. I remained in this position for fifteen or twenty seconds, Phil and Sally holding onto the belt loops in my pants. We were at an impasse.

"I'm afraid the line's going to get cut on the keel," I huffed.

But soon the fish began to move again. I reeled in a few feet of line.

"He's tiring," Phil said. "He's fighting us and the current."

I turned the crank again, only to lose everything I'd gained when the fish overcame the drag. The long rip of the drag was like the world being laid open with a zipper. For minutes we pulled at one another in silence as the fish rose and descended. Sally broke this silence occasionally, the strain of a possible future too much, and screamed, "Don't let him get away! I love him!" After a while the angle of the line as it entered the water lessened. The fish was plainly coming to the surface. I cranked as fast as I could. Phil shone a flashlight out into the water, a dozen feet from the boat.

"God, God, God!" Sally yelled.

I couldn't see him. My eyeglasses were still below. "What is it?" I yelled. "What is it? I can't see."

"It's huge," Phil said.

"My glasses, Sally, and the net, Phil. It's up in the head."

I worked the fish closer to the boat. Without my glasses, I could make out only a glimmer, a rumor, the reflection of a star on dark water. With my glasses on, as Phil dipped the net into the water, I could see the fish was about three feet long but couldn't tell what species. We pulled the fish aboard with a great heave and dropped him thrashing to the deck. As the fish ate his way through the net and Sally's screams, I recognized him as a blue. "Don't let him bite you!" I yelled. We were all barefoot, and since the fish was three feet long and the cockpit only six feet wide, and since the fish and our feet were often trading places, I sent Phil below to the toolbox for a hammer. My brother had never hit a fish with a hammer before but guessed the head was a good spot to aim for. The problem was a fish's head is curved and often wet. The hammer caromed off the slick fish to rebound off my smooth teak deck several times and I started to swear.

"Well, he's moving," Phil defended himself.

Finally a strike left the blue's eye dull and he lay still on the deck. I reached down gingerly and picked the big fish up by the tail, lifted him into the glow off the power plants. He vomited a half-digested, foot-long mackerel onto my foot and *Yonder*'s deck.

"Oh, God," Sally whispered.

"We killed him," I said.

"I think I'll go put my pants on," Phil mumbled. Porch lights were snapping on in all the houses along the coast of Maine.

We curled the blue into a cooler and went back to bed. It rained that night, and we woke to a viscous fog, a crush of weather where I thought fish could live on thick air. The rest of our eels had somehow escaped, having popped open the bait bucket lid and flushed into the river. How would we find them in all that water? A couple of days later I put Phil and Sally back on an airplane with the big fish story. My sister couldn't wait to tell her husband. I'd held the blue in my arms as I stood on the bathroom scale. Alone, I weighed thirteen pounds less. Beverly had grilled the big fish for my brother and sister's farewell supper. He tasted like silence, as if he weren't there.

The next day I rowed back out to *Yonder* and found that we'd left the Styrofoam soup container down below in the sink. The remaining sandworms had crawled out and rotted on the upward curve of the porcelain. When I first opened the companionway the smell forced me back to the rail, where I, like the blue, vomited. As I leaned there, spitting and drooling into the river, absolutely sure that I was alive, I thought that someday I would tell this story.

15

EVEN THEN, THE BOAT was only a means to an end, a way to row to the homes of fish. At twelve and thirteen, Phil and I spent the summer with Grandma and Grandpa on the lake. My father bought us a ten-foot aluminum johnboat; it rang like an oil drum when we dropped a fishing rod or paddle onto its glaring surface. Selling points for my father were the chunks of Styrofoam flotation under each seat, and a hull that couldn't be paddled very fast or far. I could stand at bow or stern, or along the rolled-aluminum rail, and not come near capsizing. If we somehow managed to roll her, she floated just as high upside down. This boat, this meatloaf pan lined with foil, the square orange life jackets we were forced to wear by our grandparents, and a pair of stubby paddles were our ticket to shallow-lake adventure. But it seemed no matter how hard we paddled, the boat jackknifing continuously across the surface of the brown water, we could always turn back and make out Grandpa on the grass, binoculars raised to his eyes, and hear him whispering to himself as he counted our life jackets over and over, "One, two. One, two."

In front of my grandparents' house was a two-foot-high concrete seawall that held back the St. Augustine grass as much as it did the lake. We tied our boat to this barrier. The bow sat on a two-foot-wide section of imported sandy beach; the stern floated in an inch of water. Grandpa helped push us off every morning with his garden hoe; then he'd use the hoe to slap at the water moccasins who'd slept under the hull. For the first fifty yards or so we could use our paddles as poles, pushing ourselves forward over the shallow bottom. It took us a week to learn the best positions from which to paddle. We tried sharing the middle thwart, but if there was the slightest difference in the strength of our strokes, the boat wobbled like the needle on a cheap compass. We couldn't sit together at the bow: the boat thought we were trying to paddle to the bottom of the lake. It rose up on its flat nose, the stern three or four feet out of the water, and fought our attempts like a cat being forced down a commode. Finally we sat on opposite ends and sides of the boat and tried to coordinate our strokes. Invariably one of us would paddle harder and our course would have to be corrected by a more strenuous effort on the weak side. This process inevitably escalated, until we arrived at our destination completely exhausted, although it was impossible to arrive in anything but a dead heat.

We paddled to the abandoned World War II Marine base across the lake, up shallow creeks, and into tree-choked coves, always searching for fish. Our poles and tackle boxes seemed to vibrate louder against the aluminum hull the farther we were from home. There was a secret we chased, a way of understanding. Our lines dropped into unclear waters, and occasionally, but never when expected, a series of bumps, like Morse code, would be transmitted from the darkness. That message could only be answered by a stalling of your heart and an involuntary contraction of your muscles. We had to know the moment instantly. And the pale flash of the fish surfacing: like a bronzed girl's white butt cheek or her blanched breast popping suddenly from her bathing suit as she rose from the water, that instantaneous, that exciting, that unexpected, that gratifying. The life through the line was a continual electric shock, a death-defying tension. And from our end the fish must also have felt our anxious, perhaps instinctual, fear of losing him. If we didn't catch the fish, we'd go hungry, die, or worse, we'd never grow up.

We brought back to Grandma stringers of bluegill and an occasional bass. Phil would clean them and eat a few, but I never grew accustomed to the idea. I couldn't develop a taste. I felt guilty about the fish we killed and didn't eat. Once we left a live string of perch tied to the stern of the boat overnight; the next morning the water moccasins were gorging themselves on them. The snakes darted away, diving into the brown water, when Grandpa threw a clamshell into the bell of our boat. "I hate them dadgum water moccasins," he said. As he pushed us off that morning he added, "Don't bring home any more fish unless you're going to eat them." And from that point I've never thought of a fish as any sort of trophy. We paddled off. "Good luck!" he yelled. "Don't go too far." His binoculars swayed on the strap that hung from his neck.

I turned and watched my brother's freckling back as I paddled. For the first time in our lives he was almost as strong as I was. I really had to work to keep the boat in a straight line.

"Where do we go today, Joe?" he yelled back at me. "I want to catch a big one today."

"Let's go over there," I said. "Let's go around that point."

16

July 30, 1992–Tomorrow I'll begin a log, my first solo
cruise. I feel fairly confident, competent, although there's
many things I haven't faced, situations I can only grimace
at now. I've never yearned to be a macho solo sailor.
That's why I bought a boat that sleeps half a dozen. But
there's this free week, the boat, and the ocean, and the
summer's almost over for me here. Heather's in school
at Bates College for a dance seminar; Rob has to work;
so I'll go it alone this time. I'll feel better over the winter having made the voyage, all that water under my belt
and keel. I'd like to make South Bristol, return *Yonder* to
her birthplace, the old Gamage Yard. Food's aboard,
water, diesel, clothes, charts, and cash. I'm here too,
tucked in among the gear, ready for sleep, waiting on the
dawn that rises from water.

AND SO MY JOURNAL became my log, in the same way that a board becomes a raft: you simply throw it in the water.

Sunrise was at 5:29. That's when I woke and started *Yonder*'s engine. The rpm gauge seemed to stick momentarily and there was a whiff of burning rubber, but the odor quickly dispersed. I opened the engine hatch and everything seemed to be humming along. I switched on the loran and let it search for itself; I'm always surprised at how quick and steadfast it is in its conclusion. If only I could be so resolute. Refrigerator on. Fathometer on. Radio on and tuned to Channel 16 for Coast Guard reports. Seacocks to the head closed. With headway speed and seacocks open, the head filled to within an inch of the rim and the water slopped over onto the sole. I dropped the mooring pennant at 5:41 and with an ebbing tide and the engine at 2500 rpm, the loran showed *Yonder* making fifteen knots. I just made Memorial's scheduled opening and then throttled back to cruising speed.

At the entrance to the harbor I made a single orbit around a tiny plywood dinghy that was adrift, heading out to sea alone just like me. It was battered and torn, the bow eye ripped free. Most of her green enamel had weathered away, and gulls had often used the single thwart as a resting place. It seemed so forlorn, bobbing in the vast mouth of the ocean. But I soon broke away from her emotional gravity and headed out into deep water.

The day was clear for now, but cloudy on the horizon. *Yonder* pushed along with a repeatedly confident surge while I entered waypoints into the loran's memory as we passed buoys: 2KR at 6:31, York Harbor 7:25, Nubble Light 7:47. At the R2 bell off Cape Porpoise it began to rain and the calm surface of the sea buttoned up. I memorized the course and distance for the next two buoys and threw the charts below, and then put on foul-weather gear. Once I decided I wasn't going to beat the rain anywhere, my sense of martyrdom began to kick in and I started to enjoy myself. I was at sea alone in the rain. It wasn't a hurricane or even a steady downpour, but there was definite dripping off the brim of my cap, and my rain gear funneled water directly into my sneakers. I could have left the steering to the autopilot and stood in the relatively dry companionway, but visibility was poor there and I didn't want to end my first solo cruise by running into a buoy or another boat. Besides, the lobster buoys were everywhere and had to be dodged. So I stood at the helm in the rain, tuning a fine sense of my own seaworthiness. I was at sea, meeting and enduring the elements. I found it dismaying that putting my hands in my pockets to warm them had the opposite effect. It seemed the pockets of my foul-weather gear held water as well as repelled it. After an hour I realized the rain gear I'd bought at Eddie Bauer, while very fashionable, didn't actually repel water, only resisted it, and had at last given in. I was soaked through. I became quite chilled and looked for ice in the rigging. Water darkened the teak sole of the cockpit. Rain ran off the deck and fell into the ocean, donning the perfect disguise. I was surrounded by water. It pooled in the pores of my skin, dripped off my nose and eyelashes. From a few years spent on a farm in Kentucky I knew that turkeys could drown in the rain, and my father swore that pheasants and guinea chicks could drown in a heavy dew. I remembered my grandfather pinching closed his nostrils before he'd dip under water, and suddenly, twenty-five years later, I wondered why evolution put our nose and mouth so near one another, since one required water and the other suffocated in it. We should logically drink from our toes and breathe through our hair. We come so close to drowning every time we drink. I couldn't look up for an explanation because rain would fall in my nose, and I didn't want to drown like a turkey.

The coast, when I could see it through the sozzle, was spread out like a wet dishtowel on the counter, low and wrinkled, used and dropped. The grayness of the horizon had turned the green trees black and the white buildings green. I motored along, unable to recall any joke that would make me laugh, any success that would warm my hands, any revenge that left me able to snort in disdain. Then it began to rain really hard. I put both hands on the wheel and began to sing "Hosanna" from *Jesus Christ Superstar* as loudly as I could, sang to overcome the roar of the engine and the thrash of the smother. As I closed in on Cape Elizabeth I realized I was in new territory, and this lifted my spirits as well. I could now say, "Yes, I remember when I was off that sea-born Cape, entering Casco Bay in a driving rain . . ." and follow it up with some nautical tale of a boat through troubled waters. So then I sang, I kid you not, "Bridge Over Troubled Waters" as brightly as I could, such was my miserable existence.

Casco Bay was littered with debris: pallets, entire trees, plastic and glass bottles, shredded lobster buoys, a casement window complete with frame and crank. I weaved through this urban flotsam, intensely interested in each shattered board, tennis ball, and cigarette butt. If these were the only clues left me, what could I deduce? The city of Portland had suddenly sunk! I brought my fishing net up from below in case I came upon anything worth dipping. My scavenger heart beat faster as I neared Jewell and her shores, one side of the island facing the inner bay and the other the open sea. What treasures, I considered, could wash up there? The ocean was a carrier of the lost, and the only requirement was that the lost must float.

I'd forgotten the rain, and when it lost my attention, it had faded away. This always surprises me, when I realize I've missed something, something as obvious as the moment when water stops falling out of the sky.

I brought my charts back up from below and entered the harbor at Jewell Island carefully. Two boats were already at anchor. I dropped my forty-pound fisherman—my galvanized friend, as the Wizard called the Tin Man—overboard and let out far too much scope. That afternoon, as the tide dropped and the rain began anew, I continually had to go back out on deck to haul in another ten feet of line so I wouldn't fetch up on the scree of the narrow harbor.

I changed from my wet clothes, slipped on a pair of dry socks. I had the idea of pulling back the companionway steps so the heat off the engine could warm the cabin, but the fumes in the confined space were overpowering, so I simply put on more clothes. For a late lunch: a can of Dinty Moore chicken stew that I balanced in a hot pad over the blanket I'd curled up in. I wish I could concur with most happy campers and say it tasted like the finest meal at a four-star restaurant in Paris, but it tasted like a can of Dinty Moore chicken stew, no more, no less. As I sat there I worked on my log. I'd made the fifty nautical miles from Memorial Bridge in eight hours and ten minutes, for an average of 6.3 knots. Very respectable, I thought, especially since the wind was of no help whatsoever, but I really had nothing to compare this mark to. I ate, I read, I lit the twin kerosene lamps that bracketed the head door in the forward bulkhead. That was romantic. I blew them out. The wind that had been absent earlier in the day began to rise around three and built in gusts. I kept losing my place in the book I was reading. It told of Jewell Island, its tunnels, World War II observation towers, tidal pools. Wind fizzed through the ports, cackled in the halyards. I suddenly felt ill-prepared in my socks and so put my wet sneakers back on. Out on deck the teak was beginning to dry. Clouds scudded along, revealing sudden sweeps of pale blue sky. Rain sputtered, congealed, seemed more like sap fall or insect spit than rain, the drops so infrequent that they seemed lost. I checked the anchor one more time, bailed the rubber dinghy, and rowed to Jewell's rocky shore.

It seems to me that the greatest of explorers have been lonely people with little to lose. When they're lost they're at home, and moving on is as necessary as breathing. Jewell Island has been visited so often by cruising yachtsmen that trails vein its interior. But I'm lost the moment I step ashore, and it's vaguely unsettling. Even though I'd been lonely a few minutes before on *Yonder,* it now seemed I had much to lose. I looked back at the boat to make sure it wasn't sinking. There wasn't enough daylight left to reach for the far end of the mile-long island and its towers, gun emplacements, and bunkers. The windward shore was only a few hundred feet away, though, through an evergreen and birch forest. A trail two feet wide, rutted with erosion, flowed through pine needles, banks of moss, and rotting branches. Mosquitoes began to rise from the steaming compost. I waded through a thicket of beach roses and arrived, wet and somehow breathless, on a far shore, a round tidal pool known as the

Punchbowl before me, banked with great piles of wrack: drift logs, wounded buoys, seaweed, Bic lighters, and pale pink tampon tubes. I found a single aqua sandal, the track of a woman's heel and toes fossilized there, but couldn't think of a reason to carry it more than a few yards. I didn't think I'd ever find her. There was a huge beam, perhaps fourteen inches square and eighteen feet long. I prized it, made it mine by sitting on it for a moment, thought how awkward it would be to tow it all the way home. I picked up stones and sticks, considered them. The sea seemed to make all things fit snugly in a human hand. Shells tucked in my palm dropped free as if from a mold. Driftwood twined through my fingers like my own veins. I told myself to remember, If you're ever lonely again, get yourself to a beach, someplace where water meets rock, and wedge yourself among the wreckage and sand there, hold a smooth salty stone on your tongue so long that it feels like you've lost a tooth when you spit it out. I stayed long enough to watch the first wave of the rising tide reach the tidal pool. It left glistening rocks and then ripples reaching out across the still water. Soon the pool would be inundated, and the flotsam banked in the outer ledges would be carried in to join the rest of the discards here. Perhaps something would be taken away. At any event things would be changed, in the same way that dust blows down a hallway when you open the door. Things would never be the same again.

I walked back to the dinghy on a narrower, darker trail, root-ribbed and muddy. The trees were close around me; water still dripped from their branches. Simply by turning my body around, I'd switched my entire environment, as from one slide to the next. Instead of a broad expanse of cloud and water, there was an almost suffocating denseness of living material. What I heard was now wind, not water. Something sweetly rotted. After the day on the boat it seemed strange, the solid earth, all the time it took soil to move from one place, one shape, to another. The forest was in slow motion compared to the sea, and I felt like a fish jumping into the air as I crossed the narrow island, suffused with light for a moment but unable to stop falling.

I rowed the rubber sled to the mouth of the cove, spun around on one oar, and took a snapshot of *Yonder,* to prove that we'd both been this far, sailed to an uninhabited island. We were only a few miles from Portland, a city of a hundred thousand souls, and there were two other boats in the same harbor, but I still felt I'd been to an undiscovered country, which was both an island and a little unvisited part of myself. Like Columbus, I had known it was there, this way to not be afraid by immersing myself in my fear. That night a storm rose, and *Yonder* tipped and rocked over her anchor. I'd sleep ten minutes at a time and then throw off my blanket in a spasm of awakening, sure that I was on the rocks or scraping alongside one of the expensive yachts in the cove. I'd purchased insurance for this first season, presuming that I'd sink my boat, but the coverage for damaging another yacht wouldn't nearly be enough if I sank a gold-plater. I'd rise and look out the ports or stick my bare head up into the doghouse, scanning for any sign of another boat. The masts on my neighbors were so high, their anchor lights, blinking in the rain, seemed like pitiful stars to pin a hope to. High tide, a foot over average, was at midnight, and I was worried that I'd taken in too much scope the afternoon before. Every hour or so I'd shine my spotlight on each bank of the cove to make sure I was equidistant from them. I tried not to light up the other yachts, but once or twice the beam rode their sheers in what must have appeared from inside something like a prison break. Assured that I was still anchored, I used a dishtowel to wipe up a puddle at the base of the mast, listened to an updated weather forecast, and switched on the bilge pump till it soothingly sucked air. If I was successful at falling asleep, I didn't want the automatic bilge switch kicking on and booting me through the deck.

I woke at five-fifteen. The rain and wind had ceased. *Yonder* was so still, I couldn't tell if she was floating. Outside, someone had dropped a sheet over my boat, like a piece of furniture in a summer cottage. I hurriedly slipped on my shoes and barged my way on deck. Fog, dense as cold oatmeal. I was sure I'd dragged my anchor. The rode drooped into the water. Perhaps my galvanized friend had lost heart. I tugged till I felt, reassuringly, a tug in return. How often my worries and precautions had gone unrewarded with disaster. Finally, I made out the stern of one of the other boats and recognized a crooked birch on shore. I hadn't dragged, only swung around. Dawn arrived like an uncle who'd died years ago, and who still wasn't any more interesting. I went back to bed for some sound sleep at last.

I woke at eight to a faint "Hulloa." There was a little plastic tub with a man in it off *Yonder*'s stern. His oars, if you could call them that, were plastic too, and all of three and a half feet long. But they were longer than his boat.

"Morning," I said, and ran my finger comb through my hair while water worked up through my socks.

"Crocker design?" he asked.

Fog still lingered, but I could see the shore now, the two boats I'd anchored behind and a third that came in after dark. The man was about sixty, wore a baby-blue golfing cap, a V-necked T-shirt, and khaki slacks. The line of his jaw was hard-chined. I could tell that he was similar to my father in that he'd been up for at least three hours. He'd put it off as long as possible, but the day was slipping away and I had to be awakened. His "Hulloa" reminded me of my father yelling up the stairs when I was a child.

"No," I answered. "John Alden, built up at the Gamage Yard in South Bristol."

"You don't say. John Alden. I would have bet anybody Sam Crocker drew her up." He did a little double oar-dip spin in his dinghy to realign himself with the truth. He sat on the only thwart. Under his feet was his bailer, a plastic coffee cup that announced he was "Born to Boat." "Well, she's real smart," he said. "Just what a fellow wants." This made me smile. "What kind of power?"

"Used to be a Gray, I think, but she's had a Westerbeke 58 for the last ten years."

"That ought to push her along."

"Well, she's got a sail, but she doesn't sail too well." This was a lie. It was me, not *Yonder,* who didn't sail well. "She does about seven knots under power." This was a lie by seven tenths of a knot. He'd woken me up and I hadn't put my morals on yet.

84

"That's good enough. It must be nice to push along like that in a calm. I'll bet she's solid too, heavy."

"The surveyor estimated eighteen thousand pounds."

"No!" he scoffed.

I shrugged. "Three thousand pounds of ballast."

"Still," he said, leaving his mouth open. "You probably didn't know there was a storm last night, boat that solid. We bounced all over the harbor." He nodded toward a thirty-two-foot fiberglass sloop.

"I threw out a fairly big anchor, so I slept fairly well."

"How big?"

"A forty-pound fisherman." I threw a forty-pound fisherman out because the only other anchor I had weighed sixty pounds.

"That would do it," he said. And, dipping his oars, he closed the conversation with "Nice boat, nice boat."

I nodded and scratched my forearms, thinking I'd handled that pretty well. He hadn't used any nautical terminology I was unfamiliar with, and I'd remembered the name and size of my engine.

The fog didn't lift till eleven, so I spent the morning mounting *Yonder's* carved escutcheon. I had to work from the dinghy, which is an unfortunate platform when you're trying to mount a board square and level on another floating object. The people on the other boats had nothing to do but drink coffee, so I had an audience. I tried to coordinate my movements in a way that might intimate I'd built the boat and was just now applying this finishing touch. I'd built an entire house in Texas without once using my ear as a pencil holder, but it seemed appropriate now. Yep, just tick off a few lofting lines here, line up that bevel, plane her down, bed it, screw it, eleven coats of varnish. Even in the fog the gold leaf shone brilliantly:

YONDER
Eliot, ME

I could have put "Fort Worth, Texas," on the stern but that would have been boasting.

The fog finally lifted, and in almost coordinated movements boats started engines, weighed anchors, and left Cocktail Cove in a little nautical parade of swizzle-stick masts. I waved at the man who'd rowed over in his five-gallon bucket, and waved at the crew who strained to make out *Yonder*'s new name board.

My anchor had come up carrying a scoop of foul-smelling black mud on one fluke. Since I didn't want to use the deck as a microscope slide to analyze the contents of this mud, I let the anchor hang in the water for a few hundred yards as *Yonder* made way: an advantage of anchors hung from the tip of the pulpit. I noticed other yachts sloshing bucket after bucket of salt water over their decks, putting the seabed back where it belonged. The only drawback to washing an anchor off the bow is it's easy to forget and you might snag a buoy. The only other drawback is trying to stow the anchor in a chop between the northern tip of Jewell Island and a rock called West Brown Cow. The waves were so steep here, I was afraid my galvanized friend would smash the pulpit or rip free the pulley mounted there. I put the engine in neutral and stumbled forward, clutching the lifelines. The bow rose and fell, dipping the anchor and five feet of chain and then snapping it back up into the air. Placing my weightiest object, my butt, on the deck, I hauled in the chain and locked it under a bit. The anchor now hung directly off the pulpit but wouldn't do any harm. I decided to wait till I reached calmer waters to lodge it in its chocks. By the time I crawled back to the helm, the boat was wallowing in the waves, the tip of the mast, in a sickening reversal, performing like an upside-down pendulum. With great pleasure I applied power and turned *Yonder*'s plumb bow back into the waves.

For the first time since I'd owned her, real spray glossed the decks. Cutting across the bay to Mackerel Cove at the tip of Bailey Island, the waves rolled into the starboard bow, and *Yonder* cut into them, then rose almost unwillingly. I scotched myself behind the wheel, held on with both hands and the soles of my sneakers. As we crested each wave, I could see other boats heading out under bare poles as there was little or no wind, just the six- and seven-foot waves coming in doubled over from the east. It took little more than an hour

86

to reach Mackerel Cove Marina, tucked among wharves stacked high with lobster traps. I threaded through the many moored boats and docked at the fuel pumps alone, jumping off the boat and cleating the bow and stern lines. This was the first time I'd ever done this, and after jumping back aboard to cut the engine, I awaited the dockmaster and his congratulations. There had been a slot perhaps twice *Yonder*'s length to negotiate and I had come in, cutting and applying power, wheel hard over, to parallel park. Now *Yonder* sat patiently, sighing and pursing her lips, waiting for the dockmaster and his congratulations. I waited five minutes, ten minutes. A man with his hands shoved in his pockets as if he didn't own them came down and looked at my boat but didn't say anything. I looked at the lobster boats in the tight harbor, many with steadying sails set. That looked neat. Must get some strong weather here, I thought. The man with stolen hands finally left. I waited some more. Finally, I walked up the gangway to a grill and asked the two waitresses where I might find the dockmaster. They looked at one another and each gave a hoot, as if they'd just stomped on packages of mustard and ketchup respectively. The older one yelled, "Billy, you're dockmaster today," and the dishwasher forced his way through swinging doors in a wet white apron. He was at most twelve. With some reluctance he turned on the pumps and helped me fill up. For a twelve-year-old he was awfully quiet. Maybe it was because I embarrassed him, calling him "dockmaster." I gave him my credit card, and he took this as an insult too. Am I downeast already, I wondered. I'd read stories about fishing harbors where they liked to kick old bait down on sailboat decks.

From the pay phone in front of the grill I called Beverly to let her know where I was, where I'd spent the night. She and Rob had driven to Biddeford Pool the evening before to see if I'd anchored there again. My dad had called her, worried, and I was to report to him at my next stop. "I'm fine," I told her. "Everything's beautiful. Don't worry."

As I motored out of the harbor the last haze of the morning's fog dispersed. At the gong marking Turnip Island Ledge the rollers seemed to have increased in size and frequency. I followed two other sailboats slogging under bare poles across the bay toward Cape Small. The waves weren't wind-pushed. *Yonder's* pennant atop her mast only moved as the boat dipped and rose. Every other wave sewed a long thin white hem to its crest. I watched Ragged and Mark Islands bob by on the starboard and was pleased for my old boat to catch up with and pass the two plastic sailboats, which were obviously having a much worse time of it. I hadn't left the helm for over an hour. The footing was too insecure. Spray spattered the raised deck and ran in tears off the doghouse windows. At the crest of bigger waves *Yonder* would consider the possibility of losing steerage and then give the idea up and stay on course.

As I approached Cape Small, perhaps a half mile to sea, I heard a bright pop, a balloon burst. I looked off at one of the sailboats I'd passed. The sound could have been a sail slapping open. *Yonder* fell below the horizon and then became part of it. It was the roughest water I'd ever been in, and the helm required constant management. Then smoke billowed from the starboard locker. I throttled down. The chest-type Norcold refrigerator was in this locker and I thought the compressor must be on fire. I jumped to the companionway and released the catch on the extinguisher mounting and then switched off the breaker to the Norcold. When I opened the locker lid, extinguisher ready, I realized the smoke was steam. Mounted in a corner of the locker was the plastic overflow container for the engine's freshwater cooling system. The pop I'd heard was the pressure of the steam blowing off the screw-on cap. The engine was hot and before I could get across the six feet of cockpit to the ignition switch, the engine was screaming. Already *Yonder* began to lurch in the swells. I went below, yanked the companionway steps and attached bulkhead away to reveal the front of the diesel. More steam, the blanched, sweet odor of hot antifreeze, and beneath this odor the rising stench of burnt rubber. I stepped back up into the cockpit and lifted the two-by-four-foot engine hatch and almost fell on the engine as *Yonder* stumbled. The heavy hatch, which under normal circumstances leaned at a forty-five-degree angle against the locker, came flying back at me. I leaped out of the way as it slammed shut. *Yonder* lay broadside to the rollers now, wallowed in the troughs. Down below, the lockers beneath the sink and stove swung open and a week's food tumbled to the sole. Pretzels and grapes slid back and forth with each wave. I opened the engine hatch again and tied it back with a short piece of line. Enough light now, and I could see that the alternator belt, which also ran the water pumps, had shredded. Why hadn't my overheating alarm warned me? I had a spare belt. I worked below, squatting in the skidding pretzels and soup cans. It was difficult because the engine was very hot and every time I placed my hands near it the boat rolled and I burned my palms trying not to fall. Soon I was sick, inhaling the burned rubber and boiling antifreeze, and just barely made it to the rail to discharge breakfast. I distinctly remember thinking at the time, So this is what it's like to be seasick. It was as if someone were forcing a wet sock down my throat. As I worked I repeatedly rose, braced myself in the companionway, and judged the distance between *Yonder* and the rocks off Cape Small. The tide was coming in and the waves were working from the south and east, so I knew it was just a matter of time.

So perhaps you know I lived through this episode since this narrative is written in the first person. You're a literary detective. You're the husband rolling his eyes in the theater, whispering to your crying wife that you know he's going to make it: who could tell the story if he didn't make it? But this is only a beginning, and the end may yet be a trailing line, a blotch of ink, a series of dots, a note added by the publisher. Perhaps, and this is a personal nightmare, I've met my end and my wife has hired someone to finish my book. This very sentence could be my last. Perhaps I haven't been here from the start: writing in the first person has become a popular technique in biography.

The belt was changed, and I spilled two gallons of fresh water over the engine, managing to pour some of it into the filler neck. I crawled across the cockpit to the ignition, desperate to get under way, to turn the bow to the waves and ride them instead of being puked by them. I turned the key; the engine screamed. It screamed like a continual stomping of boots on the paws of cats and dogs. I cursed, turned off the engine, and kicked the locker. I checked to make sure the belt I'd installed wasn't too tight or too loose, then started the engine again. It shrieked. "What, what, what?" I yelled, and turned it off again. I didn't know it at the time, but a molded hose had burst and the water pump was ruined. The fluorescent green slick in the bilge should have given me some clue, but I was not only sick and stupid, but frightened. In any case there was no way I could repair the engine at sea.

I looked toward Cape Small and it didn't seem any closer than it had an hour earlier. This seemed strange. Would it be worse to be carried out to sea? I wondered. What was unacceptable was to remain broadside to the waves. At this point, in such close proximity to the two conditions, I realized how much more enjoyable it was to be frightened than to be sick, and I thought I would never again be afraid of fear, since sickness was so much more debilitating. I'd always heard that once you threw up, the seasickness would subside. But I discovered this was a damned lie. My tongue felt like a baggy-wrinkle. I looked at my charts, at my guide to the coast. The nearest boat yards were in Sebasco Harbor. On the very page of the coastal guide describing Sebasco was a photo of a sailing ship on the rocks at Cape Elizabeth. This was confidence-bolstering. I could have tried to sail to the harbor, but there was almost no wind, and I was so inexperienced, I knew I'd put *Yonder* in danger. The idea that I could sail up to a dock or mooring was so remote that I barely recognized it. I actually said aloud, "I need some help," and I picked up the mike to the radio and hailed both boat yards in Sebasco. Neither answered. It was a Saturday afternoon and no one seemed to be working. I was on the verge of calling the Coast Guard, but I knew they wouldn't send a boat out unless my life was at risk. I scanned the area for other boats. There was a small luffing sail, like a sheet hanging from a clothesline by one pin, far out to sea. I hailed both boat yards again, and then I began to consider the possibility that my radio wasn't working. I called, "Is anybody out there?" *La Vida,* out of Cape Elizabeth, returned my call. They were on a mooring at Sebasco Harbor and offered to tow me in. I readied my anchor line as a tow rope. It seemed to take them bare minutes to arrive, a big powerful sport-fishing boat that threw off broad sheets of spray as she charged through the waves. When they saw the boat lying ahull and me pitching around on the pulpit with the anchor line, they suggested I don a life preserver in case I was thrown overboard. It chagrined me that I hadn't thought of this. It chagrined me to be rescued. There was a family aboard *La Vida,* an older man at the helm, his wife at the radio, and what could have been two sons in their late twenties in the stern. They backed in on *Yonder's* lee, but the water was too rough; *Yonder* lurched dangerously toward their transom. One of the younger men took the helm and moved their boat bow to weather and backed in toward *Yonder's* port side. I couldn't throw my anchor line because the heavy galvanized thimble in the eye splice might injure. They had to come in close enough so I could drop the line over their outstretched boathook. After two attempts we accomplished this. I let out sixty feet of line as they motored slowly away and then cleated it off. *Yonder* swung heavily around, yawing for a few moments in the following seas, but soon became accustomed to her tow. I sat and watched the vibrating line dip into the crest of a wave and then shake off the water like a dog. My stomach was still uneasy and before we entered the calmer waters of Sebasco, I performed my penance, a blanching set of dry heaves, vomiting nothing but pride.

It took two turns around a mooring to snare it with my boathook. Once *Yonder* was safely tied to the earth on her raised deck, I stood, quivering, spread my arms like a cormorant drying his wings, or like someone being crucified, and yelled at the crew of *La Vida,* "How can I ever thank you?" I was as grateful as anyone who's ever been saved.

They yelled back, "We'll be out there someday. You can tow us in." I'd been rescued by gracious people.

Soon a launch approached from Sebasco Lodge. I paid a mooring fee and John gave me a ride down the cove to H & H Boatworks. The employees were having a picnic in the yard, and we made plans to tow the boat down to their shop Monday morning for repair. John dropped me off with words of encouragement. "There's showers and phones at the snack bar, and you can leave your dinghy at the float as long as you'd like. You really couldn't have broken down at a better place."

With *Yonder* safely moored, preparations for her repair made, and once again alone, I stumbled below and collapsed on a bunk. There seemed to be bile in every area of my body except my stomach. One eye was jammed into a pillow, but with the other I could see that almost everything I'd carefully stowed was now in the sole. Smashed pretzels and grapes formed an unlikely cake in the galley. A jar of spaghetti sauce had managed to roll the complete length of the cabin and burst against the head. All my tools, coated with grease and belt dust, were lying in the bilge, rusting. I lay down for five minutes of self-pity, but it wouldn't work. There were still things to be done. Disasters provide the raw material to overcome them by leaving such a mess.

I rowed in, searched out the pay phones, and called Rob and Beverly. Yes, they'd come rescue me, bring me home by land. Rob knew right where Sebasco Lodge was. "Call your father," Beverly said. "He's called again already."

"Okay," I said.

"I knew it, I knew it," Dad said. "I knew something was wrong. I felt it."

And I believed him, and I was grateful in a way.

"Do you need anything?" he asked.

"No, Rob and Beverly are on their way to pick me up. I'm going to go back out to the boat and clean up the mess. Then I'll have a shower and wait. Everything's fine. I'm going to have them check the engine over completely."

Dad tried to fix the engine over the phone. "Another chewed-up belt? Maybe the alternator is out of alignment with the other pulleys. Make sure they look at that. I just knew something was wrong. You shouldn't go out alone."

There was some solace in placing a can of soup back in its rightful place, rinsing and drying my tools, stowing my stomach. I locked *Yonder* up after looking stonily at the engine one more time. My emotions slinked from shame to embarrassment to relief. Why wasn't I smart enough to fix it, brave enough to sail? My first season had finished at the bitter end of a tow rope. I rowed in with my kit bag to a cold shower.

In the common area of Sebasco Lodge's showers, I dried my feet and slipped on clean socks. My shoes were finally dry from . . . could it be only yesterday's rain? It felt good to comb my wet hair, organize what part of the world I could.

I bought a Pepsi from a machine and walked in the dark through the cabins toward the registration office, where I'd await my in-laws. On the way I chanted a little mantra that's always made me feel better, even though it's been ten years since I've seen a classroom. "There's no school tomorrow," I said aloud, over and over. "There's no school tomorrow." Strange, how my eight-year-old heart and mind still lived and struggled in my thirty-three-year-old body.

17

~

WHEN I WAS SIXTEEN, my family moved to a farm in central Kentucky. Across the county was Harrod's Lake, formed by the dammed Dix River. Sinuous and deep, its banks tree-lined and steep, the lake seemed wild and unexplored. I rented a fourteen-foot aluminum boat and outboard motor there one Sunday, and the only difference in this boating story and all the others before it was the girl on the bow. The wind blew strands of her long hair into her open mouth. Later that day I returned the skiff to the marina, the gas tank half empty and an almost imperceptible dent in the bow where we'd beached on a far shore.

> *Wash me in the water*
> *That you washed the colonel's daughter*
> *And I shall be whiter*
> *Than the whitewash on the wall.*
> —Popular song of British Troops
> in France, 1914–18

18

W HAT WE HAVE FROM the past are the countless individual decisions of our parents to bear and raise children. Almost every one of us, for millions of years now, has determined the future can be risked, that hope and care are enough.

When the boatyard called a few days later and said *Yonder* was ready, my father offered to fly up and crew for me on the cruise home, but I was able to tell him that my father-in-law had already signed on, that I wouldn't be out there alone. This gave him some solace, until I said we'd be cruising in the dark, an all-nighter from Sebasco Harbor to Eliot. Rob's done it many times before, I assured him. It's probably safer than cruising in daylight: fewer boats to collide with. And we wouldn't be too near any islands or capes. We'd sail far off the shore.

"Just don't fall overboard," Dad said. "Call me when you get home."

"Okay." I was thirty-three years old, but there was no question that he was within his rights.

Heather dropped Rob and me off at seven-thirty Friday evening; then she was off again for her last week at school. I couldn't continue downeast because friends were coming in and afterward there'd be only a few days left to prepare for the drive home to Texas. Rob liked night cruising, and he'd still have the remainder of the weekend to work on his boat, a twenty-seven-foot St. Pierre dory.

I was shown my sparkling red engine by one of the staff at the boatyard, who had kindly stayed late to wait for us. They'd discovered a hairline crack on the backside of the crankshaft pulley; this had been chewing up my belts. The freshwater pump was replaced, the raw-water pump had needed a new impeller, the alternator was gone through, the glow plugs pulled and new ones planted, the starter solenoid healed. In addition, every hose had been replaced. All scale and rust had been scraped off and the engine repainted. I paid my bill up at the boat shed. This is a large building used for repairing boats indoors and for containing the screams of stunned young captains.

"You probably weren't expecting it to be this much," he said.

The bill was sixteen hundred dollars: eleven hundred in labor and five hundred in parts, paint, and miscellaneous rags. "But the boat was only here for four days," I said.

"Our labor rate is thirty-two dollars an hour. Everything we did needed to be done."

"You're right," I said. "I don't want to go out in an unsafe boat." Still, I shook my head in a way that wasn't very good-natured. I'm learning to sail, I thought. This will be a good incentive. And I'm going to learn to work on a diesel engine. And I'm going to carry a spare engine in the forward locker.

We walked back down to the dock and this very same man helped Rob and me cast off. "Watch your new hoses," he said. "They may need retightening."

The engine started without the usual dose of WD-40. I steered out around Harbor Island while Rob coiled lines forward. The alternator gauge needle seemed to be exploring new territory on its dial. The engine hatch didn't vibrate as it used to and there was none of that peculiar pinging I'd grown enamored of. Rob returned from the raised deck with two lines that didn't belong to me. Ha, ha, I win, I thought. A few minutes later, off Flag Island, I discovered that one of my new spring lines was missing. Still one ahead, I thought, less gleefully.

I told Rob about the bill and he winced, shook his head, and said, "Well, it's a short season."

"I think I'll take a course in diesel engine repair," I said, thinking about my bright red and smoothly humming Westerbeke. I don't know why I make my most sincere decisions to diet while on a full stomach.

Outside Mark Island Ledge, with the day's light waning, I set the autopilot for 24YL, a buoy off Portsmouth Harbor. There was only water and Boon Island between the two points. The water hardly resembled its former self, its cover a chop that I could make in a bathtub. Boon Island, on the other hand, had been sinking ships since rocks learned how. Miles off the coast in open water, its low shores are now marked with a 133-foot granite lighthouse. Even though we were almost forty miles away, I began a careful search.

By nine o'clock the day had backed out of the door and fallen off the porch. The moon before us was three-quarters, the color of a peach, blotched like a child's cold cheeks. It was my first night passage. We strained to see man-made points of light, Halfway Rock and then the monster buoy off Cape Elizabeth. As the moon descended, the sea reflected its light in shards, as if it were a dish flung on the floor. I liked the way all this light led to *Yonder*. Yet even with all this, the moon, stars, beacons, we seemed to remain in darkness. The lights from shore reached out to us but always fell just short. We were more distant. We were in a darkness that swallowed light with a liquid gurgle.

I sat at the helm for the first three hours, watching the engine gauges till they became like little moons, faraway, imponderable. I shut my eyes as tight as the valve of a barnacle. I opened them and the peachy moon skidded from the sky but never bounced. All that remained was a vast and random placement of stars, cold as the buttons of an old doll's eyes. It actually hurt to think about them, how indifferent they were to me and my boat.

Later Rob and I set the autopilot and then took shelter behind the raised deck. Even though it was mid-August, the fifty-four-degree sea was in control of all the weather within ten feet of its surface. I wore a long-sleeved shirt over a T-shirt, and over these a sweater, a windbreaker, a coat, and a blanket. I heated water in a teapot on the propane stove, and in the darkness the gas flaming around the edges of the round pot looked like a total solar eclipse.

The instant cocoa burned my tongue but felt good on my palms. I thought about how rare this night was, my presence in it on a boat at sea. It's hard to consider life when it's lived so close to your eyes. There's so much of it, from the peripheral to the point-blank, that I'm never sure whether I should try to focus on my nose or Venus, and hold my hand up between the two as a reference and guide, but am always disappointed to find that this compass points in five different directions. I tried to remember that *Yonder* churned forward with something similar to purpose on a course that I had set, but when I raised my head and peered over the deck, my eyes watered. What's out there? Some moments seem angular, specific, and others are embedded in wool. Everything's rare, I tried to remind myself. I found something hard in my cocoa, a nugget, a copper morsel from my old water tank, and spat it out, something solid into the night.

Something clunked against the hull, and I looked up at Rob.

"Lobster buoy," he said. "That's one thing about night cruising: you can't dodge the buoys."

"What do we do?"

"We don't worry about them."

"What if we hit a big log, low in the water?"

"How could we avoid it?"

"We just blunder along?"

"Joseph," he said, using *Joseph* as he always does, whenever I seem to be falling over an edge, "we'll have an answer for that."

He doesn't (I almost write the word *evaporate*) continue. This kind of unbalanced confidence is maddening. "What answer?" I asked.

"Joseph, only the circumstances can provide the answers. You have to wait for them." He looked like a white-haired Maine Buddha, huddled in the cockpit corner under a blanket.

"I'm just not experienced enough," I said. I've always been exasperated by the fact that experience requires experience, that reading and imagination can't be substituted, that lead can't be turned into gold, that girls aren't as easily kissed as mirrors.

We cleaved through dark water and it bled a white foam that congealed and puddled off our stern. Alongside, plankton glowed with a disturbed green phosphorescence. There was a splash to starboard, another, a splash to port. I stepped up on the raised deck for a better look. Between the pulpit and the tabernacle was an entrance to a netherworld. I tripped over this hatch. Something splashed again as I fell on the deck, then never again splashed.

Between one and three A.M. we listened to a one-sided conversation between the Portland Coast Guard and a woman in Cocktail Cove at Jewell Island, where I'd spent the night exactly one week before. (Between one and three that night I'd been lying awake listening to the wind and rain, occasionally rising to check my position.) We could hear only the Coast Guard operator, a young man, precise, orderly, running down a list of requirements. He asked the woman repeatedly to spell the name of her boat. He told her to put a life jacket on. We understood that she was on a yacht, anchored safely, but that her husband had fallen ill, some sort of attack. The Coast Guard got in touch with the sick man's doctor, and the radio operator relayed the doctor's questions. Where is the pain? How long ago? Is there blood in the urine? Finally, finally, a decision was made to send out a fast boat to bring the sick man into a Portland hospital. That's the last we heard. We motored out of range, or the Coast Guard switched to another channel. I continued to look at our radio expectantly, for some word, a sigh of relief. But there was only static, an occasional call for a radio check, a fisherman searching for a catch. Rob and I shook our heads and wondered. And I realized that for a while at least, I had been the old woman in Cocktail Cove, on a yacht she knew nothing about, her husband moaning at her feet. I identified with the person I could not hear. Preparation is a slow weaving through minutes placed like traffic cones before us one at a time. Every minute is distinct, unusual, unique. How can we not be afraid? Every minute is hollow, expected, another dog hair on the couch. How can we not be bored? How can all be unique and common at the same time? An eclipse, for all its rarity, is a daily event, with coronas called dusk and dawn. Beautiful and ordinary, the minutes drop into place like periwinkle shells on a beach, irreplaceable yet easily displaced. Who can tell which is important, which to save, which explains the next?

By the time we were abeam of Boon Island there was a faint light in the east. It reminded me of the way the day before began, the way most days begin, hushed and unsure. It wavered as if it might not happen. At the mouth of Portsmouth Harbor the sun rose and followed us up the river. As we dipped under the trinity of bridges, the morning, gathering confidence, leapt them. By the time we arrived at Hutton's Landing, the sun was already there, drying the dew from the weathered lumber of the dock. It was good to have my old boat back on her mooring, safe.

It was still early in Texas, so I decided to sleep for a couple of hours before calling home. I was awakened, unsure of where I was for an unrecognizable moment, by the distant ringing of a phone in a hallway. It was noon already. Rob, still in his pajamas, pushed open my door a few inches and said, "It's your father."

I moved slowly out into the hallway, rubbing my eyes, and picked up the strange lightness of a modern telephone.

"Dad," I said.

"Son, I was up all night worrying about you." He paused, and I could hear, even through my grogginess, his voice rising with relief and happiness and pride as he said, "You made it."

This one, this one, this moment, I thought, taking the phone, already heavy and slick, in both my hands.

19

DURING MY SOPHOMORE YEAR of college my family moved back home to Fort Worth. My grandparents didn't live on the lake anymore, but my parents compensated by purchasing a house in Lake Country Estates (no estates there) on Eagle Mountain Lake (no eagles and certainly no mountains there), a subdivision with access rights to an asphalt launching ramp. Because we didn't have a boat, the ramp seemed a dubious luxury: a little road that led underwater, an invitation impossible to accept on foot.

Yet behind the new house itself was a private man-made lake in the shape of a kidney, and because its concrete bottom was painted blue it seemed bottomless. It came with a diving board, a curved slide, heated, filtered, and chemically treated water, and a shoreline of blue and orange tile. Instead of a gravel beach, graduated steps; rather than rain, a running garden hose. Chlorine tablets scooted across the surface, and an algae sweep roamed the bottom. My mother caught leaves like butterflies, with a net on a ten-foot pole, before they could freckle the pool's surface. It didn't seem to matter that the water burned your eyes or tasted like the inside of a pill bottle: it was clear. It contained no sharks. But when our dog refused to drink from it, refused even to approach its nubbly banks, I should have realized it was his way of advising caution.

At a summer pool party, twenty members of the family were in the water, and twenty sat in lawn chairs that had broken free from the cocoons they'd been in since my grandparents moved from the lake. I stood poised on the diving board and told my cousin Bobby to move the inner tube farther away. We'd made a contest of diving through its black rubbery maw. Distance was now a determining factor. I leaped, felt victory in the forgiving embrace of a truck tube and an instant later my skull struck bottom. These were much shallower waters than I'd thought. I was immediately outraged, because there, underwater, something had happened. I couldn't move.

I WALKED THE SHORELINE of Eagle Mountain Lake after my accident searching for meaning, gathering up its shattered and weathered remnants in my arms. I searched for proof of a previous existence, or at the very least a life of experience, exposure to the wind and sun. Everything I collected had spent time with water, had the ability to float, and might have been carried off again at the next flood. So these planks, bits of lumber, molding, and broomstick—and I— came together at the only time in the history of the planet possible, between rains. I filled the trunk of my car with short pieces of board, stumps of posts, boxcar siding, a closet rod. A doorknob floated in on a wrecked door. I brought home a garboard, a broken rudder, a gray window sill, a length of barn siding, yellow cabinetry, cedar shingles light as dead wasps. Longer lumber protruded from the trunk, hung from the mirrors and antennas, draped over the windshield like stiff bangs. I required a great deal of material because I could only use the essence, the most telling feature of each board. The rest I burned in my folks' fireplace.

AFTER I STRUCK the concrete, I could see quite clearly the blue bottom, my brother's and my cousin's legs. I could hear muted voices and the aggravated noise of waters, splashing, jetting, dripping. The very top of my head hurt: each follicle of hair felt like a beesting. I was suspended in the water but realized I was floating toward the surface, that there was some opportunity I should take advantage of. Yet I had no idea of what it might be. Gosh, my head hurt. Look, I thought, there's my hand. What's it doing over there?

USING A HANDSAW, I cut one to four inches off the end of each board till I had a garage floor piled high with weathered butts. Except for a few short sections of lumber retaining old paint, everything else was scrap. My parents, brother, and sister wandered out to my studio occasionally and asked about my intentions. I told them all I knew: "I'm going to paint a piece of plywood, about two feet by four feet, black. Then I'm going to glue all these butt ends across it."

"Oh," they said, and went on their way, as if I'd told them I was changing the oil in my car. I'm not sure what I was about. I'd come close to death before—car wrecks, falls from heights—but nothing had ever made me resort to a glue gun. It would be thematically convenient to conjecture I was trying to build a boat, but there was no utilitarian aspect to this construct but the construction itself. The process of placing the worn knuckles of wood in random patterns on the black backdrop was pleasing. Each butt seemed to have as much character as a human face. The exposed tree rings were furrowed, the softer summer pulp having weathered more deeply. A knot in the end of a board reminded me of a child dying. The way each butt shadowed or hid in the shadow of the one next to it added meaning, defied time, made memories. As I worked, our dog, Zeke, lay on the garage floor and gnawed a butt to pass the time. When he was through I added this bone to my collage.

I REMEMBER COUGHING and the force of my coughing pushing my face up from the water. At the same moment my toes scraped on the rough concrete below me and involuntarily flexed. I looked up as I began to sink again, and my aunt Melody, the very same who knew a spoonful of water, said, "Oh, look, he's making a funny face," and then she and my mother both screamed at my cousin. In the middle of his name I sank back underwater. Then the water was dripping from the roof of the world and I was being lifted up and carried from the pool. My older cousin, Bobby, who'd always wrestled me to exhaustion as a child in my grandmother's St. Augustine grass, now laid me gently down on the concrete at my mother's feet.

"I'm okay, Mom," I said.

Everyone yelled, "Don't move him! Don't let him move!" My spine prickled and then a wave of emotion billowed through me. I lifted my arm and wiped the water from my face.

"Joe Alan, just be still," my mother ordered. I moved my feet, flexed my knee. "What did I just tell you?" she asked.

Someone had called an ambulance.

"You shouldn't move," Grandma told me, and sat down, placing her palm on my scalp.

"It tingles," I said, and smiled. "I'm okay."

My skinny mother, who's as graceful and calm as a heron in an emergency, sat down in the puddling water on my other side and said, "We'll just wait."

Phil, his hair slick on his head, leaned over, put his hands on my knees and said, "Hey, look, Joe, all the water's draining out of the pool."

"Very funny."

The ambulance arrived; a brace was fastened around my neck. I was carried from the house on a gurney, the first journey I'd ever made by this mode of transportation. My father, such was his luck, drove up just as the ambulance pulled away from our house, lights flashing.

My neck was sore, my fingertips a bit numb, but a variety of X rays and probing questions resulted in only a prescription for pain medication. I was allowed, after some three hours, to sit up on the gurney. My parents were warned to watch me carefully for the next twenty-four hours. But for the thickness of my skull, my name would have been written in water.

Is GLUING TRASH together a way to not die? Then why did I feel a little death when I finished my collage? And why again, years later, does it give me a queer sense of overcoming to look at it suspended on my library wall, this great dusty hulk of dry rot, a week's desperate beachcombing? I like to think that should there ever be another deluge, my piece would once again float, much like Queequeg's casket, and carry me to safety.

FINALLY BACK HOME from the hospital, I walked into the bathroom, still in my swim trunks. There in the mirror was the absolute riot of my hair, stiff with chlorine, styled by a gurney, a straw broom attacked by a dog. I reached up and touched it gingerly. This, I thought, is what I'd have looked like if I'd drowned. This, I thought, is what I look like when I don't drown.

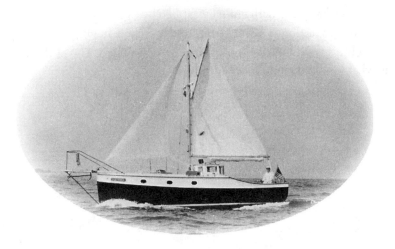

20

ON OUR LAST DAY aboard for the season, Heather and I took pictures of Old Salty, a downeast doll who once steered *Covenant,* Heather's grandfather's yacht. Old Salty's foul-weather gear was beginning to crack and flake away, but he still looked at home at the helm, happy to be at a wheel again after a fifteen-year hiatus. After we'd snapped the pictures and taken all the stale pretzels, rusty-bottomed tin cans, and ill-considered bottles of diet root beer off the boat, I stood in the cockpit as if I were lost. I couldn't seem to think of what to do next. I had to step into the dinghy sometime. There was still so much good weather left in the season. "Is that everything?" I asked Heather. She said yes, as if this were obvious. Rob would handle the haul-out later in the fall. I'd locked everything down, removed anything that might rot, closed the seacocks. It seemed as if I'd learned so little. I sighed and jumped overboard, but landed in a rubber boat.

At the float I looked back at *Yonder* and remembered we didn't have any photos of her with the sails set. I rowed back out and raised the sails, leaving Heather ashore snapping pictures. It was slack tide, and there was a good wind. *Yonder* yawed and jerked at her mooring, like a horse in the starting gates. Soon the wind stiffened, or the tide changed, and suddenly with sails and rode taut, I was sailing alone around the mooring.

On the long drive home we stopped in Raleigh to see Granny and Skipper, showing them the photos of Old Salty at *Yonder*'s helm. Heather's grandparents lived in a retirement community, but their boating memories were fresh, *Covenant* still in a frame in the hallway. We talked about the *QE II* running aground off Massachusetts that summer. It reminded Skipper of a boat story of his own.

Covenant lost her engine in the middle of Long Island Sound and had to be towed into port. Skipper, a former navy captain, still tasted the bile of this incident on his tongue. Shamefully, I relished this story. Then I said, "But *Covenant* was a fifty-two-foot Hatteras. You had two engines."

"That was the second *Covenant*," Skipper said. "The first was a thirty-four-footer, with only the one engine. Which is why we bought the second *Covenant*. I wanted a spare engine."

"Exactly." I beamed.

Sitting on Granny's couch, I turned to Heather. "I could take one more cruise. In a couple weeks when I've caught the business up. Maybe bring Phil or Dad up for a week's cruise."

"Sure," she said.

"I'd feel so much better about it over the winter," I said.

Skipper said, "Our cruising days are over, I'm afraid."

Granny put her narrow hand on his forearm. "But we don't have anything to complain about. We've been around the world twice on cruise ships."

When we left, I kissed Granny on the cheek, and for the first time since I'd known him, I hugged Skipper.

Back in Texas, I mistook water towers for lighthouses, stood on the edge of sidewalks as if they were docks, and rubbed my eyes when I saw lobster buoys bobbing in the cattle tank. Dad and Sally had brought them home for souvenirs.

IT REQUIRED ONLY a few bare seconds of thought for Dad and my mother's brother, my uncle Tommy, to commit to a week's cruise. Our goal would be the Gamage Yard at South Bristol, *Yonder*'s birthplace. We descended into Boston on a Super 80 three weeks later. A schooner was reaching out of the harbor, which seemed a good omen. We spent an afternoon provisioning: groceries at Market Basket, more tools at Sears (my father and uncle are both handy, have killed most of their life's demons with a Crescent wrench), fishing tackle at the Kittery Trading Post, and a last stop at Badger's Island for eels, shrimp, and frozen mackerel, long gray bananas of horror.

Aboard *Yonder* we tipped the mast to repair the anchor light. The bulb was out. We decided to raise the mast in the morning, after we cleared Memorial Bridge. Using the last of the day's light as if it were the last three inches on a spool of tape, I inspected everything I could imagine, hoping for a faultless cruise. I'd learned my lesson concerning storage. The boat would have to capsize before a grape could break free from its vine. I started the engine and let it run for an hour. Dad and Tommy listened to it with their heads cocked like dogs.

We ate dinner with Rob, Beverly, and Nanny that evening at Friar's Fish in Eliot, Nanny's favorite. She'd watched over *Yonder* that summer as if she were one of her children. I loved to listen to her stories, because I always knew the ending, whether the subject was her church, her garden, or flirting with boys seventy-five years earlier. She told ninety-eight percent of the narrative and closed with the words, "Well, you know . . .," leaving them expanding in your consciousness like a balloon stuck on a helium tank. She told my uncle that she liked my grandfather, even though he was very young (only eighty-five) and ate the wrong kind of beans, and, well, you know . . .

Rob would try to catch up with us at Boothbay Harbor in a couple of days, if we made it that far. Beverly promised a pancake breakfast upon our triumphant return.

We spent the night on *Yonder*'s mooring. My uncle and father fished off the stern. I watched their hands at the intricacies of line, hook, and bait. Their fishing, after fifty-some years of practice, had taken on a methodical confidence, as if they believed in the existence of fish the way a priest believes in God. Classical music played on the stereo. If there were any mosquitoes left in the season, there was just enough wind in early September to make them concentrate on flying. Mists didn't steal in but practiced petty theft. I fell asleep hoping for smooth sailing. A summer on *Yonder* slipped into the sea like rainwater, painfully, effortlessly, the way memory fell down to meaning, and meaning to illusion, a larger mystery. I was awakened by the massed snorings and fartings of my uncle and father many times during the night.

In the morning the air inside the cabin was fetid; it was as if we were being supplied with oxygen from an inner tube. Dad announced, in a victimized tone, that he was sleeping outside from then on.

"You guys make me feel sorry for my wife," I said.

"Why?" Tommy bit.

"Because you're two of my closest male relatives. Someday, I'll be treating her the way you treated me last night."

"I don't remember anything," Dad said.

"I slept right through," Tommy said.

"The fish in the very ocean were banging on the hull last night," I said, pounding on the cockpit locker. "Keep it quiet in there."

Both men smiled, looked at each other. They were brothers-in-law of thirty-five years and knew each other's faults like their own house keys, but neither considered flatulence and snoring among them.

I got *Yonder* under way as quickly as possible and then let Dad take the helm so I could move all the way forward to the pulpit for some fresh air. We cleared Memorial at seven, and a hundred yards farther on Tommy called me back to the cockpit with a mumble. There was a sweet roll in his mouth.

"What?" I asked.

"I said, Is all that water supposed to be down there?"

He pointed to the cabin sole. An inch of water sluiced back and forth over the boards. It reminded me of a fourth-grade science project, wave action in a shallow plywood box. I opened the engine hatch. Steam billowed up. Not again, I thought, not again. But this was something different. Water was at the level of the revolving prop shaft. The coupling threw a whorl of spray up. I leaned over *Yonder's* starboard side: no water exited the bilge. I jumped below and pulled the companionway steps away from the front of the engine, then lifted the boards over the bilge pump. It was running but was clogged by white lithium grease. Once this was cleared away the pump began taking up water. Now I had to find the leak. The spray thrown up by the shaft coupling dropped down on the engine block and skittered across the hot surface, sputtering. Dad was still at the helm. I hadn't told him to kill the engine because we were in the strength of the current and only yards from a granite bridge support and a flotilla of moored boats. I asked him if the engine was running hot. He bent down, squinted at the gauge.

"She's at a hundred and ninety degrees," he said.

"That's about ten degrees too warm," I said.

I checked the raw-water inlet, the filter, the hose. I climbed back up into the cockpit and looked down at the hoses leading in and out of the heat exchanger. Uncle Tommy spotted the problem: a U-shaped hose, behind the raw-water pump, had come loose. I reached around the whir of the spinning belt, loosened the clamp screw, shoved the hose back on, and then retightened the screw. The bilge began to drain. We weren't sinking anymore.

"Nothing like pumping water into your boat through a one-inch hose!" I yelled.

"That was good, Joe," my father said. "No wasted action."

I began to put the boat back together in order to give my brittle heart some elasticity. Tommy had never stopped chewing on his sweet roll. Between bites he suggested I might check each of the new clamps and hoses.

"I should have done that last night," I said, but petulantly thought, Geez, do I have to rebuild this boat every time I take her out? A sixty-foot Bronze Age vessel has recently been discovered off Dover, England. Archaeologists found a pair of leather underwear in the caulking, but this last sacrifice wasn't enough to save the ship. I'd read of a lobsterman who dived overboard and jammed a sleeping bag into a gaping wound in his hull. I had to be prepared to go as far as these men to save my boat.

Fog awaited us outside Portsmouth Harbor, standing beyond Whaleback Light, a fat mugger hiding behind a street lamp. Greasy rollers met the shoreline and disappeared like the steps of an escalator. The fog to my mind was resilient, almost impenetrable.

"Well, maybe we should wait a couple of hours," I suggested.

"We can navigate," Dad said. "I used to fly blind all the time. You just take a fix off the chart, take the distance and rate of speed, watch your compass. We'll be all right."

"What do you think, Tommy?"

"I'll do anything y'all want to do."

We were entering the mists.

"Well, we need to raise the mast. The radar reflector hangs from it," I said.

Even though we were at the mouth of a busy harbor, the only other craft I could see was a lobster boat working the shoal waters off Whaleback. Tommy and I went forward and loosened the halyards that doubled as tie-downs, while Dad throttled back and kept the bow to the belly dancing of the sea. I was surprised at how difficult it was to keep my footing as the boat dipped, waddled, and rose. Uncle Tommy is a half foot taller than I am, so I put him at the tip of the mast. As we began walking aft the spruce rose easily. We discovered some difficulty in timing our steps to the waves and avoiding the stays, halyards, and roller furled jib that hung from the mast. I soon realized this was much easier at the dock. The scene became a desperate parody of the flag raising on Iwo Jima. At the midpoint of our struggle the mast became unbelievably heavy. I put my shoulder against its trunk and began to drive at the mast as if it were a blocking sled on a football field. I heard Tommy groaning behind me. Dad left the wheel, snatched the flailing gaff halyard, and pulled. And then release: *Yonder* climbed a three-foot roller and the turnbuckle closed. Tommy pushed on the mast while I snapped the shrouds in place. I was completely winded, and my fingers worked like Lincoln Logs glued together in the shape of a human hand, each knuckle another right angle. Once the mast was secure I raised the radar reflector, a tin Christmas ornament the size of a soccer ball. Wood doesn't respond very well to radar, so the reflector high in the rigging might warn a passing coal freighter that we were about to be run down, and they could have a good laugh over it. We had to double back a couple hundred yards or so to pick up the wooden mast support. This board holds the mast on an even keel while it's lowered. I'd kicked it overboard as I'd struggled under the mast and the drapery of rigging. Thank fog we were hidden through most of this episode or the towns of Kittery and Newcastle and the Portsmouth Coast Guard station might have sent out all their lifesaving equipment.

Once fixed on buoy 24YL, Tommy went back to work on the sweet rolls, as relaxed as any passenger on a jetliner. Dad concentrated on keeping our course, his gaze fixed on the old pedestal compass. I sat on a locker near the raised deck and tried to see through the fog. After half an hour, my eyes throbbing like oatmeal at the boil, I came under the delusion that the fog was really only a thick mist, and that I could see a good ten or twelve boat lengths into the distance. Tommy finished off the rolls and went to work on a banana. I looked at the banana, looked up, and there was a long low white lobster boat dead ahead.

I yelled, "Dad, whoa," and leaped for the wheel, turning hard to starboard. Dad was turning too and we fought over the wheel's spokes. We missed the boat by ten to fifteen feet off his bow. Another couple of seconds, or if he'd been under way, and we'd have broadsided him, cut him in two. As it was, the lobsterman stood there, warp zipping through his hand, his eyes big as dog food bowls. I waved a little bent-fingered wave toward him, and he raised a gloved hand, and then he looked at his hand as if someone had switched it with his foot.

Dad said, "Here, Joe, you take this wheel. I need to go below." For some time afterward Dad had bad dreams about this incident, the white boat helpless before him.

I throttled back to about half a knot and went chastely on my way. After another hour it was plain we'd missed our mark, so we resorted to the electronics. Tommy checked the loran against the charted depths and the fathometer and it seemed accurate. My only fear beyond other boats was Boon Island, so we stayed well clear. The fog would lift and drop, dissipate and thicken. Occasionally *Yonder* wandered through bright fogdogs, blue sky above us as at the top of a well. I strained to see, waiting for another lobster boat to appear like the white whale. We ate lunch in the fog, but by one o'clock it lifted and we found ourselves off Cape Porpoise thanks to the machinery. My stomach and intestines, which were twisted like a rubber band between my esophagus and my sphincter, began to unwind. To see, to see, rather than to sea, to sea. A headache, which I hadn't known I even had, began to evaporate as well.

We rented a mooring from the Biddeford Pool Yacht Club because Wood Island Harbor promised a heave-ho night. Passing through the granite walls of the gut led us to a sanctuary of calm water, boats with reflections. I lay down on the raised deck and let my head hang out over the pool. The boat shifted and slipped, settled into the water she displaced like a plastic cereal bowl in a sink. As the sun descended I watched *Yonder*'s shadow merge with her reflection. The water seemed to accept both with equanimity. Each described her lines with alternative uses of light, ways of seeing. It seemed to me that water was a mirror much finer than mercury, in that I could merge with my reflection without destroying it. I just had to take to the water slowly. I had to wade in. Narcissus' mistake was plunging, falling for himself.

I looked up at my father and uncle. "Let's take a small boat ashore," I said.

We found a niche for the rubber sled under the gangway to the yacht club's float (there always seems to be a slot under the gangway reserved for visiting dinghies). The village of Biddeford Pool was relaxed, content, a cat on the windowsill, a dog under the porch with a thrice-chewed bone. Clapboard homes a century or two old lounged on curved streets. Tommy asked a man at a lobster pound if he could ship to Texas and the man, holding a lobster in each hand, said, "Why not just eat them here?" We walked up a narrow lane toward the public beach and found ourselves in front of a deli, so we used it, having sandwiches and potato chips, soda from cans. We knew it would be much better than anything the three of us would cook aboard *Yonder*. But this was as far as we could go. It was our first day at sea, too full of adventures. The food and my worn eyes made me sleepy. Our conversation disintegrated to the point that Dad and I listened to Tommy brag about the shoes he'd just paid nine dollars for back home. We actually looked under the table at his feet. I remember rowing back out to the boat, and Tommy and Dad calling me up to the cockpit late in the evening to see the crabs hanging onto their fish bait, but all I have in my log for the close of this first day was this: "Tommy's eating again. Do my eyes look as tired as my father's? To be snug in a good harbor, classical music down below, and a white light on my journal: where I be. Today, we squeezed through."

The next day at sea was for the most part a repeat of the last of my solo cruise, without the breakdown. We were fogged in early, making no attempt to navigate in the shoals of Wood Island Harbor, but by noon we'd rounded Cape Elizabeth. We ducked between Cliff and Jewell Islands to avoid the building seas, and just as we came through the narrows the fog rolled around the end of Jewell. We were lucky to be so near a safe harbor, and wheeled about to enter with three other boats who had the identical idea. The mouth of Cocktail Cove is tight and our entrance with the other boats, sails dropping, halyards slapping, anchors at ready, reminded me of the Three Stooges making for a doorway. In the time that it took to make three bologna sandwiches and eat them, the fog bank had pushed through.

"Damned funny weather," my father noted.

While Tommy found himself some sort of dessert I raised the anchor, and, mindful of an earlier episode, brought it aboard mud and all. We elbowed our way back out of Cocktail Cove and turned into the wind just south of Eagle Island. Here we met big waves, fresh from the Atlantic. Spray blew across the raised deck and cascaded over my father at the helm. I turned to him to see the expression on his face. It was as if he'd just met an alien being, and found her beautiful. He smiled at me with an open mouth and hunched his shoulders trying to stop the water from rolling down his neck. Tommy ducked behind the bulkhead and yelled, "Turn the bow into the waves!" Seawater had salted his half-eaten apple, and now dripped from his cap brim and nose. *Yonder* climbed and fell. At each breaker the spray flew and we all ducked as if knives were being thrown at us. The boat was wet from pulpit to rudder. For an instant at the peak of each wave, just as we began to roll off, I almost felt weightless, as if I could be left behind.

It was a careening but short turn into Mackerel Cove, where I refueled once again, trying to perfect the earlier voyage, but the dockmaster had been forced to return to school. The waitress gave me the key to the pump and asked me to lock it back up when I was through. Boy, just show up twice, I thought, and you're an old and trusted customer.

The sky was as clear now as it had been since we left Eliot, so we decided a two-hour run to Sebasco Harbor could be risked, even though it seemed to take a fog bank bare moments to build and roll in. We fought our way out of Mackerel Cove and surfed into Sebasco, a strong wind pushing on *Yonder*'s new escutcheon. It was good to come into the harbor with the engine running. We tied up at Sebasco Lodge's dock since we couldn't get anyone's attention about a mooring. I walked into the snack bar and asked for John, and the cook said the season was over, to take any mooring I wanted. She was surly in a tired way, afraid I was going to ask for a hamburger after she'd just cleaned the grill for the final time that year. I told Dad and Tommy we might as well take showers while we were at the dock, as it would be a hard row from the mooring across the windy harbor. At the showers we met a young family who told us all the boats in the harbor were clearing out. It was rough and going to get rougher that night. They were headed for The Basin.

"What's The Basin?" I asked.

"A hurricane hole just up the New Meadows River. You can follow us there if you'd like." For the second time in as many visits I'd found a boating family in Sebasco Harbor who were willing to save me. I took the last turn in the shower while a groundskeeper chewed out my uncle for docking.

"He asked me who the hell I thought I was," Tommy said. "So I told him I was just a passenger. He said we'd better get off the dock as soon as you got back and so I told him I thought we would. Sour old cuss."

"I guess they don't want people tying up," I said, pulling my socks on.

"I think we ought to stay here all night," Tommy said, his anger rising the more he thought about the groundskeeper.

"What do people mean exactly when they ask you who the hell do you think you are?" I asked.

"Snotty bastard," Tommy said, speaking of the groundskeeper, I think.

"Did you tell him Princess Di was aboard and wanted to take a royal shit in their establishment?" I asked. I smiled and started the engine, but Tommy frowned and went to look for something to eat in the galley.

We followed the young family's plastic boat into the yet rising winds and turned upriver for a two-mile run to The Basin.

I said to my uncle, "Well, we did get free showers." But his mind was made up. "It was my fault," I went on. "But I didn't see any sign that said we couldn't dock."

"Joe Alan," Tommy invoked, and the argument following didn't have to contain reasoning because all the elders on my mother's side of the family have successfully used middle names to cow children and grandchildren for generations. "Joe Alan," he said, "you don't open a conversation with 'Who the hell do you think you are?' even if we'd run the boat through his damned dock. I should have kicked his bony butt back up to dry land."

My father had a great hoot and I smiled, shook my head. It seemed that every port was a different country with its own laws and customs, which is what made The Basin so appealing. We made two doglegs up a narrow tree-lined channel and entered a broad, tranquil harbor. There was almost no sign of habitation, at least on shore. A dozen other boats were already at anchor, their hulls in calm water but their mast pennants flapping wildly. The double dogleg thwarted sea waves and the tall conifers broke down much of the low-level wind. We anchored in twenty feet of milky green water, then sat in the cockpit looking up into the wooded hills, at the clouds scowling above us, at the obviously inferior yachts close by. Seals barked deep in The Basin, and we could hear voices on the other boats going about the negotiations of cooking supper. This picked up my uncle's spirits and he began to warm up cans of stew and beans. Through the evening we listened to weather reports predicting thunderstorms for the night. We backed down on our anchor to make sure it was well set, and saw other boats laying out a second hook. By midnight it had begun to rain intermittently, but what kept me awake was the gusting wind, strumming the halyards and stays. There was also a strange knock in the storm, like an oar banging against the side of the boat, the planks of my carvel skull. I rose twice in the night to check our position. The rainwater on deck was cool to my bare feet; the grain of the teak had risen like welts. Clouds screamed along just beneath a near full moon. A swift incoming tide parted on *Yonder's* plumb stem. I kneeled on the pulpit and held the taut wet anchor line in my hand as if it were the reins to the planet. It seemed as if we were being pulled along at an incredible speed, through time itself. And the world felt oddly overturned. There in The Basin the night was lit from the sky rather than from the ground. I needed a porch light to orient myself. I scanned the other boats in the harbor and was surprised to see three or four other captains kneeling on their pulpits, arms outstretched to a quivering rode.

At the height of the storm, in high winds and driving rain, two huge trawlers burned their way into The Basin with halogen light. It was as eerie and overwhelming as spacecraft dropping into a field of sparrows. Their crews yelled and laughed, walked the decks in full rain gear. I thought their anchors would knock holes in the bottom of the harbor and we'd all be sucked down a crude drain. Two plastic yachts near the trawlers weighed anchor and moved away, their captains yelling curses about scope and swing at the commercial pilot-houses yards above them. When the trawlers shut down their engines the storm was almost quiet in comparison. I watched the two displaced sailboats wander about the harbor till they found suitable berths. Wives stepped forward in businesslike fashion and let go anchors, then stood out on deck till their husbands waved them back in.

I went below too, to another storm, to the accumulated eruptions of bodily effluence, to the coded sighs of human sleep. The only thing more strenuously put forth than my father's and uncle's groaning, snoring, and farting were their accusations and denials the next morning.

> Our disputants put me in mind of the skuttle fish, that when he is unable to extricate himself, blackens all the water about him, till he becomes invisible.
>
> Joseph Addison,
> *The Spectator*

I was stirring oatmeal when Dad called me up into the cockpit. "This man wants to know what kind of boat this is." Another old man in a dinghy was off *Yonder*'s stern.

"Morning," I said.

"She's a Crocker, isn't she?"

I shook my head. "John Alden. Built at the Gamage Yard. We're on our way there now."

"John Alden?" His jaw dropped as if somebody had slapped it there. "I used to have an Alden sloop. It was too much for me to maintain, so I traded it in on a fiberglass boat." He motioned to his boat across the water. His wife was washing down the deck. "Wood's nice, but you can't beat plastic for maintenance." His wife got up off her knees, threw a sponge into a bucket as if she were kicking a dog, and then put her hands on her hips. She seemed to be scanning the harbor for a small boat. "John Alden," he said, shaking his head, as he moved on to another yacht.

Seals barked farewell as we motored out of The Basin and into swells still running from the night's storm. Off Cape Small I pointed overboard to a spot in the water and said, "Dad, this is where I lost my engine." He looked at the ocean beyond, the waves crashing on Bald Head Ledge and shook his head with a frown. I was happy to have new water under my keel. With any luck at all we'd make South Bristol and the Gamage Yard by early afternoon.

Behind Seguin Island seals surfaced to watch us motor by. I couldn't get beyond my first impression that people had thrown their bird dogs overboard, so much did the seals' eyes resemble my black Labrador's back home. They seemed to rise often near lobster buoys, and Tommy suggested they held onto the buoys to rest.

"What do you suppose they did before men put Styrofoam out for them?" I asked.

"A lot of drownings," Tommy said, and laughed as if he'd said the funniest thing words ever allowed. I wondered if he realized how much he was like his father at that moment. Grandpa could tell the same story three times a day for fifty years and think it was funnier every telling. I told my uncle about Grandpa's cruise earlier in the summer, when he thought we were still going downeast even though the land was off to starboard and he'd seen the same sights the day before. I realized then that Grandpa saw everything new each day, and that was why the same jokes were always funny, the same people always achingly lovable.

We ticked off buoys on our way, noted the increasing numbers of boats as we approached Boothbay Harbor. Dude schooners, in a mirror image, sailed around both sides of Squirrel Island, headed for open water. Tommy toasted the many lighthouses with drafts of

The Gamage Yard

Miller beer. We finally turned inland on the Damariscotta River, toward the small village of South Bristol where *Yonder* was born.

The Gamage family built boats at South Bristol for over a hundred years, but the last boat slid down the ways in 1981. Local boats were now hauled, launched, and stored at the yard. A small chandlery perched on the dock, selling Harvey Gamage T-shirts. Two great tin sheds rested on the shore, as empty as a Texas culvert. *Yonder* was built during the middle of the Great Depression, perhaps before the sheds were erected, before government contracts for minesweepers and PT boats. She might have been built just above the high-tide mark, on a gently sloping beach, surrounded by stacks of lumber and spruce logs. Harvey Gamage, who bought the yard from his grandfather, great-uncle, and uncle in 1925, built many of Alden's designs, mostly swift schooners and ketches. *Yonder* was small in comparison to most of these yachts. Smaller, slower, and a little dumpy compared with Alden's famous racers. No wonder the old men were surprised he designed her. Alden boats went through the water heeled over so far, their owners painted the hull on a pair of tacks. Yet none of the old rudder kickers were ever surprised to find that *Yonder* was built by Harvey Gamage. She was, in some part, an ancestor to the minesweepers to come eight years later, stoutly built.

Gamage was known for building boats stronger than the naval architect recommended. He didn't scrimp on the size and thickness of ribs and planks. If a three-inch rib was good, then a four-inch rib was obviously better. The proof of craftsmanship was in *Yonder*'s return sixty years after she was built.

We tied up next to a beautiful white-hulled wooden schooner at the Gamage docks, and I walked into the chandlery, I admit, somewhat breathlessly. No one was at home. I picked out a blue Gamage Shipyard sweatshirt and then went on a search for a clerk or yardbird. I peered into the cavernous sheds and was struck by the size of a bandsaw along one wall. I could have driven my car through it. But there were no sawdust-and-shaving-coated craftsmen here, no one to walk down to the docks and gaze at their grandfather's handiwork. There were a few boats in the yard that looked as if they'd die there. I scanned the ground as I walked, searching for something more telling, a homecoming, a nut and bolt.

"Can I help?" a man asked.

I looked up and said, "I'd like to buy a shirt to go with my old Gamage boat." I pointed at *Yonder,* but he didn't even bother to look over his shoulder.

"All we do now is haul and store boats," he said.

But he sold shirts too, and he allowed us to tie up while we walked into South Bristol for a late lunch. I was dispirited in a way, walking uphill to a hamburger. There had been no old photos on the walls, no half hulls, no yard histories for sale; *Yonder*'s patterns weren't hung on a rusty nail. Even though *Yonder* was unique, the return to her ways had been similar to driving a Mustang up to the gates of the Ford assembly plant in Detroit. I told the waitress my story. She'd lived in South Bristol all her life and commiserated with me. "I miss all the activity that was there years ago. We didn't appreciate it then, though. It was just work. We didn't know it was special." With a sniff of disdain, she said the Gamage man was half the year in Florida. Then her mood changed sharply. Her nephew was launching a new wooden lobster boat the next day. There'd be a big party. "Come on down and watch her go in," she said.

"I hope it lasts for sixty years," I said, and toasted the boat and the waitress with my Pepsi. They'd both made me feel better.

"A new wooden boat," I said to my father, and he smiled.

We walked down to the Gut in South Bristol and watched the swing bridge pivot open. Cars piled up on each side and waited for a wooden lobster boat to pass through. Life was as it should be. There are rumors that the lobstermen are beginning to trade in their plastic boats for wooden ones. Cedar hulls are easier on your spine when pounding through a sea. Back at the Gamage docks I stripped and pulled my new shirt over my head. If *Yonder* was sentient, she didn't show it. I took her away from those docks one more time, and the wake she left melted away as if it were any other water.

Across the river, in East Boothbay, a huge steel ferry was under construction at Washburn & Daughty. Welders crouched on scaffolding, worshipping an intensely bright light, and somewhere in the bowels of the boat a hammer repeatedly struck a hollow steel organ.

There were several old boats scattered in the harbor and I used *Yonder* to connect the dots. I admit to a degree of voyeurism. I stood on tiptoe to see over sills into cockpits, admiring the curve of a coaming, curious about the contents of a locker. Occasionally, when I'm looking into the windows of other people's boats, my wake, like a stick breaking underfoot, alerts the owners, and I'm surprised by a head thrust from a companionway or hatch. I smile awkwardly and wiggle my fingers, as if the five feet of ocean between my boat and theirs is a complete coincidence. Or I affect the posture of a dog owner: *Yonder* is my pet Lab, and she may be on a leash, but she still somehow manages to get within sniffing range of the other dogs in the park.

We made our anchorage that afternoon in Lewis Cove of Linekin Bay. (I'd been to the same spot a few years earlier on my first cruise downeast, aboard Ralph Remick's *Sprig of Acacia,* of which there'll be more later.) It was just a short row to Barret Park, where we could alight and walk across the isthmus of Spruce Point to the town of Boothbay Harbor. Unfortunately, some fifty feet from the park, the rubber sled grounded in three inches of water and three inches of mud. I used an oar to pull us along another six or eight feet. We'd all put on fresh clothes and slicked back our hair for the excursion, but somebody was going to have to get out and tow the other two in.

My father looked at his brother-in-law. "How much did you say you paid for your shoes, Tommy?" he asked.

I immediately volunteered that I'd spent the enormous sum of $47.50 on my Reeboks. "I'm ashamed that I spent so much. It was vanity through and through, but I also hoped they'd last me till I could afford another pair."

"My deck shoes cost forty-two dollars," Dad said.

"Dad," I said, "I think Tommy said he paid nine dollars for his shoes. He got a bargain."

My uncle stepped out into the shallow water, the deep mud, and taking the painter over his shoulder, tugged us to dry land. The beginnings and endings of words could be heard under his breathing. They mingled with the slosh of his ankles through the water and the suck of his soles from the mud, and made a sound like nine dollars, over and over. This was one of cruising's finest qualities: to give human beings the opportunity to display decisiveness, courage, ability, and not least grace, in the face of overwhelming nature.

There's no finer entrance than walking into a small town with a pair of oars over your shoulder. Tourists know you're a man of the sea, merchants realize you won't steal large objects. At Boothbay Harbor's memorial to lost fishermen, a bronze dory, I read the list of names to see if there were any Joe Coomers and, finding none, hid my oars inside the memorial. I thought it might be the last place a thief would look. And here at the edge of the harbor, even if my oars were found, other men's dinghies were much more likely to be stolen. This gave me a light heart as I walked the streets.

We were lucky enough to arrive in Boothbay on an empty stomach. Harbor-view restaurants are plentiful, and since the heavy tourist season was now over, the waiters and waitresses were equally glad to see us. We took seats at a plate-glass window that looked out on a pair of dude schooners and a harbor still full of boats of every description, from gold-plated to rust-scabbed.

Dad and Tommy both ordered double lobsters and spent the meal arguing over whose turn it was to pay.

"I think I got the last one," Tommy said.

"That was two ham sandwiches and a grilled cheese," Dad countered. "The bar tab I just paid for was more than that."

"A turn's a turn," Tommy said.

"I'll get breakfast tomorrow," I offered.

They both put a bit of crustacean between their molars. Dad swallowed first. "I think you've still got some of my tools I loaned you," he accused my uncle.

"Loaned me when?" Tommy asked.

"When we had the airplane."

"That was thirty years ago."

Dad turned to me. "Did anybody ever tell you about the time Tommy and your uncle Bob crashed the airplane?"

"We didn't crash it," Tommy said, holding a claw in midair. "We cut through a power line during a landing."

"Had to replace the prop and the engine cowling," Dad said, rubbing his stomach as if he'd just eaten his enemy.

"What's all that got to do with anything?" Tommy asked, laughing.

"I just want to know when it's your turn because I'm having the biggest damned steak they sell in this town."

With that, Tommy pushed his chair back and lifted his too-large foot, encased in muddy sock and sneaker, and dropped it on the edge of the tabletop for our examination. Dad sucked at his teeth and looked for a waitress.

"No matter what it costs, I'm buying breakfast tomorrow, boys," I said.

After dinner we called the wives and made plans to meet Rob in the morning at the town dock. The tide had come in a bit while we were gone, so we were able to float away from Barret Park without the further wetting of shoes. *Yonder*'s anchor line hung limply into the cove that evening, mosquitoes banged their heads repeatedly against solid objects, and the night was so bright with moonlight, I kept waking up and thinking I'd been chosen. The snoring took up where it had left off sixteen hours earlier, but even it seemed to be more relaxed, to have taken on the rhythm of the waves. I decided I liked this little white room on the water.

In the morning, Dad and Tommy volleyed "I was up earlier" times. This didn't bother me because I used the time to get more sleep. The day began in earnest with the hiss of the propane under a coffeepot, fire and water divided by a thin sheet of earth. Then, when we realized it would take more than five minutes to work around Spruce Point and into the harbor to meet Rob, we hurriedly tried to get under way. But the boat didn't want to leave the quiet, tree-banked cove. The engine started but this was only a ruse. I went forward to raise the anchor, but it was like trying to pull a bone from a dog's mouth. Tommy came to help, and between us the anchor came up with a final release that was as relaxing as breaking wind.

Hm, I wondered, what would I do if someday the anchor decided never to come up? Such questions always pestered me, the what-ifs. It was nice to have Rob to refer to, like the back of a medicine bottle. Dad and Tommy threw lines to him at the public dock, and as soon as the engine was quiet, I asked him, "What do I do if the anchor won't come up?"

He shook my Dad's hand and said, "Had some problems, have you?"

"Oh, no," Dad said. "It's been beautiful."

I turned to him and smiled. "What about the fog, and all the water in the cabin, and nearly running over that lobster boat, and that was just the first day?"

"Those weren't problems, Joe," Dad said, and frowned at me, as if I'd just told the crowd at the sale barn our horse had gout.

"Geez," Rob said. "Tell me all about it over breakfast. I know a great place just up the street."

"But what if the anchor won't come up?" I said again, sure that this would happen the next morning.

"Cleat off the rode and try to dislodge it with power. Use the boat. You might beforehand tie a line to a fluke and buoy the other end.

Then if you get stuck you can pick up the buoy and pull the anchor up by the fluke." What a good word *fluke* was to hear. I tried to envision the knots this would require but Rob eased my mind by saying he'd rig up something after we ate.

Over breakfast we narrated the preceding three days from our individual perspectives. As early as this I understood that *Yonder* had already paid me back in full for her cost. We laughed, and lied, and ate without remembering it. Rob soaked up the stories with his toast, wincing and bobbing his head, throwing in memories of currents and coves that were on our route. We chewed on plans for a day sail to Damariscove Island, and a return to Boothbay via the Sheepscot River and Townsend Gut. Breakfast cost $16.32.

"But what if the anchor still won't come up?" I asked, watching Rob tie a line around the anchor stock. "What if," I continued, "what if the State of Maine sits on my anchor?"

"Why, Joseph." And Rob shook his head. For a moment I felt like a dog with his hind foot hung in his ear. "Just cut the damned thing loose. It's only an anchor."

I beamed. It was only an anchor. I had faced this most drastic possibility of anchoring. I felt much better. Often, if I'm prepared to kill someone, it's much easier to handle the more probable cuss fight.

As we motored out of the harbor it was apparent we had our first Maine Day, clear skies and a following wind. I raised the sails at Mouse Island and threw a short fiberglass batten out of the mainsail high into the air and then deep into the harbor. Rob stood at the helm and said, "They're cheap." And so we were off among small following white-caps. The wind was cool but out of the north, exactly what we needed to make Damariscove on one long run. I'd made it a point since the loss of the engine off Cape Small to become more proficient with *Yonder*'s steadying rig. Heather and I had spent a couple of afternoons in the waters between Portsmouth Harbor and the Isles of Shoals reaching, running, and sailing close-hauled, but the wind had been so slight we hadn't made much headway. Rob taught me another lesson on the run to Damariscove, trimming the mainsail out to starboard, and the jib out to port. Goosewings, he called it, but it looked like one wing and a stump. There was enough wind to shut off the engine and still we went along briskly. My father was mesmerized. He kept touching the sheets, testing the wind's strength. He climbed up on the raised deck and put his palm against the taut sail itself.

"This is wonderful," he said. "Why haven't we been doing this all along?"

"There's been too little or too much wind," I said. "And even if we'd had perfect conditions, we'd just now be off Wood Island Harbor. We're only doing about two knots."

"Is that all? I would have guessed more than that."

Rob fired up the Westerbeke again and said, "Let's do what this boat was built to do: motorsail."

Yonder cut through the lop, and I noticed her movement was much easier, much more settled, as if she were running down a furrow that had already been plowed. I remarked upon it. "Nothing better than a steadying sail and a big engine in greasy water. Keeps the passengers from mutiny."

Rob wanted to visit Damariscove for its long and varied history, and I'd go anywhere land and water met. The island had been inhabited by Europeans before Jamestown and was a major port for the English fishery as early as the late sixteenth century. It was now owned by the Nature Conservancy. Architectural improvements consisted of a few weathered cottages and a Victorian Coast Guard station transformed into a private residence. We anchored in the cove on the southern end of the island, off the old station. I tried to imagine a couple dozen square-riggers crammed into this wet, narrow defile, loading fish and fur, and the shoreline crowded with drying stages, a pervasive stench of spoiled guts wafting on the air. The trees that had once covered much of the island were for the most part gone. We rowed ashore and waded through waist-high brush and dry stiff grass to high ground. Trails often existed only from the knees down and you had to trust your feet to follow them. The views were unhindered: southwest to Seguin Island and east to the impressionist mirage of Monhegan. It was a good climb for my father, bound with heavy clothes, ten years since a double bypass. We split up at the top, Tommy and Rob heading north to the head of the cove and an old ice pond, while Dad and I went as far out into the Atlantic as we could go on foot and then followed the battered granite, collecting lost buoys. Once again Dad seemed mesmerized, wary in a way, but also grateful. His byword from this point on, whenever we considered an anchorage, was that we should find an island to walk on. Dad and I rowed back out to *Yonder* with our cache of wounded Styrofoam and then retrieved Tommy and Rob from the opposite bank. They didn't want to walk back around. Dad said if it was him he'd get a motor for the dinghy. That way we could explore all the coves too shallow for *Yonder*'s three-and-a-half-foot draft. I could see he was working out a set of plans, a course of action, but I didn't yet know what it was all about.

We had lunch there in the cove, with the granite and the brush and the grass paying no attention to us. Waves lapped at the boot top, and a single gull asked for potato chips. Rob sat back against the bulkhead with a beer and a sandwich someone else had made, and offered forth, "Now, I ask you, does it get any better than this?" Which wasn't really a question but a sigh. I could have said, "Yes, kissing my wife is better, or finishing an acceptable chapter." But they all might have thought I was lying, and who wanted a liar in their midst at a time like this, so I just sighed too and threw a chip to the polite gull.

On the return leg we had another fine sail, a reach that took us deep into Sheepscot Bay. At the tip of Cape Newagen we saluted a lighthouse known as The Cuckolds, and I wondered how many sailors rounding these rocks were unaware that their name was being called. Soon we were in a traffic jam in Townsend Gut, waiting along with a dozen other boats for the bridge to pivot. It's a true shortcut, but I guessed there were many crews, like us, who came through just to say they had. And so back into Boothbay Harbor, where we dropped Rob off and refueled at the docks of Carousel Marina. The attendant was friendly and talkative, asked where we planned to spend the night.

"I suppose we'll slip back around the corner to Lewis Cove," I answered.

"Why not stay here?" he said. "It's off season and the moorings are half price, only seven dollars. We've got showers and a chandlery if you need anything."

We did need showers. I turned to the crew. They looked beat, windburned and dehydrated, empty bags blown up against a fence. I weakened. We took up mooring number 12 with the boathook. It seemed fairly luxurious, right there in the middle of things, restaurants and bars only a short row away. One of the best views in the world for only seven bucks. We took turns showering. There were clean stalls with a personal paper floor mat for only a dollar. I asked the lady if I couldn't just use my dollar as a floor mat, but this was against the rules. But I figured I could take about forty thousand showers there and still come out cheaper than buying a yacht with a built-in shower. However, things began to take a bad turn. As we were stepping back aboard *Yonder,* my father took me by the elbow and said almost gleefully, "Tommy's stopped up the head."

"What?" I said.

"He hasn't gone to the bathroom since we've been aboard and now he's stopped up the toilet."

"Joe Alan," my uncle called from below.

"Jesus, Jesus, Jesus," I wailed. But it was no use. Short of dismantling the beast there on the boat, which none of us wanted to do, the head was out of order for the duration. I stood on the old bronze pump handle, but this only caused the rubber seals to bulge, allowing fine jetlike sprays of effluent to paint the ceiling. "We'll have to row in and use the toilet at the marina," I said. "But right now I've just had a shower and I'm staying clean as long as possible." I closed the door to the head and hung a dead mackerel from a nail to combat the smell.

That evening we ate dinner at the most expensive place Dad could find without walking too far to find it, the Black Orchid. He picked out a steak-and-lobster combination and encouraged me to order anything I liked: appetizer, entrée, dessert.

I ordered and Dad said, "Why don't you have two of those?"

This was too much for my uncle. "He don't want two of those!"

"I'm going to have a couple of desserts myself," Dad said.

Tommy warned, "Now remember, the head's clogged up."

And so it went. It was hard for me to believe that they'd been having this same argument for thirty-five years and that they still enjoyed it. And why did the waitress seem to enjoy it as well? Was I losing my mind?

Not yet. It wasn't completely gone till three o'clock that morning. Parties, bright lights, tour boats, drunks: we were trying to sleep in the eye of an entertainment hurricane. A ghastly odor emanated from the head. We kept it behind the closed door for the most part but occasionally swung the hinges to squeeze off a round of Lysol down its throat. We were off the most expensive mooring I've ever paid for by five A.M. but by that time, everything was quiet.

"The best night's sleep in Boothbay didn't cost us anything," Dad said.

"I wonder," I said, "if I'd paid that guy full price for the mooring, maybe he would have put his hand on my shoulder and told me to go back to Linekin Bay."

What was pleasant, however, was to wake up every morning, wipe the dew from the helm and the instruments, have the engine start on the first crank, and set off into an accepting sea. We began each morning with a half-dozen layers of clothing and a mug of hot coffee. My eyeglasses fogged over each time I lifted the mug, but unlike when driving a car, I had the leisure to let the lenses clear in their own good time. It was hard to complain about the cold when we knew we'd be back in Texas in three days, breaking a sweat on the walk from the air-conditioned house to the air-conditioned car. It seemed that in Maine the whole outdoors was an air-conditioned luxury, as remarkably free as walking around the vast shopping malls back home.

As soon as the sun rose over the doghouse, Tommy broke out his tackle box, baited a hook, and trolled. And although we thought we were one of the first out of the harbor that morning, we ran into a fleet of small fishing boats west of Seguin Island who looked as if they'd been at it for hours. Tommy caught a mackerel as we skirted the boats, and we realized that the fleet on the surface was following another below.

"Mark this place on the chart," Tommy said. I saw that a mark was already there.

"It's called Halibut Rocks," I said.

"Wrong fish."

Things had changed. I crossed out *Halibut* on the chart and renamed the rocks for mackerel. And so we three men will know them for the rest of our lives. It was a bit of heresy, but the great thing about being on your own boat at sea is it's hard for the masses to persecute you.

Unless you pull into Cocktail Cove for lunch on a Sunday. We dropped anchor at eleven-thirty and there were twelve other boats tucked in the harbor. By the time we ate grilled-cheese sandwiches and lingered over Pepsis, there were twenty-six boats in the harbor. We thought it time to make a break for the open sea and found a quieter anchorage a couple hours closer to home at Richmond Island.

On the way *Yonder* was buzzed once by a Cessna pontoon plane and twice by what Dad said was a sub chaser, perhaps out of Brunswick Naval Air Station. I told the crew that everyone wants to get near a good-looking boat. I was so close, I was inside.

There was only one other boat in Seal Cove, anchored near the long breakwater that connected the island to Cape Elizabeth. I respected their privacy and dropped my galvanized friend, at high tide, in a rocky inlet farther east. I whispered to the anchor as it fell, "I wouldn't cut you away for anything, sweetie. Don't you have a worry."

Tommy was anxious to get ashore. The coast was pulverized to beach near the breakwater, but we were jumbled-rock men, so we rowed toward a stand of conifers on East Point and the ruins of a granite mountain below. This end of the island was so wave-worn, vulnerable as it was to the direct brunt of Atlantic storms, that the rocks were relatively free of sea wrack. Great driftwood logs had been thrown high up into the stand of trees to rot at the feet of the living. Tommy at last found a smooth timber he could relieve himself over. But as he dropped his trousers, a sheep, male or female I knew not, began bleating wildly and advanced toward him out of a grassy meadow. It wasn't a bleat of fondness or even love, but of some awkward passion. Tommy pulled his pants back up. The sheep halted his advance. Tommy dropped his pants and began to squat. Again the tormented bleating and anguished advancing. Dad by this time was laughing as hard as the sheep bleated. The sheep moved to within a dozen feet of my uncle and stood on the rocks above him. Was Tommy trespassing on the sheep's territory? Had the sheep never seen a human ass before? At any rate, as soon as Tommy finished, the sheep relented or lost interest. The delicate moment was gone.

Dad found three new lobster buoys, all with the same owner's color scheme. There was a bit of warp hanging from each which had plainly been cut. What were the odds that boats had slashed three lines without harming the buoys? It seemed a sure sign of a lobster war, lobstermen fighting over territory. Each buoy cut free was at least one lost trap, a financial burden that might chase a competitor from contested fishing grounds.

Our last dinner aboard was a mixture of three tins: bean-and-ham soup, vegetable-beef soup, and new potatoes. Its tastiest ingredient was heat. I brought my log up-to-date while the crew fished with slices of mackerel. And then, as the sun set, I rowed back ashore to get a snapshot of *Yonder*'s silhouette. That night Dad and Tommy both slept in the cockpit. I thought at first they were doing this to give me a night of respite from the snoring, but it was actually the proximity to the head they were concerned about. I pondered unbolting the toilet bowl from the sole and dropping it overboard. As the tide ebbed, rocks began to sneak out from shore toward *Yonder*'s precious hull. Touch us, they called, kiss us. I watched the boat and rocks as I might my daughter and her beau on the front porch, ready to leap through the screen at the least indiscretion. I lay in my bunk that night, my face so hot from windburn that my own hands felt cold on my cheeks. I was as constipated as *Yonder*'s head. I was completely surrounded by an odor as foul as puppy breath. Yet I was content, felt that I'd accomplished more than my abilities should have allowed. I went up on deck to check on the rocks one last time, to pee over the gunwale. As I did, Dad shifted and spoke. I've never yet become accustomed to someone speaking to me while I pee. It's always hard to answer, difficult to comprehend language.

Dad said, "You know, Joe, I think I'll get me a boat."

"What?" I said.

"I've been going to get one for a long time."

"Since when?"

"For a long time."

"What kind of boat?"

"A big motorsailer, one your mother would be comfortable on."

I said, "Hunh." But wanted to say, "It's too dangerous: you and Mom out on a boat alone. Your heart's bad. You'd be raising sails and lifting anchors. I couldn't be there all the time."

"I really like this," he said. "Look at these stars."

"I'd worry about you all the time," I said, putting myself away.

"Ah, Joe," he said. "You worry too much."

We were in Eliot by one in the afternoon the next day. The only noteworthy item of the journey was that my uncle ate the last slice of bread. "I can't believe he ate the last piece of bread," my father would muse over the next few months. Then he'd look off into the distance and shake his head. While Dad and Tommy cleaned the boat,

I unbolted the head and rowed it ashore, dropped it on the dock at Hutton's Landing. I pried out a roll of Soft-N-Nice from the flapper valves, my last bit of nautical maintenance for the season. Tommy had a big laugh at my expense over this. I told him he shouldn't eat sesame seeds anymore because his body was unable to digest them, a sure sign of intestinal breakdown. My uncle, like his father, laughs easily and never seems to come wholly undone unless he feels that someone has let the species down. This cruise gave him his last restful moments for some time to come: Grandpa, since his return home from Maine, wasn't eating much.

Dad had pointed out boats he liked as we motored up the Piscataqua. I didn't encourage or discourage him, hoping that this might just be a flush of emotion, that it would fade away once he was back at home in the plains, feeding his longhorn cattle.

But things come back to you. A dog dies along the roadside and you watch his body fade into the grass over weeks till he's gone, indistinguishable from the soil. And then years later, he comes back to you, as fresh as the wound in his side, and you know you have to do something. You have to go see the girl, buy the boat, write the book, allow to exist some old uncertainty.

21

~

In 1492 when Columbus crossed the Atlantic, America
was 20 meters nearer to Europe than it is today.
James Hamilton-Paterson,
The Great Deep

So I THOUGHT I'd better get under way before it was too late, too
far to go. "Be careful of all those foreigners who live over there," my
grandmother warned me. I never considered a boat to cross the Atlantic, took instead an airplane, an odd fish adapted to thin water. I'd
been out of college for a year, and felt it time to explore another island. I believed the Atlantic existed on that flight, but I never saw it.
The plane left Dallas at a midwinter six P.M. and arrived in London
at nine the next morning in a blanched Dickensian fog. There'd been
a black void and then a blinding light, and I felt as if I'd been deloused
with some new microwave technology.

I met my girlfriend in Edinburgh, and then for three months, it
seems to me now, we looked for water, by way of an occasional museum or author's home. We climbed Arthur's Seat early on and saw
the Firth of Forth in the distance, a vast expanse of water crossed by
minuscule freighters. The city, dark and sprawling, steepled and
crenellated, beautiful and terrifying, seemed also, next to the sea,
insignificant.

We took trains to St. Andrews and Berwick-upon-Tweed not be-
cause we cared about golf or ancient cities but to be near the ocean.
At St. Andrews we spent most of the day walking the West Sands.
(". . . I thought of writing on this whole voyage, very diligently, all

that I would do and see and experience . . ." *The Diario of Christopher Columbus's First Voyage to America,* abstracted by Fray Bartolomé de Las Casas, translated by Oliver Dunn and James E. Kelley, Jr.) From my journal: "2-26-83 Pockets of shells, the tide is coming in, wind but slight and fog over the bay so everything is gray but the white caps of the waves. A half-dozen dead seabirds on the shore, so abandoned in their deaths, sprawled amid the other debris of the ocean. And then I remember the shells in my pocket once held souls too. Two miles of sand to the rocky point, and I don't think anyone could ever be bored living on the ocean, wave after new wave, never the same, and so much possibility in what may wash up on the shore. The whole world, the rest of your life, could be washed up on the shore."

I picked up a small wooden wheel, perhaps a net buoy, the wood saturated with the sea, the grain packed with sand. I placed it on a steam radiator to dry that night and the next morning didn't recognize the buoy, split and shriveled, as different from itself as the dead gulls I'd seen on the beach the day before.

It was obvious at Berwick-upon-Tweed that I'd been reading too much Hemingway, but also clear that I was struck by the simple architecture of a town meeting the sea: "3-12-83 Berwick was a fine town with a long concrete pier and a lighthouse. We walked out on the pier with the ocean on both sides of us and sat under the little red and white lighthouse and watched the waves over some rocks and then a tug, orange with white lettering—PILOT—churn out to some kind of big cargo ship and lead it in along the pier and past it, where it made an exact 180-degree turn, the big ship did, and then moved on into the mouth of the River Tweed. That was a good thing to see. There were some men fishing on the end of the pier. They didn't catch anything while we were there, but that would have been too much to ask for.

"The pier made room for a little beach where it ran out from the coast. It was just a little sandy beach, without any shells or drift of any kind at all, before it ran into a line of cliffs and then was of course no beach at all.

"Down to the Tweed itself, below the train station, to what's left of the old castle and wall. This not much but the Tweed is fine, green and slow and seemingly unsuspecting of any sea around the next bend."

I crossed the English Channel on a ferry with perhaps four hundred schoolgirls. They chased each other in an endless blur of blue sweaters and plaid skirts, still young enough that the most interesting thing about crossing the ocean was the ship's snack bar. I sat on deck in a down coat, writing in my journal, trying to be so affected that I wouldn't remember thirteen years later how anxious I was: "3-16-83 The Channel is a great wide sheet of inscrutable [I'd been reading Conrad] crepe paper, more calm than smooth, and our passage is smoother than a train ride. Out of Newhaven Harbour and four hours to Dieppe. Gulls off the port and we throw them halves of malted milk balls and they bank and dive and refuse them. Gulls must not have sugar beaks. Our ferry is the *Valencary,* a blunt instrument. Gray skies, it's true, but a calm slate-gray crossing, and ships on the horizon, and the promise of the coast of France."

In the cities we visited inland, I walked the banks of the Seine, the Rhine, the Arno, the Tiber, and am proud today to say I sneaked down quays, got down on my knees, and stuck my hand in all these cold and filthy streams. I found it hard to feel as if I belonged on those foreign streets, but my hand plunged into water let me become involved. Here too, over the water, was open space, a familiar sky.

In Amsterdam: "3-23-83 I've always leaned toward water, like a dousing rod, and they've got plenty of it here. As many canals as streets and just as orderly. They're green, although they say they change the water four or five times a week. We took your typical glass-top tourist-boat tourist-canal trip in the morning and it was good, better than swimming, twice as dry."

Our boat, the *Vincent Van Gogh* perhaps, took us through narrow bridges and locks, showed us the one-meter-wide house, a variety of gables and furniture hoists, Montelbaan Tower and Mint Tower. I was most intrigued by the boats moored along the canals, though: a boat cats lived on, a boat hippies lived on, a boat ordinary humans occupied. These long low barge homes were completely different from the tall narrow staircases on the street above them. I'd lugged my sixty-pound suitcase up four flights to my hotel room, so I understood the boats' advantages. At last the tour boat exited the canals and carried us into the open harbor. Spray and light rain speckled our glass enclosure; I was able to stick my arm out the window and feel the spume off the crest of a wave, and I was as happy as I'd been in days, immersed in light and water.

I was so taken by the cruise in Holland that when I arrived in Switzerland I booked an excursion on Lake Lucerne from Lucerne to Vitznau. We boarded a monstrous double-decked steamer, the crew and all four passengers. My girlfriend and I climbed to the open upper deck for the view. A third of the way across the lake, a uniformed and bearded mate stuck his head up through the stairwell and frowned. He repeated a sentence several times, and by his tone and expression I understood that I'd raped his mother and beaten his dog. Finally, he held out his hand for me to spit into, but instead I put our tickets there. Then he said, "These are second-class fares. You are on a first-class level. Follow me." He turned and walked away as if I were on a leash. At the companionway he realized his leash was broken. He reiterated the mother-beating and dog-raping accusations.

(". . . the Christians, being forewarned, attacked the Indians . . ." Ibid.) "How much more is a first-class ticket?" I asked. "Or are you all sold out?"

"Let's just go down," my girlfriend said. "It's cold up here anyway."

"Durn heathen," I said.

It was the first time in my life I wanted to buy a business so I could fire an employee. I make this remark only to note the first occasion I thought of purchasing a boat.

In Venice, we hired the whole fleet: water taxi, water bus, gondola, simply because we found that while a particular destination as the pigeon flies may have been a half-mile away, it was an hour and a half as the Venetian walks. If it weren't for the wakes of the taxis and police runabouts, I wouldn't have believed the water in the canals was liquid. There seemed to be no current or tide. Between San Marcos Plaza and Lido, seaweed was mired in a gelled surface, like veins in pork fat. We expected to see waves on the far side of the island, which faced the Adriatic, but there too the sea was flat, emotionless. It was as if the ocean had forgotten this bay, given these slack waters up to the continent rather than cleanse them continually. I'm sure the ocean was just as aghast as the Venetians that Venice was sinking.

I remember our obligatory gondola ride chiefly because of my repeated desire to usurp the helm and tour the less crowded canals. It felt odd to have this fellow pushing me and my girl around in a boat. ("Here the men could no longer stand it; they complained of the long voyage." Ibid.) And why wasn't anyone fishing?

In Florence, I watched a bronzed man in a rowing scull scoot back and forth between the Ponte Vecchio and the Ponte alla Carraia, like a water bug trapped in a shrinking pool. It was as poignant as anything in the Uffizi.

The yachts in the harbors of Monte Carlo and Nice must have been so distant, economically, and so far out of human scale that I considered them the way I did banks or apartment buildings. I hardly remarked upon them in my journal. But one of my last entries is from a walk along the Côte d'Azur, along a trucked-in and smoothly surfaced strand. And it's telling of where my attentions lay. Yachts weren't given a fair opportunity. "Cannes. 4-18-83 Still too cold for nudes on the beach." ("Soon they saw naked people . . . the women wear in front of their bodies a little thing of cotton that scarcely covers their genitals." Ibid.)

In Europe, only the water was as comforting as home. Whenever I felt the least insecure, I sought out a bit of river or lake or sea. I thought it must be the same water that flowed out of Eagle Mountain Lake into the Trinity and thereby into the Gulf of Mexico, a branch of the Mediterranean. Then, turning back to the mainland, I was able to see Europe as just another island, people surrounded by water, a place to leave from and come back to. (". . . to go around these islands there is need of many kinds of wind, and the wind does not blow just as men would wish." Ibid.) I'd return. What were another twenty meters to me? Only the distance we've come in five hundred years.

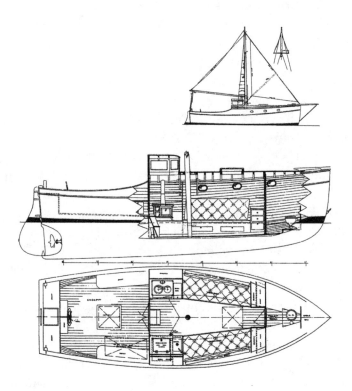

22

HOW IS IT THAT moments come but years go by?

In the binder of paperwork that came with *Yonder,* among manuals and old receipts: a single typed page of major repairs made over the preceding ten years, a handwritten, torn and taped (trapped under the tape, four fine hairs of a cat) scrap of notebook paper listing the names and dates of ownership of the previous eight captains, and a photocopied page from *Motor Boat* magazine dated November 1934. To these I added a fourth item: a set of Alden's original plans, design number 584, ordered direct from the archives of his company, still in business some fifty-eight years later. As I studied these documents over the long, waterless Texas winter of '92, I realized I was taking them too personally. They seemed to hold me responsible in some way, for I knew not what, other than, perhaps, to carry on, to hold preciously this legacy.

PLANS WORTHWHILE

Here is a little ship. There is no use calling her anything else. Designed by the well-known Boston architect, she is exactly the sort of boat for the chap who is tired of express cruisers, polished brass and calm waters. At first glance she looks like many of the Down East fishing boats. Why not? If the commercial fishermen decide that a certain type of craft works out best for their use, why wouldn't a similar boat work out for an owner who wants to go to sea and catch fish for fun instead of profit?

The husky mast with the heavy shrouds and ratlines, the coal stove, the raised companionway and the swordfish pulpit are all earmarks of a boat that can go out and take whatever the weather offers and come back home again with nothing worse than salt grime on her decks.

A picture of this boat is shown on page 8 of this issue and carries further proof that she is all that a little cruiser should be.

She is 28 feet overall; 27 feet, 1 inch on the waterline; 9 feet, 8 inches in beam and has a draft of 3 feet, 6 inches of water. In the cabin there are berths for four, all snugly arranged so that cruising in any sort of weather is comfortable and enjoyable. There is even a connection in the little companionway shelter so you can steer from there when it is really cold or rainy.

There are 3,000 pounds of inside ballast to give her plenty
of draft to hang on in broken water as well as to keep her motion from being a bit too lively for stomachs that are not used
to the sea. The Gray engine has a reduction-gear drive.

[*Motor Boat,* November 1934, p. 25.]

Home in Texas, Grandpa's dyspepsia and lack of appetite seemed
to have been brought under control. I showed him pictures of the
season's cruising.

"I liked sitting up there on that little house," he said.

Grandma leaned over his shoulders, wiping her hands on a dishtowel. "To this day I can't understand not knowing I was sick till I
was sick. It just came over me all at once."

"It didn't bother me at all," Grandpa said. "That little boat was
just as smooth . . ."

And that was the end of his sentence, except for his smile and
the period of a clap to my shoulder blade. I don't think he often bested
Grandma where stamina and resilience were concerned, and he
seemed to rather enjoy himself with this recollection.

"I'm sending the boat to a yard for the winter for some upgrades
and repairs," I said. "Next summer we'll cruise all the way to Canada."

"I can't wait," Grandma said, and tugged at a fistful of Grandpa's
red hair to watch his head come along with it at that peculiar angle.

THE ARTICLE IN *Motor Boat* made it apparent that the trade of the
period respected *Yonder*'s design. I placed a classified in *WoodenBoat,*
looking for an original magazine. I wanted to see that picture "on page
8," the boat as she was brand-new. But the only response was from
a dealer in Chicago who said his November 1934 issue of *Motor Boat*
carried no such article.

"I don't understand," I said. "I have a photocopy here in front of
me. It was clearly torn from a *Motor Boat* magazine."

"I don't know what to tell you," he answered.

"What's on your page twenty-five?"

"Some ads, part of another article."

"It doesn't make any sense."

"HEY BOSS, I need a few days off." It was Grandpa, calling me at home. He worked for Heather and me, five days a week, at our antique-mall business.

"It will have to be without pay," I said. "You had too much time off this summer—lying around on yachts, I heard." He held his hand over the phone, but I could hear him laughing and telling Grandma what I'd said. My sense of humor was designed to make my family laugh. If anyone else ever laughs at anything I have to say, it's only a mutation. "Why do you need time off?" I asked.

"Well, they found this thing on my forehead and they want to take it off," he said, somewhat unsure.

"What kind of thing?"

"Well, you know I'm always having things burned and frozen off . . ." And here he launched into a story I've heard a hundred times, how he told the skin doctor to look for cancers on the end of his nose because it wouldn't hurt to have a beak like his shortened a bit, and he laughed again at the end of this story, because he's so funny and has always enjoyed having a long nose. ". . . and well, they cut a piece of this one out. What do you call it?"

"A biopsy," I said.

"A biopsy, and now they want to cut it all out."

"What is it, Grandpa?"

"Horsefly," he yelled. "What is it again? I can't ever think of that word."

"Just give me the phone," I heard her say.

"Joe Alan, Dr. Goldman says it's a melanoma, and that's the worst kind. So he's going in Thursday and they'll cut about four square inches of skin from his forehead and eyebrow, and replace it with skin from his back." Then she whispered, "He's trying not to show it, but he's scared to death. His mother died of a melanoma."

"Tell him he'll have to make up all the time he misses," I said.

143

. . .

Work done on Compromise

1982—New Westerbeke diesel

1982—Re-covered decks with marine plywood and Dynel (Bud Mcintosh)

1983—Replaced horn timber, engine beds, floor timbers from beds aft, sister-framed entire boat, replaced much planking, refastened complete hull (assistant to Gordon Swift)

1984—Replaced entire cockpit, built new lockers, replaced cockpit cap rails (Gallant Boat Works)

1985—New rudder (Gordon Swift) and bowsprit (J. Foley)

1986—Removed 1500 pounds inside ballast, recast and installed in keel (Gordon Swift)

1988—Removed galley and rebuilt to specs, replaced one plank in topsides, replaced raised deck drip rail

1991—Removed interior and replaced floor timbers forward of engine beds, replaced butt blocks in bilge, rebuilt interior to specs (Ethan Cook)

On one of the last days of summer I'd sat in a metal lawn chair in the shade of Paul Rollins's boat shed, petting his dog, Molly (my dog's name was Molly, too), and talking about my boat. If you can possibly manage this feat, I mean petting a good dog in the shade of a boat shed while talking about old boats, I would recommend immediate action. Do not permit the desperate course of human events or the inexorable march of nature to delay you. There are three things worth doing: making something new, caring for something old, and finding the lost. The fourth thing is your hand deep in dog fur, talking about the first three. I showed Paul the list of things done.

"These men who've worked on your boat: she's been very lucky."

"My father-in-law says they've been working around here for years."

"I worked with Bud. He's a master."

"Everyone's taken care of this boat," I said. "She must have had some good owners over the past fifty-eight years."

"What can we do for her now?" Paul asked.

I'd made a list. The plywood locker lids were beginning to delaminate, the grain lifting. I wanted these replaced with solid mahogany, as well as the drawer faces down below. A broken lifeline stanchion needed to be recast. The galley smokestack truncheon, a block of rust, needed to be recast in bronze. The doghouse, still covered in canvas and now rotting, needed to be re-covered just as the raised deck had been ten years earlier. The prop had to be repaired and balanced. I wanted the gear and throttle controls, now mounted just above the sole, to be repositioned and raised to a more convenient level. As it was, I occasionally brushed against the throttle with my calf and the engine would suddenly and dramatically drop to an idle. I became used to this after the third or fourth time, but guests found it unnerving. Lifelines needed to be replaced, spars and mast wooded and varnished, instrument panel canted for better viewing, hatch rebuilt, the complete hull sanded and repainted. And finally, the most important item: something I knew I needed the first day I took *Yonder*'s helm, and which the arrival of the Alden plans confirmed had once been designed in. There was originally a short, six-inch step beneath the wheel, which would allow a fellow of my height to look over the raised deck and see straight ahead. No sign of this step in the rebuilt cockpit, but the previous owner was easily six feet tall, and so perhaps was Fritz Schaller, the owner who had the cockpit made over. Frederick Mason, the original owner, and perhaps even John Alden for all I knew, may have been my height, which is five feet eight inches during a spring flood tide. I handed Paul the list. He read it.

I said, "Well?"

And he said, "We'll do what we can for her."

HOME FROM THE HOSPITAL, Grandpa lifted up the gauze so I could peek under. I clinched my teeth, trying to let the skin around my mouth remain slack.

"It looks like a patch in a sail," I said, and smiled. "Does it hurt?"

"My back hurts worse than my head." He sat in his pajamas at the dinner table, taking turns lifting a spoon to his mouth and touching his forehead gingerly. "They say it will heal up and look all right, but I don't have any hair on my eyebrow anymore."

"You'll have to be careful," I said. "You'll always look like you're winking. You'll have half the women at the antique mall thinking you're interested."

"Oh, Lord," he said, and shook his head. "I'll be glad when I can get back to work."

A few weeks later, back at work, the ladies didn't have to corner him for their hugs. He met them at the door. "How are you, Grandpa?" they asked, cooing.

"Oh, you can't beat it," he said, rubbing at the gauze over the patch of skin. But his strength hadn't returned. For years the employees had lost Grandpa and then found him again in some antique armchair in a back aisle of the mall, testing it prior to sale, sound asleep. They'd touch him lightly on the arm and he'd open his eyes and say, "This one passes."

He went with me on a supply run to Sam's Wholesale Club, but grew so tired walking the concrete aisles that I sat him on a crate of oranges while I finished. Then at lunch, in a Luby's Cafeteria jammed with other old people, I realized halfway through the meal that he hadn't taken off his cap. Not removing your cap at a table for my grandfather was roughly equivalent to not believing in God.

"You think we might get a sudden rain shower in here?" I asked, smiling, and pointed to his head.

He didn't smile back. It was one of the few times in my life he hadn't laughed at something I said. "Aw, Joe Alan," he said, looking at his plate, "these people don't want to look at me." The gauze was now off the wound, which glistened with Vaseline. The patch of skin, taken from his back, was pale as bone from a lifetime of being hidden from the sun by a khaki work shirt.

"It doesn't look that bad," I said. "When you're outside, take off your hat and let it tan. It will look just like the rest of your skin."

"I think that's what started this whole mess," he said, and then added, "I just can't eat another bite."

"Grandpa, that's liver and onions you're leaving on your plate."

"I can't think of anything more shameful, and it's good too."

And so it began, or so it ended. Within weeks he couldn't work, spent day after day at doctors' offices, ate less and less, until, just before Christmas, he was finally diagnosed with pancreatic cancer and given a few weeks to live.

IN THE MIDST of winter I dreamed dreams of summer's anxiety: I'm docking *Yonder* at a current-racked pier, no one knows how to handle lines; a Coast Guard inspector boards and wants to know where my supply of black ink pens is kept, repeating over and over that it's for my safety; I'm motoring off Whaleback Light and find my bow and prop bumping against some sort of submerged buoys and vainly attempt to avoid them; and finally the boat is sinking, water over the sole, then over the decks, and the mast slips under the waves, but I am strangely dry.

SITTING ON THE tile outside the hospital room, my aunt June told us that Grandpa had many times said that the first person he expected to see in heaven was his father, because he'd never seen him in life. His father died when Grandpa was still in the womb.

Above my desk are three old photos of my grandfather's championship baseball teams. He got work during the Depression by pitching for company teams. I thought of having him sign a baseball before he died, so that someday I could teach my children how to play catch with it. I thought of having his nine grandchildren sign a ball and placing it in the casket with him.

Around each corner, a word, some memory, imagination; my heart brimmed with pain. I watched my grandmother watch my grandfather sleep.

She said, "He looks just like his mother."

Why must we grope our way into darkness? My grandfather is the hero of many of my books, and it seemed unfair that he would die and these characters would live on. It seemed absurd, shameful, that books lived longer than lives. My grandfather was being diluted, becoming his daughter, becoming me, my children, the silent literature of genes that noted only the facts.

My father told me not to take it so hard. He'd thought Grandpa would die a half-dozen times before. "He's lived a good long life."

My mother walked around in a daze, saying, "I thought he would live forever."

But none of us would have regrets. Everyone told him, aloud, how much they loved him, and we'd been doing this for eighty-five years.

He wanted to leave the hospital and go home.

I asked Grandpa on Christmas Day if there was anything he wanted, anything he wished to do: fly in a hot-air balloon or see a chorus line of naked girls. He shook his head.

"I'm glad I know what's wrong with me," he said. "I didn't like not knowing." When Heather and I were in the living room alone with him, he told us he wasn't afraid to die, but before he could explain why, something caught in his throat and then he didn't want to talk anymore. I knew he'd always considered himself a lucky man.

He'd told us it would be over his dead body before he would be moved to the hospital bed in the second bedroom. But when he learned Grandma wasn't sleeping, he consented. I made him smile suddenly one evening with a lament of married life and I took this home with me like some precious gift, a marble too blue to be believed. He earned a pill for pain every four hours and an injection in the hip every evening. He became so weak my uncle Tommy fed him water a spoonful at a time. "Here, you like pudding," my aunt June told him, prodding his lower lip. Grandpa raised the lids of his eyes with our requests and nodded or spoke a few words. His skin was the yellow of a smoker's stained fingers. He seemed to have little to say, and we were all afraid to ask what it was like to be dying, afraid he'd ask us to save him. He'd been a fireman most of his life, but now there was no one to rescue him.

At last he wouldn't acknowledge us. He stopped speaking and only with the greatest reluctance opened his mouth for a spoonful of water. At times his feet would go blue, his hands and arms swell with retained water. With a movement that seemed almost absent-minded he'd raise his hand and touch the patch of skin on his forehead where his ordeal began. Ironically, it was finally healed. My mother, her brother and sisters, spent all their nights at their parents', leaving their mates at home. Once again they were a family under one roof as they'd been at childhood. His breathing became heavy; he began to cough and choke. We lost all communication with him save the heat off his body.

He waited, as we counted them later, ten days to a time when all the women had left the house. Aunt June had gone home for a shower; Mom and Melody and Grandma had gone to Wal-Mart. My uncle Tommy had left the room for a few minutes and when he returned, Grandpa was gone too. I wish I could say what happened next.

LATER THAT WINTER I flew to Maine, rented a car, and drove up to a snowbound York and Paul Rollins's boat shed. *Yonder* was inside, looked like an old woman who'd just taken out her teeth. She'd been dismasted, stripped of paint and varnish; hardware that wasn't missing hung loosely by screws. Her hull looked like a great bruised pear. Paul was ill, and had been for weeks. There'd been lots of dust created, but I'd come at the wrong time.

AT THE FUNERAL HOME, Brother Roberts asked Grandma about Grandpa's last thoughts, and she told him the last thing he said to her was, "Kiss me, kiss me." Well, I put a new baseball, still wrapped in its tissue paper, in the crook of Grandpa's right arm, in case he should ever want to get up a game, and so I'd be able to play again with a light heart. I've never been religious, and this was the only thing my grandfather ever took me to task for, shaking his head at my obvious ignorance. I think he thought he had enough faith to take me across the river in his wake. He helped teach me how to swim. I like, at times, to think of my grandfather as a little boy, carrot-topped, nothing in his hands but a baseball, meeting his father for the first time, beginning a human life all over again, but this time knowing the love of his father as I have. I like to think of him taking his father's large hand and turning around to wait for us.

Bay Queen	1934	Frederick Mason–deceased
"	1943	E. Y. Stimpson
"	1943	Leland Reynolds
Compromise	1958	Arlen B. Whitney
"	?	Thomas Underhill
"	1967	R. Borck
"	1973	Donald R. Schaller
"	1987	Ethan Cook

I sat at my kitchen table and added my name to the list of owners:

| *Yonder* | 1992 | Joe Coomer |

I ran my finger over the word *deceased* next to Frederick Mason's name. "Heather!" I yelled across the kitchen and up the stairwell.

"What!" she screamed.

"Maybe I could find Mr. Mason's children."

"Who's Mr. Mason and why would you want to find his children?" she yelled down the well.

I walked to the bottom of the staircase. She arrived at the top. We both had our hands on the long smooth oak rail. "He's the man who had *Yonder* built back in 1934," I explained. "Maybe there are stories. His children could tell me about him."

I found *Yonder* that spring glistening in the sun, already immersed, waiting for me at the dock on Badger's Island. There was mahogany everywhere; bronze and brass flashed in my eyes; the water at *Yonder*'s hull was bashful. This cost me a thousand dollars more than I thought it would, but I was getting used to that figure by now. Paul showed me his handiwork, noted areas for future maintenance, and helped me get under way.

I motored upriver alone, but by the time I arrived at Hutton's Landing, my grandfather was on top of the doghouse. He told me he'd stay there and watch the evening come in. I lingered for a moment, unsure, but he had a cup of coffee, so I knew he'd be warm.

That night, as I was going over *Yonder*'s bills from foundry, yard, chandlery, and haulers with Rob, he shook his head and said, "Well, maybe next time she needs refastening you should just give her up and build a new boat."

"No, I think I'll just carry on," I said. "As long as I'm able. I know it's unreasonable to like a dumpy old boat so much, but I can't help it."

The pharaohs favored boats for their postmortem transportation. The Vikings buried their chieftains in a wooden hull. King Arthur set forth to the hereafter with a sail of fire. I walked down to the foreshore in the gathering darkness, watched *Yonder*'s silhouette undulate against an electric sea, and thought about how young I was, and how long I'd live in the lee of my grandfather's life.

23

In a boat, I have always noticed that it is the fixed idea of
each member of the crew that he is doing everything.

Jerome K. Jerome,
Three Men in a Boat

JUST WHEN I THOUGHT it was safe to go back in the water, my
brother invited me on a two-day canoe ride down the Brazos River.
We would put in just below the dam at Possum Kingdom Lake, Phil
and his seven-year-old son in one canoe, me and my cousin Chad in
another, and we'd have a leisurely float downstream. "The water
should be up," Phil said.

You look back on events and try to ascertain the exact point
where everything went wrong, where you should have sensed the im-
pending doom: a rock sliding out from beneath your foot, or the way
someone's mouth remained open after they finished a sentence.
Phil's offer seemed genuine. I looked forward to a day on the water
with his son, who had an annoying resemblance to the little kid I used
to beat up twenty years earlier. I was twenty-seven years old and a
newlywed. The morning itself was warm, soft, like your wife in a
sweater just out of the dryer. We drove into west Texas through
Weatherford, Mineral Wells (famous for its spring waters, but almost
any water out here is famous), and Palo Pinto, lulled by the dry earth,
the low ranges of spare mesquite, jackrabbits resting unafraid in the
middle of the road. It's always hard to imagine a river issuing from
these loins of rocky mesa and stunted cedar. But it's there, like a steak

in a dog food bowl, a coin between your toes. The Brazos writhes in tortuous bends several hundred miles to the ocean, as if it were looking for somewhere else to go, any alternative to going to sea. Possum Kingdom is the first of three dammed reservoirs in its course, all of them convoluted, tentacled: centipedes attacked by ants. But this is only on a map. On the surface the river and its lakes are always a mystery, disappearing around a point of land, beckoning: around this bend is the fabled city of gold, or girls sunbathing on a sandy spit. I'm losing my lead here, though. I was looking for that point of departure where adventure became commuting and leisure a struggle. Perhaps it was at the canoe rental camp. We loaded our gear, sleeping bags, tent, fishing rods, food, and water into the back of the transfer truck, beneath steel canoe racks. The camp was just off State Highway 4, tucked along the bridge next to the river. The transfer truck would carry us twenty miles upriver and drop us off, and we'd float back down to the camp and our car. Simple enough. If I'd only paid more attention to the canoes themselves, mounted upside down on the truck's racks. Here was the sign. But we were so busy, loading, deciding who'd ride in the cab and who in the bed, paying rental fees. Impressed into the hulls of these two aluminum conveyances were the seals and promise of every obstruction a river can offer. These boats looked like the crushed fuselages of airliners, or cars smashed at high school fund-raisers: a dollar for three whacks with a sledge hammer. Long welds had healed terrible gashes. Each boat's stem, like a fighter's nose, had been broken and flattened. The bottoms were corrugated; the turn of the bilge was for the worse. What remained of the original red paint only made the canoes seem bloodshot and varicose-veined. All these things I noted as the day progressed. Bumping along in the back of the truck, I was too busy playing shove with my nephew, trying to make him smile, trying to apologize for all the crummy things I did to his father when he was my little brother (which for the most part he deserved).

Canoeing was a new interest for Phil. He'd kept a Sunfish for a season or two, but the lack of a trailer was a drawback to its success. I was glad to see him give it up anyway: he'd once returned from a sail with a knot on his forehead as big as the bowl of a tablespoon. While he was out on the lake alone, his boom jibed; instead of ducking first, he'd looked first and, consequently, was knocked overboard. Getting struck on the head was nothing new for Phil, we all did that for him, but falling overboard was. So he traded the Sunfish for a fiberglass canoe. And this probably should have been another sign, that my brother rented a canoe rather than use his own on the Brazos, but his excuse was the problem of transfer.

My nephew, little Phil, cached himself among the sleeping bags and gear in the back of the truck so that when he became airborne he'd have something soft to fall back into. The driver of the transfer truck either owned the business or made his salary by the trip. He took the turn off the state road onto the gravel of Fortune Bend Road as if it were simply more straight highway. My brother looked back through the cab window at his first-born son and only brother, caroming off the truck's rails and rack, and smiled. I made frantic signs at him to shoot the driver. The gravel road, rutted where it had been wet, a washboard where it had been dry, shook the old truck as if there were pennies in it. Little Phil and I reached up, caught hold of thwarts in the overturned canoes, and tried to save ourselves by hanging in midair.

"Clinch your jaws together," I yelled at him. "Maybe it will keep your teeth from chipping."

"You look like a baboon, Uncle Joe," he answered.

The canoes were held down by a single strap over the cab. As we skirted Shut In Mountain, nearing the headwaters beneath the dam, I watched the driver carefully to make sure he didn't release the tie-down in preparation to slamming on the brakes at the water's edge. But once we arrived at the bank of the river he acted as if he had the next millennium at his beck and call.

"Yeah," he said, his hands on his hips, "wish I could go down with you boys today." He untied the single strap, and then his hands went back down to his hips and got hung up there while we unloaded the canoes and gear. His last bit of help was this offering from the cab, just before he sent half the dust of Texas airborne on his return leg, "Maybe they'll start letting a little more water out of the dam later this morning."

The most important element in running a river, and I feel secure in this assertion, is a supply of water sufficient to float a boat. As I stood in the dust of the driver's leaving, my own mind suddenly became buoyant. I turned to the waters of the Brazos River, sparkling and quick over a gravel bed, and tried to judge how many inches over my ankles it might come were I to step in. However, my fears were quickly put to rest when the canoe of the two Phils, with sleeping bags and tent aboard, skimmed over the gravel, bustling downstream. Chad and I ordered our bags, food, and cooler amidships, hurrying to little Phil's excited whoops. Then we jumped aboard and pushed off. Here my fears were quickly resurrected. The canoe clung to the gravel, locked in a coital embrace with the planet. At this juncture I realized that while I and my brother were of the same size, Chad, known as Lumpy to his high school buddies, outweighed little Phil by some two hundred pounds.

"You're going to have to get out and push," I told my young cousin.

"My feet will be wet for the rest of the day," he said.

"Take your shoes off."

"What's wrong with you pushing?" he asked.

"Older-cousinitis," I said. "Paid-for-the-canoe-rentalitis."

I looked downriver. The canoe of the two Phils was bobbing over a stretch of rapids, becoming smaller and smaller in its happiness. Finally, Chad, sure that he'd been invited for just this purpose, stepped out and pushed the canoe to deeper water, if you can call another two inches of water "deeper." I steadied the boat with my paddle while he stepped aboard, and suddenly we were off. To this day we argue over the events of the next few seconds. Not fifty feet from our point of departure we rolled the canoe, dumping food, clothing, cooler, and bodies into the eight inches of water. As we gathered up sandwiches, soda cans, and ditty bags, snagging them from the current, we asked one another how we'd best like to be re-membered. "My fault?" we said. "You were the one who was too high," we said. The canoe, now light and puppylike, kept trying to catch up to its brother. I held on with one hand and pitched supplies back in with the other. Again we boarded, Chad in the bow and an indignant captain in the stern. Both of us tried to shift our center of gravity ever lower. By the time we were approaching the short stretch of rapids, I was already in a better frame of mind. I'd been able to dip my paddle a half dozen times. Yet as we entered the shoals the hull began to grind, to bump, and finally called it quits by clutch-ing a rock and hanging on. Well, we were both wet already, so we climbed out, whereupon the canoe let go, and we all three waded to deeper water.

My brother and his son had fetched up on a gravel bar to wait for us.

"That was something," he said as Chad and I stroked on by. Lit-tle Phil hacked with laughter.

"Funny this," I said. "We lost all of our ice, and the sandwiches and extra clothes are soaked."

"You need to stay low in your boat, boys," Phil said.

Chad and I both flipped water his way with our paddles.

Even though it was spring, the sun was now hot. I took some small pleasure in watching the white meat of Chad's back roll to scarlet as the day bore on. The canoe itself became too warm to touch with bare skin. By ten I wished that I'd brought a hat and sunglasses, that the sodas were cold instead of lukewarm, that my clothes weren't so humid, that Chad would paddle more.

In the middle of a deep slack pool, I said, "Keep paddling."

"Yeah," he said. "How do I know you didn't stop paddling an hour ago?"

Oh, to be falsely accused. "Chad, I've been paddling, and I'll be damned if I'm going to paddle your carcass all the way down this river."

"If you've been paddling all the time, how'd you drink that Pepsi

I handed to you?" He hunched his shoulders, as if to catch something I might throw at him with his shoulder blades, and started to paddle again. I made a mental note to leave him at the next sandbar.

We portaged over half a dozen more shallow runs that morning, while Phil and Phil diddled on the far side. No rapid on the Brazos could carry our combined weight. I looked back upriver often, hoping the dam would burst.

We beached at Chick Bend among huge boulders fallen in the river's path. The water moved around the rocks carefully, deep green with concern. Other campers dived and swam, but somehow, now that I'd fallen accidentally into the water, all the joy of wetness had been lost for me. We ate the less sodden of sandwich corners and shared a single dry bag of cookies. Our two-day supply of food was now completely depleted. The soda cans were as hot as spent ammo casings. Chad said, "You know, my shoulders sort of hurt. Am I red, Joe Alan?" The decision wasn't hard to reach. We'd push on, forget the overnight camping, drive home that night.

We added bruises to our canoe in the afternoon. Deeper water was often obstructed from above by tree branches. As we dipped under an overhanging willow, a spider did enter my open mouth, and when I spat him out, he crawled over my lips, nose, and eyelashes, and finally paused on the inside of my eyeglass lens. I have a bit of astigmatism as well as being nearsighted, so the spider must have been appalled at this new image of his river world through my lenses. Perhaps as appalled as I was to have a massive spider obscure my vision. I forgot that my paddle wasn't a part of my arm, so when I went slapping for the spider, the paddle dropped overboard and, being much lighter than Chad, the canoe, and me, it decided to make a break for the open ocean. We chased that paddle for half a mile before it hung on another shoal. Once it was taken up again, Chad hinted that since he'd just paddled for half a mile alone, the next half mile might be my concern. This made me feel flowery toward all mankind.

Years later I would read John Graves's elegy, *Goodbye to a River,* and feel a sense of shame in that my own journey down the Brazos was so contentious and overwrought. However, Mr. Graves went down with plenty of water, his only passenger a puppy. My elegy would be written for my cousin.

As we neared our destination, I began to realize that this canyon of waters, with its banks of cottonwood and oak, was one of the few places in Texas where the sky wasn't bigger than the earth. Here a human life could be contained, have a sense of purpose whose example was the river itself, continually pushing toward the sea. Above, on the mesas and plains, there was no question of human insignificance; intent might not have any more bearing than accident. The question was whether to take the river to the sea or live on its banks. I thought I could be content doing either.

As we approached the high bridge of State Highway 4 and our landing, the current became more insistent. The river widened, then narrowed into a foam wall whose inclination was opposite that of the flow, as if the water were a big dog that didn't want to go any farther. The canoe of the two Phils shot through with bow and stern alternately high and low, my brother's back straining with the paddle. We followed. Chad soon rose up on his knees, turned to me, and in letters too small to be read, said, "Rock." We hit the stone with bow-point accuracy, Chad doubled over as if he'd been gut-punched, and I was flung across the cooler. The boat paused as if awaiting some decision, and with a mind made up, the stern swung around and took its turn leading us downriver. We managed to straighten up in front of about thirty-five onlookers at the camp and then dragged the corpse of our boat ashore, where our driver met us, his hands still tangled in the barbed wire of his belt loops.

"Didn't expect y'all till tomorrow," he said. "That was a hell of a run, twenty miles in that water in one day. You'll have to come back when the dam's open and we have some real white water."

"Next time," I said, "I'll want wheels on my canoe."

He grinned, his hands came off his hips an inch or so, and for a bizarre moment, I thought he'd fly.

My little brother, who didn't want any twenty-year-old apologies, slapped me on my own burned back and said, "Wasn't that great?"

Chad said, "I want to thank you, Joe. I've never done anything like this before. I really appreciate it." This made me feel a bit guilty about watching his back toast.

Little Phil, still brimming with energy, was at the bank throwing rocks at the river. This seemed like a good idea.

24

If rightly made, a boat would be a sort of amphibious animal, a creature of two elements, related by one-half its
structure to some swift and shapely fish, and by the other
to some strong-winged and graceful bird.

> Henry David Thoreau,
> *A Week on the Concord and Merrimack Rivers*

. . . to me a three-day fair was of more importance than
anything—except, naturally, my father and my dinghy.

> Kenneth Roberts,
> *Boon Island*

BETWEEN DING-DONG and dingle—between the pealing of bells and
a small wooded valley—lies a little boat floating like a curled leaf on
a pond, intent on the delivery of a bug from one bank to another.
Through the languid change of seasons, long past its usefulness to
men, it goes about the work of transporting deadfall and dust, pollen
and seed, across a clear span of waters, charged by the wind, performing simple acts of evolution, tendering species. In its hold, among
the wrack and mud, is a pool of rainwater, and from time to time a
dog drinks there, a frog is born, a bird bathes. Over years the old salt
in the strakes dissolves, is replaced by a graceful rot that radiates heat,
and finally with only the rippling surface of the water as witness, the
boat slips, and winks, and sinks. All good dinghies go to heaven.

Among *Yonder's* equipment at purchase was a ten-foot inflatable
dinghy. Worn and patched, with leaky valves and fraying seams, it

tended to collapse when dropped into cold water from a warm dock. Its designer didn't trust any pilot, not even the owner, because the boat's oars were bolted to the gunwales. The dinghy was so light, so exposed, that I was once caught by the wind, rowing from the dock to *Yonder*'s mooring, and blown halfway across the cove. I had the singular intimation of how it felt to be swept out to sea. Advantages were stability, a shallow draft, the carelessness with which one dripped paint on its surface, and the boat's ability to make equal headway whether the bow, stern, or gunwale was in the lead. But finally, its texture and form were so out of period with *Yonder,* left such an aesthetic oil slick in her wake, that I soon began searching for another more suitable dinghy. *Yonder,* plump old aristocrat, required a sleek poodle on her painter. The rubber sled, even after a short daysail on her leash, resembled a dead, wrinkled, and hairless shar-pei dragged mercilessly down the sidewalk home.

What's required of a dinghy? Before beauty, utility. My needs were for a small boat able to provide the tender necessities of a cruising yacht: to haul passengers and cargo safely from shore to ship, to follow *Yonder* truly when under way, to be a tour boat through scenic shallow passages, and finally, as a last resort, to save the crew's lives in the event of the mother ship's sinking. The coast of Maine makes additional requirements: swift currents necessitate a sharp bow to knife through them, and high tides sometimes make for long foreshore portages, so if a boat can't be carried it should at least be light enough to drag. The great number of dinghies overcome their shortcomings by adding an internal combustion engine to their butts, and go through their lives with a drooping stern and an upturned nose, as if they were too good for oars and water were beneath them. But an engine, for all its speed, makes for very slow going in shallow water, and for some reason, when the motor won't start, the dinghy it's attached to forgets that it can go on alone. The most stranded person I've ever met was an old man who'd motored two miles into Stonington Harbor in his twelve-foot Zodiac. His outboard had died, his milk was going bad, and even if he'd had an oar, it would be midnight before he'd reach his wife and yacht anchored off an outer island. Oars rarely take you so far from home that you can't return with them. Oars cost thirty dollars a pair, an engine anywhere from eight hundred to five grand, and then it's useless until you feed it dollar bills in the form of gallons of gas.

"IF YOU FELT this way about engines, why didn't you buy a pure sailboat?" Heather asked.

"Because sometimes the wind doesn't blow. Oars work in any kind of weather."

"I think it would be fun to zip around in a little outboard."

"Fun?" I said.

"Fun."

"Fun?" I said.

"What life is for," she explained.

"But outboards, and boats that will take them, usually aren't very pretty."

"What's pretty have to do with a dinghy?"

My jaw dropped, revealing my prostrate tongue. It laid there like a corpse in a casket. It was true. I didn't care if my dinghy was wise or strong or even buoyant. I wanted a work of art, a sculpture whose base was seawater. I'd long salivated over the sheerly graceful, lapstraked and varnish-slapped tenders occasionally presented in *WoodenBoat* magazine, oars perched on their gunwales like the wings of an insect, transoms as shapely as leaves.

Unfortunately, nothing of the kind seemed to be available. A month's perusal of want ads, chandlers, and boat yards produced two dozen dinghies built of plywood, fiberglass, and aluminum. No one was building production boats out of mere boards anymore. The most common fasteners were tape and wire, rather than screws and rivets. The boats themselves seemed to be ashamed of curves, and anything that might resemble a bow was resolutely chopped off. Apparently the boats I'd caressed in magazines were one-of-a-kinds, lovingly restored, or built with the free weekends of a lifetime by a devoted postal worker.

My last hope was the WoodenBoat Show in Newport, Rhode Island. Rob and Heather and I made the three-hour drive from Eliot. I doubted there'd be anything at the show for me, but I thought I might be able to get some direction from the builders there. Perhaps someone knew someone who knew of a builder who knew of a boat . . . At the show I walked through a display tent, bought a pair of dividers and a paperback copy of Childers's *Riddle of the Sands,* and emerged into the bright sunshine with my hand to my brow. I blinked. There before me, balanced on a pair of sawhorses . . . Heather put her hand on my forearm.

"You're jumping up and down," she said.

"Lookee," I explained.

"Oh my," Rob said. "That's a corker."

I found myself standing next to the boat, unaware of how I'd arrived. I reached out to touch it in the same way that I'd reach for a wounded bird. Here, in design and construction, was simply a work of art; ten and a half feet long, plumb-stemmed with a wineglass transom, nine copper-riveted strakes to a side, delicate oak ribs and keel. Her hull flared at the center thwart, as if she were five months pregnant. I reached across the U-shaped stern thwart and shook Chris Stickney's hand. He'd built her, and a handful just like her.

"Is this your design?" Rob asked.

"Oh no," Chris said. His eyes moved like birds hopping over one another on an electric line. He had a full beard and dark hair that he combed with his hands, a rumpled shirt, and a cautious smile. "I don't really know who the designer or original builder was. I think it's from the turn of the century. I found the old boat and took it apart for patterns. She's built with hackmatack knees, oak keel and ribs, and cedar strakes, and the top strake is aromatic red cedar."

I bent down and took a whiff. The top strake smelled like a souvenir shop in a national forest. This boat even smelled good.

"The transom's mahogany, of course, and these thwarts are fir, but you could have mahogany there too for a little more."

"How does she row?" Rob asked.

"Oh, she pulls right along," Chris said. I liked him when he didn't embellish.

"You're not from down here, are you?" Rob asked.

"Oh no, shop's up in St. George, Maine."

Rob slapped the bow thwart. This provenance, apparently, was good enough for him.

"All the fastenings are bronze and copper," Chris went on. "She weighs about seventy pounds, so you can pick her up if you have to. I put two rowing stations on her. She'll carry four easily, but if there's just two, I like to row from the bow."

"Can you put a motor on?" Heather asked.

Chris snapped his head around, as if someone had just stabbed him in the neck with a kitchen knife. "Well, I suppose you could mount a two- or three-horsepower, but she'll row as fast as the motor would push her."

"Really?" I said.

"Oh, she's real quick."

"Is this one for sale?" I asked.

"No, but I can build you one."

"How much?"

"The base model, with paint inside and out, galvanized oar locks, is eighteen hundred and fifty dollars. You can have varnish, mahogany thwarts, and bronze oarlocks for about another four hundred."

"When would she be ready?"

"Possibly by the end of the season. I get a lot of repair work in the summer, lobster boats mostly, and I like to get those guys back on the water since it's their living."

"Let us walk around a bit, Chris, and I'll get back to you, one way or the other," I said.

"Fair enough. If I'm not here, I'll be off getting a sandwich."

I shook his hand again. His grip was loose, relaxed, careful not to offend, like a doctor's. It only took one more turn through the displays to make a decision. On the waterfront we found another fairly turned tender, but she wasn't for sale. Her owner had bought her some sixty years earlier. "I thought it was a lot of money then," he said, "but now I know she was a bargain." I thanked the man profusely for saying this in front of my wife.

There was yet another lapstrake dinghy inside the main display building, but when asked the cost, the builder, who was incorporated, told me his boat had been a special order for a great yacht, and another just like her would cost around eight thousand dollars, more if I wanted mahogany. I pushed old ladies and small children to the ground on my dash back to Chris Stickney's booth.

"Chris," I asked, still winded, "how can you sell this boat for that price?"

"Well, the materials aren't that much, and I charge fifteen dollars an hour for my time."

I ordered mahogany thwarts, a bright finish, bronze oarlocks, a towing eye, and a rope gunwale guard so that when *Yonder* and *Hither* met, they'd leave each other without any impression whatsoever. I wrote a deposit check and Chris invited us up to St. George to see the shop. "Any time," he said.

I stroked the strakes one last time, as finely tucked under one another as a bird's feathers. Holding these wings taut, it was unmistakable now, was a delicate yet powerful skeletal pattern, the backbone and ribs of a fish. This was a boat designed after a wing and a fin, a creature of two elements. It also resembled Chris Stickney's cupped human hand.

A week after the boat show, in what I momentarily thought of as a bit of tragedy, Rob's next-door neighbor, Jeff, held a barn sale where I and two of Heather's cousins purchased a nine-and-a-half-foot wooden dinghy; the price was ten dollars each. We named her *Trinity*. The boat was tucked in a corner of the barn, covered with a fibrous mat of straw and cobweb. As Tom and Richard and I carried her out into the sunshine (she was as light and dry as an old insurance policy), I thought, Now here's a fine piece of irony: you look for an old dinghy for a month and it was never more than a hundred feet away, at a price of thirty bucks, and now you've paid two thousand for a boat that won't see the water till next season. I tried to console myself by noting that this dinghy clearly wasn't the work of art that *Hither* would be. Still, the difference between thirty dollars and immediately available and two thousand and wait till next year seemed rather like a severe reproach for my impatience. We carried *Trinity* up the hill to Rob's house, a man at each corner.

"Don't weigh much, does she," I noted.

"She's dry," Richard said.

We swept the straw from her hull, and I measured a half-inch gap between each of the three long boards on her bottom.

"She'll swell up," Tom said.

"Some idiot put her together with iron nails," Richard said.

Turning her over to sweep out the interior, we found a bronze plate. "She's a factory job: Baltzer Boat Works—West Medford, Mass. They used their bronze allotment in the wrong area. The name plate's going to last longer than the boat."

Rob loaned us a hammer to tap down the nails that had sprung, and gave us a pair of oarlocks to replace those missing. He looked at the long wide gaps in the bottom and said, "She might swell up."

"Couple coats of paint and she'll be fine," Tom suggested.

"Hey, we couldn't go wrong for thirty bucks," Richard insisted.

Tom and Richard painted *Trinity* that afternoon: sky-blue interior, white hull, red stem and gunwale. I wrapped the boat in canvas when she was dry and soaked her for two days. At the end of this period I could still read two lines of newsprint through each seam in the bottom. I rammed cotton into these cracks and followed it with seam compound and another coat of bottom paint. On her maiden dunking in the river she sank in four minutes without a soul aboard. We looked at her, a foot below water, and putting our hands in our pockets decided to let her swell some more right where she was. After three days we raised her and took our maiden rows. Water still issued in an unnerving stream from the three corners of the boat, but there was time for a hurried row out from the float, around a nearby mooring buoy, and back in before your knees got wet. More unnerving than the ocean boiling in was the attitude of the dinghy.

One had to align one's self on the exact centerline of the boat or she threatened to roll. Ralph Remick, Rob's good friend and a boat builder, whose *Sprig of Acacia* is moored beside *Yonder,* suggested *Trinity* might be too narrow for a flat bottom. This would make her "quick."

"It feels like I'm trying to balance on a bicycle that's standing still," I said from ten feet off the dock.

"That would be a good definition of *quick,* Joe," Ralph said, nodding.

"But this is a factory-built boat," I said. "Wouldn't they test the first one before they built more?"

"I think," Ralph said, "you'll be able to get her passable dry with a bit more cotton and caulk, but she'll always be narrow. That's probably why she was in a barn rather than in the water."

"I wouldn't put my grandmother in this boat on a bet," I said disgustedly, my spine describing a sinuous path to keep my butt dry.

That night I asked Rob, "What if *Hither* is quick, too? I'm paying two thousand dollars for a boat I might hate."

"*Hither* will be fine. She's got a rounded hull and a little keel. She'll be very stable."

"I hope so."

"I know so."

"At any event, I don't feel so bad now about the difference between thirty and two thousand."

"There's no comparison," Rob said. "You just wait."

IN MID-AUGUST, at the end of our first season on *Yonder,* Rob and I drove the three hours north to St. George to check on *Hither's* progress. Phoning ahead, we were given to understand that while work was under way, the boat probably wouldn't be ready till October. I told Chris this was fine, since I couldn't use her till next summer anyway. He explained there'd been more repair work than he'd expected, and he liked to take it when it came along. I'd run my business the same way, I told him, and reiterated the solemn fact that I wouldn't even be in the state of Maine for another nine months.

Still, gracious spirit that I imagined myself, I was put out when we arrived and found that my boat, after two months on order, consisted of four pieces of lumber: oak keel, hackmatack stem knee and stem, mahogany transom. The boat ran its full length, true, but was on the narrow side.

Chris said, "I know she doesn't look like much, but these are the important pieces. There's a lot of handwork in them, and everything builds off of them. From here on the work will go much faster."

He showed us the patterns that would mold the hull's shape, and a rather weathered-looking stack of cedar that the strakes would be cut from.

"I was lucky to find this cedar," Chris said.

"Why?" I asked, wondering if it was good or bad luck.

"Well, I know it looks warped and gray, but it's a good length and the few knots are small and tight. It's good boat lumber."

Chris's shop, open wide to the summer, was uninsulated. A large wood stove dominated the floor. Rob asked about working there in the winter.

"I can raise the temperature twenty degrees in the winter in four hours. Then I can work in the forty-degree weather inside."

Rob and I shuddered. It took some dedication to be a Maine boatbuilder.

That October I flew up to watch *Yonder* being hauled for the winter, unable to hold myself back. Since I hadn't heard from Chris, I called and he apologized and explained there wouldn't be any use in driving up because *Hither* hadn't really progressed. He'd gotten more unexpected repair work. "I'm glad to get it, and I knew you'd said there wasn't any hurry for your boat."

"I did say that, didn't I," I said listlessly.

"I'll send along a photo when there's more to report."

Still, I was glum. November passed. December too. January went without word. But in mid-February an envelope arrived, stiff with the words "Photo enclosed. Do not bend." I ripped open the letter and found a photo of *Hither,* fully planked, overturned on a pair of sawhorses. The aromatic sheer strake was still clamped in place, red as a freshly slapped cheek. There was a big dog lying on the floor beneath the boat, sweeping the shavings with his tail, seemingly satisfied with the workmanship and the safe cover of an overturned rowboat in a busy shop. Chris suggested that if I thought the progress warranted it, I might send along another bit of cash toward the total. He thought the boat would easily be finished by mid-May when I arrived. Happily I sent along the check.

In March I somewhat unexpectedly found myself in Maine again, lured north by the Maine Boatbuilders' Show in Portland and a desire to inspect *Yonder* and *Hither*. Rob, Ralph, and I found Chris in his shop, the old stove roaring, *Hither* just as I'd seen her in Chris's photo, the same dog sweeping the chips beneath her.

"Can we turn her over?" I asked.

"Sure. You can help me lift the station molds out."

We did so, and I was shocked to find the boat completely empty. There wasn't a rib in her, much less thwarts. Rivets, screws, and bedding compound held her shape. The lumber was as pale as the sole of my foot. Chris said if we'd come after lunch, we'd have caught him working on her.

"Chris," I said, "I'll be back in seven weeks, ready to put her in the water."

"She'll be ready and delivered, waiting for you."

I picked *Hither* up by the stem. She was as light as a bleached bird bone. I smiled with satisfaction. The dog wagged his tail, so I reached down and petted him too. This made me feel better.

Chris said it had done some good, at least for him, to have the boat go so long a-building. He had possible orders for two more from boat shop dropper-inners. Perhaps it was his earnestness, or the long cold winter, that made him seem so gaunt. I almost hadn't recognized him when I first walked in the door. The shop was cold. He worked alone, from job to job. I asked if he needed another advance to finish *Hither*.

He looked startled. "Oh no. I'll pick up the last check when she's finished. I'm just sorry you can't take her with you right now."

Ralph, whose compliments carry weight, commented on the fine, careful craftsmanship, the way the hood ends were let into the stem. Rob drew directions to his house on a shingle, and Chris said he'd call before coming.

A couple days before Heather and I left on the drive from Texas to Maine in May, Beverly called to say *Hither* was in the living room.

"In the living room?" I said.

"Oh, she's much too beautiful to go out in the barn. She's the most beautiful thing you've ever seen. Rob's already had Ralph and Ernest and Jeff up to see her. It's a long walk around her to change channels on the TV, but we wouldn't have it any other way. I think she'd make a wonderful coffee table if you decide you don't want to get any of that old dirty river water on her."

Little *Hither* went over on Thursday, May 20, 1993, after I'd crushed a can of Big Red, bottled in Waco, Texas, on her stem. I stepped aboard gingerly, pointed her toward *Yonder* in the distance, and stroked, stroked, stroked, and with a resounding jolt rammed my old boat. Could it be possible? I turned and looked at the motorsailer above me, turned and looked at the distance I'd covered. "This is a ROWBOAT," I whooped. I moved further out into the river, leaned left and right to test for quickness, and finding her as stable as the kitchen table, took a bearing and pulled for all I was worth. *Hither* skipped across the water, pointed true, and held her way in an amateur's hands. I bounced up and down on the thwart, buoyed up by lumber as lithe and alive as a deer.

Heather was yelling from the float, "My turn, my turn!" Reluctantly, I rowed home and passed her the oars.

"Be careful," I said. I helped her into the dinghy as if she were mounting a cardinal or a trout. She rowed around *Yonder* and came back to the float grinning.

"This is my boat," she claimed. Nanny came down to the point on Rob's arm. "Look at our new dinghy, Nanny!" Heather yelled.

Nanny paused, the words working forward slowly, with the sureness and decision of ninety years. "That's no dinghy, dear," she reproved. "That's a tender."

"That's right," Rob said, helping her to a seat on the dock bench, and then turning to Heather. "Now, dear, get out of that boat and let your old father have a turn."

The last we saw of him he was headed upriver toward Dead Duck Landing to let all the old boys gathered in their lawn chairs have a good gawk. It was a fine sight, to watch someone who'd been rowing on the river for fifty years stroke off in a new wooden boat.

It was the beginning of a new season: *Yonder's* sixtieth, *Hither's* first, and my second. *Hither* and I would have to rely on *Yonder's* experience to get us across the bar. I hoped *Hither* and I would both live as long as *Yonder* had. I hoped heaven would wait. We wanted to rot before we sank.

25

I MET MY WIFE in the high desert of New Mexico, alongside a
bustling, optimistic creek that mated with the Rio Grande, a river
that makes, through dry lands and dry villages, the narrowest of es-
capes to the sea. To impress this girl, to show that I had secrets, I carried a seed in my shirt pocket, and when the time and place were
exactly right, I tossed the kernel into a small clear pool of the creek:
from beneath an overhanging bank a small trout shot forward, took
the seed, and instantly retreated. I held my palms out and open to
show that it was I who'd created this magic, called forth four inches
of desert lightning.

"He lives here," I told her.

She asked, "How long does it take this water to get to the ocean?"

"We'll go there and ask," I said, asking if she'd go. I dropped a
short stick into the stream. "We'll look for this stick."

It's a six-hour drive from my home in Fort Worth to Port Aransas,
Texas, and the Gulf of Mexico. I was twenty-six years old before I
arrived. What took me so long? We found a tiny room in a hotel just
off Holiday Beach, and after throwing our luggage on the bed and
putting on jackets, we ran to the shore. It was March, the week after
spring break, still cool and windy. At the end of a board sidewalk we
both came to a dead halt before the beach. The Gulf, low and brown,
emptied itself in murky froth onto a field of litter, a sandy landfill.
Plastic bottles rode the crests of waves; paper clung to the wind. A
four-wheel-drive truck churned past us, its tires bursting the air blad-
ders of beached men-of-war. At intervals along the shore there were
the remains of driftwood fires, charred aluminum cans and wads of

foil at their centers. Rags and torn clothing were mired in the sandy foreshore; cigarette butts fed on them. Shredded plastic bags were tangled in the sea grass of the dunes, like dried sexual effluence matted in pubic hair.

"What happened here?" Heather asked.

"Spring break?"

"Even the shells are broken."

"The cars driving on the beach."

We went back to our car and went farther south down Mustang Island, a long low barrier of sand, pulling off occasionally to inspect the litter. Finally, driving as far as we could into the Padre Island National Seashore, and then walking for an hour, we found a sand dune that was free of trash. Here we spread a blanket and watched birds skittering through the fallback of small breakers. At dusk, the lights of distant oil platforms began to twinkle. We drove slowly back to our concrete-block room. Above the door to our hallway, a sign we hadn't noticed earlier:

PLEASE WIPE TAR FROM
FEET BEFORE ENTERING

Of this ocean I hadn't the heart to ask how long, how far, to what end. It was a different fear this time that wouldn't let me go near the water. We'd given the stick I'd dropped in Pot Creek almost two years to make it to the sea, but it was nowhere to be found.

26

OFF THE ENTRANCE TO Portsmouth Harbor, five miles to sea, lies a huddled group of rocks, the Isles of Shoals. First noted by Captain John Smith, who humbly named them after himself, these tiny islands have a long and varied history, much of which describes the shoals of fish in the surrounding shoal waters. In renaming the islands, the inhabitants decided the fish were more worthy and descriptive than Smith. The Isles had great eras of fisheries and hotels, were the home of poet Celia Thaxter, the subject of painter Childe Hassam, the site of suffering and murder. Currently, the Unitarians hold conferences on Star Island, and the University of New Hampshire studies the marine environment from Appledore; summerhouses and a few lobstermen fill niches in the rock and brush. But what draws us on our day sails with friends isn't the human history, but the idea of islands.

"Where will we go?" guests ask.

"To the islands," I tell them, and their faces become full, like sails on a reach, as if they'd remembered something to do with joy. In return my own head bobs happily along like a buoy free in the current. To the islands: declaration, verb, destination, a lifetime's worthy pursuit. It's so convenient that they're only five miles away, an hour's cruise from Whaleback Light if the ebb is under way.

Heather stacks Moe's sandwiches under her arm like firewood, and our guests carry enough soda and cheap trinkets to barter with the inhabitants of the islands. We find that most of our guests, being from inland, have never been on a sailboat before, much less one that's sixty years old. Stepping aboard from the float at Hutton's Landing, they do one of two things: sit down solidly on the nearest locker or scamper over the decks and rigging as if the boat were a schoolyard jungle gym. As a conscientious captain, I ask if everyone can swim, and show them the whereabouts of life jackets and other safety equipment. They take this information with a slow studied gulp or complete indifference.

"Why are you showing me the fire extinguisher?" Hillary, a friend from high school, asks.

"Just to be safe," I explain, and try to reassure her by saying, "I've never yet had a fire on board."

"I'd just as soon remain ignorant of possible disasters, if you don't mind," she says. "You're the captain. Just take care of me."

On another day sail, I pointed out the location of life jackets to my aunt Linda, whom I suspected of being on a fatal dose of Dramamine, and she said, "Should I put one on now?"

Once we've been under way for a few moments, most of our guests find *Yonder* a stable platform, and with their eyes on the swift current of the river and the wake astern, inquire into the operation of the head. Heather instructs them in the simple hand pump operation and thoughtfully closes the door since the head faces the helm. The door has a very tentative latch, and occasionally in the yaw of a bow wave it will swing open, away from the head's occupant, and I must look far out to sea for a polite moment.

After the head has been explained, and the galley discovered ("Oh, Joe, you have a little kitchen!"), and the instruments understood, most of our passengers settle down with a pillow and blanket to sight-see. Heather and I give the standard tour: Portsmouth's brick façade, the nuclear sub at the shipyard (here we learn political affiliations), the old prison (they can't understand why the navy hasn't turned it into a hotel), the lighthouses. It's at the entrance to the harbor, where we meet the ocean's first swells, that everyone remembers we're on a boat again, rather than a bus. Hands grip coamings and lifelines, gluteus maximus muscles grope vainly at the smooth mahogany. Here, those prone to motion sickness utter small words: oh and uh, wa and hoo.

"It will smooth out a bit once we're beyond the harbor mouth,"

I reassure them. Sometimes this is the truth, often it's a brutal lie.

If the wind's not blowing directly from the Shoals, we'll raise all sails and make our wandering way to the islands. Depending on the humidity the Isles can seem just off the bow or a faint mirage on the horizon. On the way other sailboats heel past us to show they can, or perhaps for a better look at an old boat. *Yonder* rarely heels. It would take a terrific gale to make her keel defy gravity. Under raised canvas we sit like passengers on a ferry and dare our sodas to slide off the locker tops. *Yonder's* sails often hang off the gaff as indifferent as a chain-link fence. Here, between shore and shore, I turn the helm over to frightened guests and tell them to aim for the lighthouse on White Island. They take the wheel as if it were a spinning saw-blade, and scan the water ahead for mines.

"What if I hit something?"

I say, "The water's ninety feet deep here. The boat only uses three and a half feet of it."

I give Steve, another friend from high school, the main sheet. I give it to him as a gift. He takes it in both hands and pulls, feeling the power of the wind through the sail and the boom and the line, and he grins the same way he did when we were seventeen and I told him I'd kissed Allison Kaiser.

Bart, a friend from Texas, stands at the helm with a bright yellow downeaster covering his head. The skies are clear, and we're beating toward Appledore.

"I don't get it," he says. "The wind is blowing toward us but we're moving into it."

Heather and I try to explain, but finally we too admit that it's impossible. And for a few moments we all allow ourselves to inhabit a miracle.

Once the strangeness of sailing has worn away, our guests, exhibiting a remarkable adaptability, resume the activities they're prone to on dry land. Jay reenters a mystery novel he began on a couch, and Margaret lays out her paints and brushes, begins a watercolor immersed in the medium. And everyone, everyone, like the band on the *Titanic,* returns to ordinary conversations, as if we weren't in imminent danger of drowning. Marsha tells us about her students. Charlie is at work on a new novel. Tom shows Heather a line-dancing step. Aunt Bonnie and her friend Nancy tell Heather how strange her ancestors were in New Bern, North Carolina. And Boofer, Bonnie's Shelty, moves from Bonnie's lap to a view of the ocean to a somewhat anxious search for grass. Before they realize it, we're in the lee of islands.

As tour guides we have little to say, other than the attenuated history I've already presented. Even this isn't necessary. Each of us comes to an island with a complete imagination. History is an intrusion that ultimately won't last. The Isles will, and as long as there's a bare rock above sea level at low tide, people will visit and make a past and present and future for it that's more enduring because it's personal.

Each of the Shoals is skirted by a wide ring of bare rock, stark testimony to the heights of waves. The stone is cracked and broken, a natural battlement. We always arrive between storms, when the waves and the rock politely reassess each other's properties, and time after time come away reassured.

I usually take *Yonder* through the narrow gut between Appledore and Malaga Islands and then completely circle one of the Shoals to reemphasize its islandness, its vulnerability and solitude, its mandated self-sufficiency. Most of the trees are gone from these islands; a low fragrant scrub almost overwhelms narrow paths and small patches of grass. The houses seem embedded in the brush and wild roses. Rounding Star Island we enter Gosport Harbor, formed by boulder breakwaters between Smuttynose, Cedar, and Star Islands. On weekends the harbor's crowded, but if we're lucky enough to arrive on a weekday, we can choose our anchorage, and then, after the engine is shut down, we become an island among islands and are privileged to know the luxury of dry, sure footing and yet be surrounded by the sea. The stainless-steel cries of the seagulls, at first appalling and overwhelming, soon become merely white noise, but their untiring flight, loose in the wind yet unbearably anxious, never spirals down to any common haven in my imagination.

Here in the calm harbor we unwrap the sandwiches and eat as if we're gulls, wary of each other, famished with our flight from Portsmouth. Boats come and go; the ferry *Thomas Laighton* arrives at the Gosport pier on Star Island and unloads Unitarians. Lobstermen make their rounds, hauling traps that seem to place their fragile hulls bare inches from the islands' rocks. Waves resound off the windward shores, and spray fills the air with a fine mist of animal, mineral, and vegetable, so thick I sometimes feel I could survive on the atmosphere alone. Feeding the gulls with the last bits of our lunch, everyone seems to feel they've arrived.

The Unitarians graciously allow visitors to walk on their island; there's a young man at the dock to take your painter. The old white Victorian hotel, somehow imposing and welcoming at the same time, dominates the landscape, but there's a score of smaller buildings that make up the town of Gosport. We wander among these for a while, pause over old tombstones and monuments, but then turn back to that point where this place is defined, the rough rock and more abrasive sea. A slow walk on the fractured shore and you'll be retracing your steps in less than an hour. There's nowhere else to go. Once you come to understand the scrub and the rock and the gulls, the only path left is inward, and so poets are written on islands, and artists are painted there, and the rest of us are merely overwhelmed by beauty and fear. No man is an island? Every man is an island, but like the Isles of Shoals, we stand alone together. Our guests step off the boat at the end of our journey as if they've been somewhere.

27

DURING THE FIRST five years of our marriage my wife and I built a house, started a business, and restored a 1936 Ford convertible, and I wrote a book. Nowhere in the previous sentence did you read the word *boat*. But boats were there, hundreds of them, squeezed into the two- or three-week vacations Heather and I spent in Connecticut and Maine each summer. My father-in-law made sure of this. He appreciated the house and the car, the business, the book—but, well, they were none of them boats. So off we'd go in search of my education and derelict wooden hulls. He was fond of old boats and I was fond of anything derelict. In the evenings after dinner and on free Sunday afternoons, on lunch hours and stolen hours, we'd search boatyard after boatyard along the New England coast. Rob and Beverly lived in Waterford, Connecticut, at the time, so we were within striking distance of dozens of marinas, repair yards, and museums. Rob, as if by inspiration, would turn down a rutted alley, rougher than frayed cordage, and find a boatyard at its bitter end. We'd saunter through these yards, down gangways, and out onto the docks as if the keys to every boat there were in our pockets. I came to heel over near old speedboats and cruisers with portholes, but he was a sail man and, while polite, would often scoff at my choices. We'd both grimace, as if we'd bitten down on a bug, when we passed through the shadow of a plastic boat. This was an instinctual abhorrence that we somehow shared, in the same way that we instinctively loved Heather.

In a yard at the end of a patched blacktop road my heart was unlaid. Heaved ashore and lying on her port side, a twenties-era cruiser had collapsed, buckling her planks. A few strakes had sprung from the stem but still hung there like the whiskers on a dead cat. The ribs were exposed and I looked in: frayed line, loose lumber, a mass of rusted chain. The deck had been robbed of all its hardware and there was a gaping wound where the engine had once beat. I looked for a name on the stern, but this had been stolen too. She still had something of grace, a simple line that remained elegant. There's a dry pond in front of our home in Texas and I wanted to take her there and right her up in the bottom of the tank. It didn't seem fair that she'd come to this end. The house I'd just spent two years building was wood too, and so I felt for her, this old boat built by some other fellow sixty years earlier, all her water pride up on a beach. It almost seemed as if my home were lying there on the pebbles, weathered and stripped and skeletal. It made me sick. Unlike an old car rusting in a field, which could be restored by effort and replacement parts from others of its kind, a rotten boat was doomed. At great expense the lines might be taken and the boat copied, but when the season-to-season maintenance had faltered, the original was forever lost. Most of the older yards had one or two of these dismal chances lingering on the foreshore, and perhaps another on rusting stands at the yard's verge, its bow burrowing into low branches and brush, its cockpit full of leaves. In their derelict misery they all retained a trace of their former beauty and utility, but their very abandonment, their hopelessness over many seasons, brought to them something more: a hoary wisdom, a weathered visage, an acceptance of dissolve. I think this is why so many artists paint old boats and old houses: they resemble human faces. Weathered grain and cracking paint, a hogging hull, are similes for our condition, our losses, our memories.

Rob had sold his first wooden motorsailer years earlier to a Kittery family, and to his dismay watched it sit on blocks over seasons and rot away, till the new owners finally cut it up for firewood. They'd never once put the boat back in the ocean, and the rain and sun and wind took their toll. Since selling the boat Rob and his family had lived inland, in Wisconsin and Colorado, and so he'd spent years ordering fact sheets from yacht brokers, and builders' plans for small boats. Over a span of ten years he watched his friend Ralph build his boat and so became intrigued about building and sailing his own ship. The move from Connecticut back home to Maine provided the opportunity to satisfy both desires, to save a wooden boat and to build one. A neighbor had begun a project he couldn't finish for any number of reasons. Behind his barn was the weathered bare hull of a twenty-seven-foot St. Pierre dory, a Glenn-L design. Rob had always been enamored of these boats, and purchased the hull and some lumber stock, with plans to marry them to an Atomic 4 engine.

I came upon this enterprise for the first time in midwinter. The workshop behind Rob and Beverly's home was a collection of lean-tos stacked against a small carriage house that had been partitioned into three separate rooms. The dory was in a shed adjoining one of the rooms in the carriage house. The shed was about four feet shorter than the boat, but Rob had made accommodations for the bow by leaving the barn doors open and building a roof over them. To keep out the weather, he'd covered the open end with plastic. Therefore, his only winter access to the boat was through a window from the shop to the shed. Using an old crate for a first step, he could then stand on the window sill, cross a small gangway to the dory's gunwale, and then step down into the hull. The only insulation in these buildings was cardboard nailed to the rafters and studs. Rob kept a small cast-iron wood stove burning with scraps from the boat's construction, so heat and construction necessarily kept pace. Since the saws and the boat were on opposite sides of the window, the entire deck, cabin, interior, and rudder, and all the mechanical equipment, passed through this open window a piece at a time. There's a metaphor here, a boat being built through a window, but I don't yet know what it is. Working under bare lightbulbs and in the smoke of a smudge, in a group of buildings designed for horses rather than dories, he had the boat ready for launching over a couple of winters. We were lucky enough to be there. Using house jacks and round fence posts to load the slab-sided, hard-chined ship aboard a borrowed trailer took several hours, but the haul to Dead Duck Landing was worth this effort alone. Heather and I followed behind the trailer and boat in our car and so were privileged to see the snapping necks and craning heads of passing motorists. A twenty-seven-foot dory, sky blue and shaped like a crescent moon, moving down a small Maine road at forty-five miles an hour, is a true joy to behold, like watching a cow on roller skates or a building bowling. At the landing, Beverly broke a bottle of champagne over the stem, and *Long Reach* slid into her namesake, a boat saved and made at the same moment.

28

Marlow ceased, and sat apart, in the pose of a meditating
Buddha. Nobody moved for a time. "We have lost the first
of the ebb," said the Director suddenly.

Joseph Conrad,
Heart of Darkness

SOME DAYS THE greatest satisfaction to be received from a boat is
attained by leaving it on the mooring. I call them piddling days, when
the page of minor maintenance and upgrading chores moves inside
my skull as if under sail. These are the only days I don't mind going
to sea alone. What futile imagination leads me to believe that if I just
replace the gaskets in the head, my life will be perfect? That if I back-
splice the bitter ends of the halyards, women of all nationalities and

races will deem me sexually desirable? These days are most enjoyable when each individual fix requires at most fifteen minutes, a day full of little orgasms of maintenance satisfaction. But this is how an average day goes:

I spill yesterday's rains from *Hither*, load her with my canvas bag of tools and another of new gadgets and replacement parts, and row out to a boat that needs my care and that happily has no telephone. As I recall, there are a couple of Pepsis and a bag of pretzels still on board from our last day sail and this is somehow more comforting than it should be for someone fifteen pounds overweight. The water laps at *Hither*'s strakes like a litter of excited puppies. They tussle with my oars at every stroke, and I can't help but smile. Lifting the canvas bags over *Yonder*'s freeboard and dropping them on the new mahogany locker tops, I notice that a seagull or cormorant has left a starburst on the cockpit sole. I'm in such a good mood, I give the bird the benefit of the doubt, that it was sick, or at least that there was no malice aforethought. Then it's back to the dock for the new cabinet doors I've built and the big new mahogany head door I contracted out. The door is almost six feet long and twenty inches wide; wrapped in a blanket, one end sits in my lap as I row and the other is two feet over *Hither*'s stern. At the boat, I delicately drop the cabinet doors into the cockpit and then stand up in *Hither* to lift the head door over the coaming. First I lay the blanket out on *Yonder*'s locker so I won't scratch the mahogany (newly varnished mahogany draws sharp objects like a dartboard). Then I pick up the door and lift it up over *Yonder*'s gunwale, and we're both, the door and I, met by a malicious gust of wind. I decide not to let go of the sparkling two-hundred-dollar door, and so we are blown into the river. *Hither* begins to float away in the current. I swim as fast as I can dragging a door and catch *Hither* ten feet off *Yonder*'s stern. Once I have hold of her rope gunwale, the coldness of the water knocks the wind out of me. Still, without any air in my lungs, I'm able to squeeze out a few words describing the event. Intent on saving the door before my life, I throw it aboard *Hither* first. It's then I notice the dinghy has shipped some water, water to the level of the thwarts. I try towing *Hither* back

185

to *Yonder,* but the current is too strong. We're all being swept up-river and out into the strength of the tide. I move back alongside the dinghy and throw myself on top of the head door. It takes a few moments to rearrange my body and the door, but I'm finally able to get the door out of the way, my butt on the center thwart, and the oars in the locks. Then, taking my plastic 1993 Dallas Cowboys Super Bowl souvenir cup in hand, I begin to bail. It only takes two cupfuls to realize I'm not gaining on the water. *Hither* is completely swamped. Only the tip of the transom and bow and the oarlocks are above water. I sit on a thwart that is six inches under the surface of the ocean. Still, I don't seem to be sinking. I take the oars in my hands for a tentative sweep. The blades never come out of the water, but *Hither* moves against the current. I sweep and sweep, my hands splashing, and we continue to gain on *Yonder. Hither* carries no additional flotation. Her cedar alone buoys the boat, the head door, and me to a level at which I can row and still breathe. Arriving alongside *Yonder,* I pitch the door over into the cockpit, damn the new varnish, and then climb over the side myself, painter in hand. It is a simple job to pull *Hither* up after me, balance her on the cockpit coaming and spill the ocean from her into *Yonder's* cockpit and my canvas tool bags. Dropping her back overboard, I watch my Super Bowl cup float away. Then I stand in the center of the cockpit and drip. I'm still stunned and have a mad fit of betrayal because I feel that something should have been done a long time ago about the coldness of the ocean here. Well, at least the sun's shining. Stripping down, I wrap a towel around my waist, and distribute my salty clothing across *Yonder's* raised deck.

It turns out that the cabinet doors, although I built all four using the old ones as patterns, don't fit. All need planing, so back they go overboard into *Hither.* I can't mount the door to the head because I've forgotten the hinges. At this point the towel around my waist becomes an extraordinary bother, flapping about, bunching up when I squat. I'm a couple of hundred feet offshore and working down below, so I decide to do away with it. Moving on to the next item on my list, I unbolt the head—yeep, the porcelain is cool to the touch—

and disassemble it on the sole. It hasn't worked at all well since my uncle gagged it. The repair kit—a pair of brass balls and several rubber gaskets—only cost me seventy-four dollars. The head's pump is cumbersome and many of the bronze fastenings are pink with corrosion. I find myself using hammer, chisel, hacksaw, and an assortment of gripping pliers to take the thing down to its constituents. Here, occasionally losing my grip or balance, I begin to feel remarkably vulnerable in my nakedness, loose as I am among the unpredictability of tools. I wrap the towel about my middle again and, ripping one edge, am able to draw it up between my legs and tie it off, fashioning a comfortable and protective diaper. Thus able to continue I replace the head's worn gaskets and valves, then quickly and with some agitation remount the urinal. After caressing the cool porcelain and bronze over the course of a long hour the toilet's perfect functioning has become of fundamental importance, reluctant as I am to test the diaper. In pumping the head this first time, the increased pressure provided by the new ball bearings and gaskets sends jetting forth to the ceiling from the vented waste line a stream of seawater mixed with my own urine. A second pump of the handle produces the same result. I put my thumb over the vent and pump. This seems to halt the flow, but on the backstroke a quarter-inch circle of the skin on my thumb attempts to enter the waste vent and drag the rest of my body with it. With a sigh I remove the vent and throw it overboard into *Hither* too. It will have to be replaced. And so I transform a leaking but useful head into an unusable one with only an hour's labor.

Perhaps now is the time for a snack. When I pop a pretzel into my mouth, my mouth spits it back out into my startled hand. How could the pretzels have gone stale in only nine days? There are Pepsis in the refrigerator, but since it doesn't run twenty-four hours a day, the sodas are at body temperature and unappetizing. I should have put them in a mesh bag and hung them over the side to cool in the river when I first came aboard. For the thousandth time in my life I pause a few moments and attempt to invent time travel.

I meet with more success on the next project. Cutting a six-inch-wide rectangle from brass sheeting, I form it into a tube and clamp this to the exhaust on *Yonder*'s stern. Only an inch of pipe had extended through the transom at the waterline; when we were under way the exhaust sometimes threw a few drops of water up over the stern onto the helmsman's back. Now, with my new, patented extension in place, that impertinence would be a thing of the past. Problem solved. I do a little soft-shoe across the cockpit to my drying clothes. They're still wet.

I've ordered a custom awning to cover the cockpit, and in preparation for its arrival I attach hardware and a shock cord to one side of the boom. This will be used to tie the awning away, beneath the boom, when it's not needed. I manage to attach the hardware and run the shock cord through it, but meet a problem at this juncture. I tie a knot in one end of the shock cord, stretch it tight, and tie a knot in the far end. This works for approximately twelve seconds, when the knots in the rubber cord, under stress, slip off the ends of the line. I look at the ends of the shock cord, trying to figure out how the knots disappeared. I try again, doubling the knots, and this time I watch them. With great patience and the skill of Houdini the knots free themselves before my eyes. I've stretched the cord too severely and have already cut off the excess. There's not enough slack to tie the kind of knot that might hold, were I to know what kind of knot this might be. I pitch the cord overboard. I'll have to purchase another length.

I've bought enough brass screening to replace that in three of the portholes. The screen is held to the port by a bronze wire band. Prying this out with a screwdriver, I'm able to free the old rotting screens to use as patterns. The new brass cuts easily with tin snips, but as I attempt to put the screens in place, the warp and weave begin to unlay. The edges dissolve in my hands. I'll have to cut the screens an inch or two larger, install them, and then trim them down to size. Of course, I'll have to do this another day because I've already cut up my complete stock of screen with assembly-line efficiency.

At this point I go below and take a nap. It is a complete success. I wake up having forgotten all the day's frustrations and remembering only the magnificent achievement of the exhaust extension.

To conclude the day's work, I decide to raise a gift from my sister, a yellow-and-blue burgee that carries *Yonder*'s name with some elegance. I've been saving this bit because I know it will give me great satisfaction to see it fly at the tip of the mast. There's no pulley at the masthead and since I don't want to mount the flag permanently, I'll have to fasten one there. I've found just the thing, an old galvanized artwork of pulley hardware. Attaching the flag to a short oak staff, and taking that in my teeth, I begin to climb with pulley, screws, screwdriver, and halyard in hand. *Yonder* has no ratlines, so I have to pull myself up the bare mast, reach out and grasp the lower shrouds, throw my leg over the spreader, and then hang from the upper shrouds and the anchor light to screw on the pulley. As I'm doing this—and I'm somewhat proud to be able to do this, because I'm bleeding from only two places—a sleek fiberglass ski boat snoops up alongside *Yonder*. I usually give a wave at these sightseers, who've come to gawk at an old boat. They're usually very complimentary. But since my hands and my very teeth are full at the moment, I just continue to work. At this point the captain of the ski boat, tanned, wearing sunglasses, an absolutely gorgeous woman in a bikini at his side, yells up at me in a poetic cadence, "You're a better man than I, Gunga Din." The burgee staff is in my teeth, and I am still wearing my diaper. He laughs, the woman laughs, he gooses the ski boat, a rooster tail of spray is flung across *Yonder*'s deck and my clothes. I watch the hunk of plastic skim away at thirty knots.

Epilogue: On our next outing, taking *Yonder* up to half speed, I am suddenly drenched by a thick stream of seawater. The lengthened exhaust shoots water into a wall of our wake and the ocean, now with a better angle, vaults back over the transom into the cockpit. Heather screams. I beat the extension off with an oar.

29

Sprig of Acacia

Drink no longer water, but use a little wine for thy stomach's sake and thine often infirmities.

I Timothy 5:23

MY FIRST CRUISE was aboard Ralph Remick's *Sprig of Acacia,* a thirty-
two-foot double ender with a gaff-headed mainsail, a fore staysail,
and a jib. When Ralph wasn't working on his own boat he worked
on submarines for the United States government at Portsmouth
Naval Shipyard, designing and building what I thought must be some
of the most deviously intricate ductwork imaginable. The result of
ten years of weekends and evenings was a boat whose sheer is, bar
none, the most graceful I've ever seen. Ralph built with wood, and

the first time I stepped aboard *Sprig* I found myself fondling the tenons and dowels, the cherry and oak, as if I were rubbing on someone else's girl. I didn't mind rubbing on someone else's girl, but I didn't want to be caught. Perhaps I felt this way because whenever Ralph was around *Sprig* his concern for her went beyond care to compassion and even to an empathy for wood. With *Sprig*'s mainsheet in his hand he collected and spilled all the wind she could abide, knowing just how much he could leave to chance. I liked Ralph because he lived in a chance he built. The universe never knew *Sprig* till he made her, made her in the womb of a pole barn behind his boyhood home; her long gestation required a patience and perseverance that most don't possess. Ralph often talked of mistakes he'd made with the boat, regrets, but after that first cruise I knew that his only real miscalculation had been left at home. The temporary pole building *Sprig* was built in butted into the side of the old family barn. In building this temporary shed Ralph temporarily forgot the length of the bowsprit, and so when that step of construction arrived he had to cut a twelve-inch-square hole in the side of the barn for the sprit to project through. To this day the hole survives, high up on the wall, with a hand-lettered sign adjacent: "Think Ahead." This sign may have been a moment's humorous self-recrimination, but it also must have been Ralph's philosophy over the long shaving curl of ten years.

It was the first time I'd ever been to sea on anything smaller than a three-hundred-foot ferry, yet strangely enough, since I had no responsibilities, I had no anxiety. I knew Ralph would sooner drown than let *Sprig* come to harm, so I felt sure I'd remain safe as long as I kept a firm grip on the boat. Rob, and Heather's brother, Tom, were along for the cruise as well. I pretended nonchalance whenever they joked about a Texan at sea, but when we let go of the mooring pennant, all the Conrad and Melville I'd been storing up inside of me threatened to free itself in an undigested form. Ralph gave me a cracker and said it would pass, and it soon did. At first I was chagrined that I had no idea what to do on the boat. Rob and Ralph rushed from bow to stern drawing in and letting out lines. I hadn't read my Conrad closely enough. I remembered I'd never once turned to the glossary of nautical terms in the back of *Moby-Dick* at college, knowing the professor was more interested in the symbolism of the white whale.

"How long did it take you to build this boat?" I asked Ralph.

"Oh, off and on, Joe," he answered, "the greater part of ten years." I made a little joke. "Sort of like Ahab's obsession with the whale."

"Well, I wish there were a better reason, but it was a plain lack of funds that kept *Sprig* so long under roof. I'd save a little, buy a stick or two of lumber, build a little."

When we reached the mouth of the harbor we tacked for the open sea. I'd been as far away as Rome but this was farther by far. I couldn't see the end of water. The waves were cold and clear and often, and if I said there was a bottom to the sea, it would have been only hearsay. The sails were full of wind, sprung and spankin', and I felt myself rising from the deck and reaching up to touch the firm side, feel the warmth and resistance of it, like the belly of a pregnant woman. We rolled over, under, and through the waves, leaning into them, and my own muscles strained with *Sprig,* with the grain of the lumber, with and against a liquid world: water, wind, sweat, and tears. The uneasy motion of a sailboat's hull under power became a smooth, rapid descent through snow. We swept past tugs, an oil barge, a cable ship, and two freighters anchored outside the harbor, then, turning downeast with a freshening wind behind us, ran for Boon Island. The day was brilliant, but the water in the distance was the color of dusk. We seemed a boat painted by Winslow Homer, heeled over, wary, suffused with light.

"Boon Island," Ralph pointed, and added, "Once home to Christian cannibals." Did the Christianity make the cannibalism worse? We had peanut-butter-and-jelly sandwiches for lunch, then pretzels and Cheese Bits, then beans and slaw. I yearned for the sinewy toughness of a dead sailor's triceps.

Ralph turned the long tiller over to Rob and moved about the boat, testing standing rigging and hardware. Knots flew from his fingertips like butterflies. He shaded his eyes and followed each stay and shroud up to its attachment point high on the mast. And although his hands knew every fastening, his eyes searched as if he were on another man's boat and he couldn't understand why things went together in such a fashion. I knew this expression because it's the same way I look at the house I built in Texas or read one of my novels. It's not second-guessing or distrust of one's abilities, but the lingering sour taste of handing your work over to time and the elements. I think it must be something like watching your daughter come home from a date with her lipstick smeared, or using some new word or expression that leaves your own mouth like an insect.

When the sun began its quick descent the wind quit too, unable to work without light. We chugged through a darkening gap between shoals into Wood Island Harbor and formed up behind a line of other cruisers.

Ralph and Rob, once the anchor was set, both began to cough, so they had something gold in a cup to heal that. Then we were all to bed, as if it were our last chance. Tom and I bunked in the open cockpit. There were stars above, the flash of the lighthouse to starboard, and many gulls on a rock off our bow. There were waves breaking on the outer shoals, and waves lapping against *Sprig of Acacia,* and waves.

In three years I'd be here in *Yonder* with my grandparents; three years later and they'd both be gone. Did the waves suspect this outcome? Which of all those millions of blinking stars was I to believe?

Rob coughed down below, and Ralph, his old friend, said, "That's a terrible cough, Bobby. You better have another touch."

"My God, I'm swimming in this bunk as it is, Ralphy."

I listened to the waves, but only understood them to say, softly and softer: now, now, now.

> For any ceremonial purposes the otherwise excellent liquid, water, is unsuitable in colour and other respects.
> Sir Alan Patrick Herbert,
> *Uncommon Law*

Cold cereal for breakfast. I washed the dishes in icy, soapy seawater and rinsed them in icy fresh. Then the sun rose up out of the Atlantic, cold as a dish. It was the first time I'd been immersed in the same element that the sun seemed to rise from, each of us at sea level. Nary a breeze, as my grandfather was fond of saying, so we used the forty-two-horsepower Perkins to push us from the harbor. The surface of the water seemed as taciturn as a window, a trompe l'oeil copy of itself, yet waves still forced themselves to break on Wood Island. Seals emerged from the still surface as we passed, only to submerge before the roll of our wake broke over their heads.

As we rounded the twin lighthouses on Cape Elizabeth (home port of the boat that would rescue me in three years) the city of Portland emerged like a deranged jack-in-the-box: a pack of cigarette boats raced by, a lethargic oil tanker loomed before us, a sailboat slinked out of the city with nothing on but a billowing red spinnaker.

Ralph asked for wind. "My boy, let's away from here."

"Sin, sin, sin," Rob said.

The wind arrived, our best air yet, and we raised all sails (which sounds much better than "we raised three sails") and drilled through small wave crests. Ralph aimed for the gut between Jewell and Cliff Islands so Tom and I could see Cocktail Cove and the movie location for *The Whales of August*. The boat moved through the sea, and there were Ralph's hands on the tiller, his feet on the rim of the cockpit well. It was almost inconceivable. How could it be that men could do such things?

"Ralph," I asked, "how did you know where to begin?" I bumped the boat so he'd know what I was talking about, but I think it's a fair enough question to ask anybody without reference to anything specific. Any answer will satisfy me.

"Well now, Joe, there's a gem of a fellow, Bud Mcintosh, a real craftsman. If I didn't go by once a week and ask him a question, he'd show up at the barn wanting to know why. He was my mentor, and I couldn't have built *Sprig* without him."

"And here she is," I said proudly, in case Ralph had forgotten.

Crackers for lunch with a Fiddle-Faddle dessert.

Cocktail Cove looked like a marina after a hurricane: rafting boats, and dinghies scooting about assessing the damage.

We made an early day of it pulling into Harpswell Harbor. As Rob and Ralph set the hook, a light rain began to fall. Tom and I waited below a bit guiltily, but there was nothing for us to do above, and it seemed such a shame to get wet in a rain when we'd avoided it all day in the ocean. Ralph cooked that evening and we all offered advice, because he seemed to work so much better with wood than with food. He placed before us plates of turkey ham, green beans, and macaroni. We praised him on the colorful presentation, thinking it might be our only chance, but it tasted good too, suffused as it was with salt air and our weariness.

Our trash bag, unwelcome aboard, rode sullenly in the dinghy. But here in Harpswell it found a friend, a big gull that sat on the dinghy's stern batting his coy eyes. How did the gull know, boxed in by the instincts of millions of years of evolution, that herring now came in black plastic rather than skin? We shooed his mooning away. Rob had spotted a Dumpster on the beach. Tom rowed ashore, while I held the garbage in my lap. Tom let me take the oars for the journey back to *Sprig*. It was the first time I'd ever rowed. I'd paddled a canoe, of course, but rowing is accomplished, or attempted in my case, with two oars and backward. I learned how it was for Ginger Rogers. I rowed out into the harbor like a poisoned wasp scuttling across the kitchen linoleum on his back. Tom tried to help. "Pick a point a hundred and eighty degrees from the direction you want to go and stay on it. You won't have to keep turning around. You have to pull evenly with both arms." He tried to assuage my embarrassment by putting forth possible explanations. "You're right-handed, so you're pulling harder with your right arm. It's perfectly understandable." I orbited *Sprig*, moving closer in a tightening gyre. Rob and Ralph shouted encouragement. I was tiring.

"Throw us a damned rope," I yelled finally. "It's getting dark."

Just before bed Rob lifted his glass to *Sprig*. In the glass was more of the thin gold cough syrup. He said it was a poor substitute for a proper toast, but Ralph averred that any toast in *Sprig*'s direction was proper and had his dollop of cough syrup too, even though he'd been cured the night before.

That night I read twenty-five pages of Willa Cather's *One of Ours* with a weakening flashlight. When I switched it off, the stars were in the sky again, just like the night before. It seemed amazing that I had another opportunity to look at them. Later, a mosquito called me, and I saw that the Milky Way was above us too, transparent and lovely as an old man's memory, and then of course a gull was murdered nearby, then waves.

> And Noah he often said to his wife when he
> sat down to dine,
> "I don't care where the water goes if it
> doesn't get into the wine."
> G. K. Chesterton,
> "Wine and Water"

I awoke to a rivulet of dew running into my nostril, the runoff from a full pond gathered on my sleeping bag. My exposed pillow felt like the belly of a dead fish. Still snorting, I ducked under the bag, where it was warm and dry, but then the yelling began. Tom and I sat up: Rob and Ralph emerged from the companionway with the expressions of dogs called by their former owners. Across the water a low sweep of lobster boat was leaving the harbor towing a fleet of four weathered dories, each a different color. It was a Maine postcard, or it would have been, but for the yelling. The captain, seemingly alone on board, raved so loudly that we thought he was bluffing. The content never reached us, only the bloated buffoonery of his yelling, which seemed petulant and selfish surrounded as it was by morning. It reminded us that there were humans still about, though we'd been sailing away for two whole days.

I had oatmeal and apple juice for breakfast, and this evil mixture fermented in my stomach for much of the morning. Luckily the sea was calm, and once again we headed out under an iron sail, as Rob put it.

The seals were more plentiful here, or at least easier to sight on the enamel finish of the ocean. Something peculiar inside me wanted to rub the fur on their bellies the wrong way, and I tried to attract them with attempts at their language, but was never successful enough to see the whites of their eyes. The seals always came to the surface as if it were a street corner and they were lost. I cupped my hands around my mouth and yelled, "This way!"

The *Sprig of Acacia* made her slow way across the remainder of Casco Bay. At Cape Small, where I'd stall on my first attempt at rounding, *Sprig* puttered contentedly along, the ocean giving way. In this passage the sea was a realistic painting of itself, rather than the Cubist representation *Yonder* and I would meet. At Seguin Island we mixed with a flotilla of other motoring sailboats bound for and retreating from Boothbay Harbor. The light airs made us all only as big as our propellers, which gave Rob the opening he was waiting for. He was sure Ralph's propeller wasn't large enough. He'd worked out the calculations. Ralph allowed as this might be so, but installing a larger prop would mean rebuilding the rudder and notching into deadwood.

"It needs to be done, Ralphy," Rob said earnestly, and pointed to the bow, the bone in *Sprig*'s throat.

Ralph wavered. "I've been thinking of ordering a big drifter for these light airs."

"I'm going to buy you a larger propeller and then you'll have to change over," Rob committed.

"I just don't know, Doctor," Ralph said to the dead air around the boat. Rob's father was Dr. Hutton, and somehow the name stuck to Rob too.

We met *Appledore III,* a dude schooner, coming out of Boothbay Harbor. Her sails were as listless as a light fixture in an empty room, and her tourists sat on deck beneath them like broken bulbs.

"Sometimes you can't even buy wind," I said.

"I think you could get another half knot with the right propeller," Rob affirmed.

Ralph winced, but said, "Maybe so, Rob, maybe so."

We anchored in Lewis Cove, across the isthmus from Boothbay Harbor, still mapping out my future cruises in *Yonder*. Boothbay Harbor was at peak season: Maine T-shirts, fudge and saltwater taffy, plastic lobsters, and miniature buoys were being traded for money at an alarming rate, with real consequences for America's future. There were lines to purchase dude schooner tickets, lines to eat, lines to see seals, and lines to pee. We stood in the line to call our wives. As I held the phone the densest fog I've ever seen rolled into town as if it had been paid for by the tourists. Just behind it was night. We picked up a few supplies at the market, and then we began our slow walk back to the dinghy, each taking turn to say the word *soupy* in a lovely and affected way. A church on the eastern side of the harbor, marked by the word *Spire* on the chart, was shrouded at first, then silhouetted, in a thick whiteness of light through water. The fog seemed to buffer the building from the world, and if I were a religious person, I'd have thought we'd been brought to this time and place on the planet for a purpose. We walked on by.

Crowding into the dinghy, we began a search for *Sprig* in the dark cove. Bumping along from boat to boat, we finally found her with the aid of the one boat in ten with an anchor light. Once aboard we found every porous item waterlogged. Our sleeping bags were wet through. Shoes left on deck glistened like baby alligators. Even the bunks down below were sodden.

Then Ralph, his voice rising, "Aw, Jesus, we left the cap off the bottle, Doctor!"

Rob said, "Give it to me." He turned it up.

Ralph waited, his hands clasped in the vice of his armpits. "Well?" he stammered.

"I think it's all right," Rob said with a sigh.

Ralph took the bottle and quickly screwed the lid back on. "That was a close one, Doctor. We'll have to be more careful. Don't want to mix this stuff with water."

"Fog like this can cut a drink in half before you get it to your mouth," I said.

Tom and I woke in the middle of the night and found another boat alongside *Sprig*. The only thing that held the two boats off each other was the thickness of the fog. We called Ralph and he told us to just push him off with the boathook. I went forward and tugged on the slack anchor line, and it finally went taut. The anchor was holding well. Another boat was a mere three feet off our port bow. I showed this to Tom and he said, "What is going on?"

"Maybe they anchored in the fog and didn't see we were so close," I suggested.

We woke again an hour later and the positions of all three boats had changed. We pushed the other boats away one more time. We were fogged and befuddled. An hour later and the boats had all traded places, as if they were cards in a sidewalk con game. My attempts at sleep were thwarted by a large something feeding and splashing around the boat. By morning all the boats around us were on taut anchor lines and at least fifty feet distant. Tom and I found this hard to believe. Rob explained that low tide, around two in the morning, had allowed the nearby boats to roam on too much scope. But I was there, and I know that the thickness of the fog and the splashing fish, which sounded as if it came from above me somehow, were more pertinent to the answer. That morning the dew tasted of salt.

Oatmeal and cantaloupe for breakfast, then a morning to read because the fog persisted. Finally, Ralph determined there was a half mile or so of visibility and we motored out into the haze. Just outside, two porpoises formed two links of the Loch Ness Monster, and then a seal surfaced so near, I could make out his lashes and the tired curiosity of his eye. It seemed to us now that the seals were plotting our course. We passed the great rocky weatherbeaten shore of Pemaquid Point and a much-photographed lighthouse. In the foggy distance these sights looked like a grainy postcard from early in the century.

By early afternoon we were at New Harbor, a working harbor without much room for yachts, but one of Ralph's friends lived here and made room for *Sprig* at his dock between his two herring boats. Ralph's friend told us he didn't get to Portsmouth to fish in the win-

199

ters anymore, explaining that he was too old and his wife too smart. Then he and his crews left for an overnight search for lobster bait.

For dinner we rowed across the narrow harbor, cutting between lobster boats and trawlers, to an old farmhouse above the cove. It's now the Gosnold Arms, and you can have a fine thick steak there and look out on the boats selling lobsters and mackerel and herring.

While Rob and Ralph took the dinghy home to *Sprig,* Tom and I walked around the port to the center of town. At the head of the harbor, resting on the mudflats of low tide, was a ravaged, salvaged, and abandoned wooden trawler. The ocean moved through her every twelve hours. I looked for something I could carry away, something I could save, but the old boat was as smooth as a granite boulder on the beach.

Back at the pier we wandered through the debris of a fishing life: mounds of old nets, coils of abraded line, battered buoys, a weathered dory, rusted chain, bent anchors. It all said ceaseless, backbreaking work, cold hands, wrinkles like nets around the eyes. It made me tired to look at it. In the dusk I could have mistaken the pier and floats, with their worn accumulation of cordage and wrack, as merely picturesque rather than as testament to a life wresting life from water. The Maine fishery is in decline. All before me and much more was the cost of taking herring, in order that other fishermen could trap lobster. We've inserted a human between every link in the food chain and wonder why there's less and less for each of us. Why is it that we hold the aftermath, the ruins of the Roman Forum and those of the Anasazi, blatant failures, as some of the most beautiful places on earth? I think it's because we're all knowledgeable of being bound there, and the act of our own falling is poignant and often graceful. The last man of our species will hold a herring in one fist and a lobster in the other and not know how to bring them together.

A quiet night on deck, the harbor numbed with fog.

> *Fharshon had a son,*
> *Who married Noah's daughter,*
> *And nearly spoiled ta Flood,*

By trinking up ta water:
Which he would have done,
I at least pelieve it,
Had the mixture peen
Only half Glenlivet.
W. E. Aytoun,
"The Massacre of the Macpherson"

With our morning's oatmeal we all had fog. There was a bit of
fog between every spoonful, cleansing the palate like the rarest of
sherbets. I felt like a colorless, gelatinous fish brought up from great
depths. Since the fog effectively acted as a paste, gluing us to the dock,
I slinked up to the one-holer on the pier. I don't know what I thought
I'd see on raising the toilet lid, but it wasn't the mud of the foreshore
at low tide. This was exactly what was in view, some twenty feet
below that horizontal porthole. Never row under a dock. There was
a shard of mirror above the toilet; part of my head was reflected in
it. I thought then that it was very lucky we're started out on mirrors
so early, or I would have frightened myself. I'd been four days without a shower; my skin was the color of a dusty sunset, my hair a
horse's tail dragged through its own feces.

By noon it was decided the fog wasn't going to lift. Rob and Ralph
plotted a course on the charts and punched coordinates into Ralph's
new loran. It was the first time he'd used it. With at most a hundred
feet of visibility, we picked our way through shoals and small islands,
bound for Tenants Harbor. Tom and I sat at the bow, listening for bells
and foghorns. A breath of wind occasionally made shapes in the fog,
but dead reckoning and the loran guided us from buoy to buoy. Beneath the fog the ocean was the color of stainless steel, blemished by
many fingerprints, like the hood over a fast-food grill. We anchored
safely at last among dozens of boats. I was more impressed than ever
with Rob and Ralph's seamanship, and also that of the little electronic
box. I thought I might buy stock in this loran company. I could see
everyone in America with a loran on their belt, helping them make
it safely from refrigerator to couch.

201

There were so many boats in Tenants Harbor, locked in by the fog, that it had been difficult to find room to swing. Dinghies buzzed through the moorings, carrying screaming children. The little market on shore was packed with women who wanted fresh fruit and vegetables. Tom and I bought a bundle of grapes, while Rob and Ralph went elsewhere for a wedge of blueberry pie. But the pie didn't taste as good as it once had because the buxom waitress they'd been served by on an earlier voyage, who was now almost legend, was no longer working.

I finished *One of Ours* as the last light the fog allowed diffused. Down below, Ralph lamented, "That's the last of it, Doctor."

"No!" Rob shot back.

I could almost hear the bottle being turned upside down and shaken. "I'm afraid so."

"But how could that be?" Rob asked.

I leaned over in my bunk and spoke to the companionway. "If you break the neck off the bottle, you can work a sponge in there and have one last suck."

"This isn't a time to joke, Joe," Ralph said, his voice heavy with the wisdom of the sea.

Then I felt sorry for them and offered, "We'll be in Rockland tomorrow. Maybe there'll be a store there."

"That won't help my cough tonight," Rob said. "I've got a cough."

I woke long before dawn and there were stars above, high above, remnants of themselves through the mist. Something small and frightened splashed around the boat. Swim, I thought, swim. In the distance, farther away than the stars, I could hear a bright crashing of water against rock, waves coming home to applause, arrival after arrival, celebrated by spray and spume and the snapping synapses of my own brain.

> Throw the lumber over, man! Let your boat of life be light, packed with only what you need—a homely home and simple pleasures, one or two friends, worth the name, someone to love and someone to love you, a cat,

a dog, and a pipe or two, enough to eat and enough to
wear, and a little more than enough to drink; for thirst is
a dangerous thing.

Jerome K. Jerome,
Three Men in a Boat

It would be our last day on the boat, and still the fog persisted.
Oatmeal. Points into the loran and out we went. Fumes from the
diesel engine somehow lingered in the cockpit. Averaging two to
three knots, *Sprig*'s beautiful sails straitjacketed in their covers, we
nudged the ocean out of the way. At times the fog would lift and we'd
see a dude schooner in our path, or a fleet of Outward Bound dories,
or a massive Russian freighter, the hammer and sickle on the smokestack and flying off the stern (sailors played volleyball surrounded
by old fishing nets). Then visibility would drop again and we'd wait,
thinking all of these obstructions could surely avoid us.

"We'll smell the Russians before we hit them," Rob conjectured,
and sure enough, when we swung downwind, the stark horror of
shipboard fish processing confronted us and everyone hung over
Sprig's gunwale trying to breathe diesel fumes.

Ralph was despondent about the weather and began to chastise
his boat. "I've jammed every nook and cranny below with lead and
she's still not on her waterline. There's no more room for ballast and
the only thing I can find with a heavier specific gravity than lead is
platinum. I can't afford platinum." (Ralph tells me now that gold, irid-
ium, and osmium would also work.)

"Move your fuel tanks and put a block of lead there," Rob suggested.

But Ralph wouldn't be comforted. Realizing he was in the perfect mood for the question I'd wanted to ask, I put my hand on the
tiller and said, "Ralph, have you ever come close to losing her?"

"Just once, Joe," he said. "She broke loose from her mooring
there at Hutton's Landing. I was at work at the shipyard when someone called to say *Sprig* was laid over on the beach. Aw, Christ, my
heart just stopped beating. To show you how out of my head I was, I

didn't even stop to clock out. I raced down there and true enough, she was lying on the beach. She'd washed up and laid over in the mud as softly as you'd want. The shore of that whole river rock and ruin and she went aground in the one place she wouldn't be hurt. My old heart still flutters when I think of the mooring chain letting go—it was a swivel that parted—and *Sprig* free in the current."

We rented a mooring in Rockland Harbor that evening. Ralph's friend Ernest would drive up in the morning and take our place as crew; we'd drive his truck back home. We took showers there at the public landing. I felt so clean, I wanted to run naked through the Lobster Festival the city celebrated that evening. Late into the night, lying in our bunks, we listened to festival announcements made over a loudspeaker on shore. As the evening progressed the lobster dinners went from ten dollars to five. At last, wonderfully, a master of ceremonies took the mike. A beauty pageant floated out to us in bits and pieces, bikini flotsam: "She's eighteen . . . a graduate of . . . her interests are . . ."

"How beautiful they all must be," Ralph said, a little wistfully.

But somebody had to win. A rock band, playing tunes from Kansas and Boston, couldn't keep the fog from descending once more. Headlights spewed cones of light out over the harbor. And then, when I thought everyone in the world was asleep but me, fireworks burst high above *Sprig,* magnificent in size and density, effervescent, like the farts of God, and the fog was painted with fire. Sparks fell away, were quenched in waves, and a more acrid fog, yellow with sulfur, reminded me of my childhood summers in Texas, pedaling on my bicycle in the fog behind the weekly mosquito control trucks as they made their rounds through the neighborhood. This was the end of my first cruise. I was drunk.

30

THROUGHOUT THE LATE SPRING and early summer of my second season I looked forward to a cruise to Mystic Seaport on the Connecticut coast. *Yonder* had received an invitation to participate in the museum's annual Classic and Antique Boat Rendezvous, which was to celebrate motorsailers that year. *Sea Fox,* at sixty-seven feet, would be the largest motorsailer there, and *Yonder,* at twenty-eight feet, the smallest. *Plantina, Kiaora, Burma, Nor'easter,* and *William Hand* would fill the scales in between, and fifty other old boats—runabouts, launches, and yachts—would be our chorus. *Yonder* was recalcitrant. It was as if she believed I was taking her to a nursing home. "Don't you want to go see *Nor'easter?*" I asked my boat. "Some people say Mr. DuPont put three million dollars into her restoration." *Yonder* wasn't impressed.

The boat show was scheduled for the last weekend in July. Heather and I had spent almost two months preparing. Beyond the work Paul Rollins had seen to over the winter, *Yonder* had a new coat of Grand Banks beige applied to her decks, and the entire interior had been scraped, sanded, and painted or varnished. The new door to the head was in, the head itself polished, and from sole to deck beams a soft pink mist paint would comfort the bowels.

The pink paint was a concession to Heather's help. Her exact words were "I'll paint the head if I can paint it pink."

We were standing in the paint section of Jackson's, about to come to blows, when Lisa, who was assisting us, agreed with her. As we mixed a color with four parts of pink per million (five parts was just going overboard), another customer asked Lisa if he could paint his red hull with blue antifouling paint. Lisa answered, "If you don't mind a purple bottom." Perhaps a soft pink head wasn't so bad.

In addition to all this makeup, the new awning had arrived. It covered the entire cockpit, protecting the occupants from sun and rain. Since the awning hung from the boom, it couldn't be used while under sail, but it would be very useful sitting at the dock at Mystic for three days.

We'd taken many day sails, and a test cruise up to Boothbay to make sure all the mechanicals were in order. Nevertheless, a week before the show, and three days before we had to get under way, the heat exchanger collapsed. This device uses seawater to cool the fresh water that cools the engine. A couple of days at Patten's Yacht Yard in Eliot solved this problem, so we had a day to spare. But when I tried to leave Patten's dock *Yonder* wouldn't budge. Jamie Thompson, our mechanic, thought the starter solenoid needed to be replaced. He'd have a new one on by nine in the morning. Still *Yonder* wouldn't turn over. Using a deadweight hammer and his boot, Jamie freed the starter itself. It urped a cupful of powdered rust into the bilge. I raced the starter to a rebuild shop, but they just pulled a sheet up over its head and said it would be dead for at least a week. They didn't carry a replacement. Hansen Marine in Marblehead, Massachusetts, was the closest Westerbeke distributor. I was there shortly after noon and paid what I thought was the appalling sum of $583 for a new starter. I could roll with the DuPonts. It was that or miss the show we'd been working toward for two months. With this major investment, *Yonder* allowed that I might not have the worst of intentions for her. Jamie worked late to get the starter in and *Yonder* spent the night before the cruise on her own mooring.

As we loaded supplies the next morning, Beverly said she couldn't pump the head. It was seized. While everyone else provisioned the boat I took the head apart, found no blockage, and so put it back together. It worked. These were my hands up in the air. "You're going to Mystic," I said aloud.

Rob, Cutter, and Beverly joined me for the cruise down, and

Heather would take their place for the return. We were under Memorial at 7:05. Beverly was seasick by 7:40 and for most of the day. Cutter spewed at 1:38.

"We can go back, guys," I offered, my fingers crossed behind my back. They both huddled under blankets, their eyes dull as moth wings.

Off Cape Ann, the dragger *Anne Marie,* working way off to starboard, suddenly went to full throttle and began a slow turn toward us. She crossed our wake not five feet off *Yonder's* stern. I thought we'd trespassed on some ancient trawler burial ground and they were trying to frighten us, but as they passed we saw there was no one at the helm. Both men aboard were in the stern, working over their last haul. When they looked up and saw us, they both immediately started for the pilothouse, jerking as if they'd just burned their fingers on a match, but then realized the danger had already passed and went back to work on their drag, which was full of rocks.

On its way into Boston Harbor a megayacht crossed our wake like a French society matron stepping over *merde* on the sidewalk. She used two black helicopters for shoulder pads, and five or six pounds of gold leaf to proclaim her name was *Platinum.*

At the entrance to the Cape Cod Canal we realized we were running against the ebb. We'd already been twelve hours on the water, and *Yonder* could only manage a knot and a half against the current. We slogged on through. Twice huge freighters bore down on us. We moved to within feet of the rocky bank. It was like trying to avoid a bullet coming down a rifle barrel when you're in the barrel. Halfway through, darkness caught up with us. For some reason the running lights refused to come on. I took off their caps and placed a flashlight behind the lenses in the port and starboard lamps, and hoped we'd be seen. At last, after four hours in the canal, we turned into Onset Harbor. Rob was at the helm while I used the spotlight to find buoys. Working from the chart to the light, I miscalculated (there were fourteen buoys from the Canal to the anchorage, not thirteen), and we turned to starboard seeking the anchorage one buoy too soon. A voice in the darkness, an older woman's voice, hailed us. It seemed to come from on shore.

"You're in too close," she yelled. "You need to go further into the harbor."

I was on the pulpit, holding the anchor chain in my hands. I quickly turned and told Rob we'd been warned off, and then I turned toward the voice again and yelled back into the darkness, "I don't know who or where you are, but thank you."

"Go back to the channel and then past one more buoy, then turn in," she yelled.

"Are you here all the time?" I asked. "Or just when I need you?" But she never spoke again.

In the morning we took on fuel and found that we'd used twenty-six gallons of the thirty aboard. We'd driven *Yonder* hard.

Beverly and Cutter faced the chop in Buzzards Bay the following morning, true martyrs. Never has anyone suffered so much to reach a beauty pageant. Beverly was queasy all day, and Cutter urped at 4:17. What are logs for but to mark these occasions? I could give waypoints and miles made, but none of these are as exciting as watching a fellow human being realize that an event over which they have no control, an event frowned upon by all polite society, is suddenly and viciously upon them. As members of this polite society, the first instinct is to find a toilet, the most internal, private space in the home. On a boat, the very nature of seasickness requires the event to be a public one, and so polite society is replaced by human empathy. Rob and I threw the urpers crackers and wet hand cloths from as far away as possible on a twenty-eight-foot boat.

We pulled into the pond at Cuttyhunk Island to rest and make lunch. Sunbathers lounged on either side of the gut that led into the dredged harbor. The channel was about seventy-five feet wide, and the catamaran we squeezed past seemed to take up sixty-five feet of this. Inside, delicate waves rolled through the water as evenly spaced as clapboards. The wind blew so hard, we had to take the grill below to light it, and then three of us carried it back outside as if it were a criminal transferred from one institution to another. The chicken breasts were an inch from the flames yet still took half an hour to cook through. We had to hold on to our sandwiches with both hands, lest the chicken teach the bread to fly.

At sea again, the waves fattened, the wind belched. Rob took the helm while the three of us hid behind the raised deck to avoid spray. The waves were taller than anything I'd ever been in before, and more jumbled, a box of Scrabble letters thrown into high grass. The stem collided with a sloping wall and then another wave would hit the boat on the quarter, sending *Yonder* up and over sickeningly. When Rob shook his head, I knew it was nasty water. We saw one or two other boats working along like cats on a leash for the first time. Our goal for the day had been Point Judith, but after three hours of this turmoil we turned into the Sakonnet River and found a berth for the night in Sakonnet Harbor. The place seemed to be deserted, so we took a slip and tied off. I went ashore, searching for someone to pay, but the girls at the nearby convenience store said the dockmaster wasn't around much, so I shouldn't worry about it. This seemed agreeable. When he showed up at ten P.M. with fifty dollars written on his palm, I felt trapped. We were exhausted, still moving with the ocean's swells, although the boat was anchored at three corners. I'd been asleep for an hour. I gave him the money as if he were a troll under a bridge. It makes a bad name for all of Sakonnet when one of its citizens acts this way.

Yonder made Mystic easily the next day in six hours of pleasant motorsailing. We felt it was our due, although we knew that bad weather could last for weeks on end at sea. After waiting an hour for the bridge to the back harbor to open, we entered a slip at the Seaport all knees and elbows. Boats of inexplicable age and sheen lined the museum's quayage. Hundreds of people were milling about. Many of them paused to look down on *Yonder* and smile. I was most interested in finding a schedule for the next day's parade and taking a shower, so Rob happily answered the onlookers' questions. A New York businessman, tired of the demands of his Concordia, wanted to buy *Yonder.* "She's just what I need," he explained, and left his card. By the time I returned, Beverly, like a magician, had produced a vase of cut flowers, which made the cockpit into a glamorous little living room. I swung out the awning for a ceiling. Cutter drew a poster board proclaiming *Yonder*'s designer and builder. To the bottom of this I added, in honor of our smallest-boat status, "The Little Motorsailer That Could." Our neighbors, the Clintons, sailing *Kiaora,* were met, and we exchanged tours of our boats. Michael McMenemy, who'd invited us to the show, and whose boat, *Burma,* had been a cover story for *WoodenBoat* magazine, took me in hand to explain the parade schedule, and then he graciously gave Rob and me a tour of his magnificent ship. Two children were oiling the bronze aboard, a pleasant alternative to the dress-whites crew on *Nor'easter* polishing its hardware to a blinding gold.

The next morning, Saturday, Rob took *Hither* out for an early row and found himself a subject for Benjamin Mendlowitz, the noted marine photographer. The idea that Rob and *Hither* might be the month of July in some future edition of the *WoodenBoat* calendar, a calendar he'd lived his life by since its inception, seemed fitting and proper, and, well, really neat. Rob gave me Mr. Mendlowitz's card and related a mesmerizing conversation whose core was if *Yonder* were ever up Brooklin, Maine, way, he'd like to take some photographs of her.

"Liar," I called my father-in-law.

"No, really," he insisted.

But I'll never get to Brooklin, Maine, because the pleasurable idea of it, the open-ended invitation of it, will only last till the first blink of the shutter. I'd rather be on my way than have been there.

The parade began after lunch, so I spent the morning at the waterline washing ocean grit from the boot top, and at the tip of the mast hanging dress flags. In between these two points I got a bad taste in my mouth. Two pleasant men with clipboards asked permission to come aboard.

"Yes and you're welcome to," I said, holding the awning back.

They gave their names, quite openly, and then said, "We're your judges." (When I returned to Eliot later, I found my information packet for the show. It had come from Mystic to Maine via Texas. The packet explained about the judges, the parade, the prizes.) Take it from me, this statement caught me completely off balance. I'd brought *Yonder* so she could be celebrated along with the other old boats, as survivors, proof of their designers' skill, their builders' artisanship, their owners' maintenance, and proof of the viability of good luck. I didn't want a ribbon, nor could I believe anybody else would want one.

"You're my what?" I asked.

"Your judges," they said, somewhat uncomfortably.

I turned to my mother-in-law. "My God, Beverly, they're book reviewers."

"Oh, let them do their job," she said.

I stood at the helm, my teeth gnashing one of the spokes on the wheel, while these two men looked up *Yonder*'s skirt. They were polite and complimentary, but their clipboard was a pile of stones. The show had turned into a contest, and I didn't feel like *Yonder* had to jump over bridges for anyone.

But as soon as the parade began I was friends with the world again. We took our place behind the mahogany runabouts, leading the motorsailers, which were followed by the remainder of the fleet. I kissed my wife and said, "You know, I've never been in a parade before."

She patted me on the head and said, "Well, it's about time."

The bridge raised its one arm in salute and we passed under its armpit to cheers and waves. Reports of cannon fire echoed off the riverbanks, air horns were impudent, bells were taken in hand by anarchists. Self-appointed judges lined the shore, but their placards only carried ratings of 9 and 10, so every boat got an A. One yacht carried a brass band, another a drum corps. A sailboat crewed only by women in period costume received the most adulation. In a jealous fit I asked my wife to take off her blouse. At the mouth of the harbor the runabouts formed a circle, and since no one had told me where to go, I headed out to sea while all the boats behind me turned and filed back toward port. I thought this was very funny in a Stooges way, and gunned *Yonder* to a quick-step to resume our place in line.

Back at the Seaport I rammed *Yonder* into her slip as if I were loading a musket, rather than have fifty priceless antiques pile up and sink at my stern.

That afternoon, as we dressed for dinner, Beverly called me up to the cockpit. "Here's a man you'll want to meet," she said. She was smiling as if she'd just found a nickel in her underwear.

I shook hands with an old man, his hair the color of bone buttons. His face was weathered, but supple and friendly. "This is my boat," he said. "I owned it fifty years ago. I almost had a heart attack when I saw you in the parade."

"Are you Mr. Mason?" I asked.

"No. Leland Reynolds. I bought her from a fellow who bought her from the man who had her built. I only owned her for a year during the war. I was always buying and selling boats back then. I can't believe she's still here."

I smiled, because his astonishment was so personal, and completely authentic.

"Did you know the original owner?"

"No, but I'd see the boat out in Buzzards Bay. The fella would tow his children in two small sailboats out to the bay so they could sail in open water. That's the reason for the heavy sternposts."

"Do you remember who you sold her to?"

"No. I was always buying and selling boats. She looks just the same. Just the same. I can't believe it. You should have seen me when I first saw you. I told everyone around me, 'That's my boat.' "

"Would you like to come aboard?"

"Oh no, I don't know if I could climb out of there if I climbed down. I just wanted to see her a bit closer to make sure. It's been fifty years."

I wrote down his address in the log and told him where our home port was so he might come up for a sail someday. When he left, I turned to Beverly and she was holding her hands in prayer, but instead of "Amen" she said, "Wow."

"Amen," I said. "That was worth the whole trip."

"I'll say."

"Did you see his eyes?"

"I did. Did you see his hands touching the boat?"

We smiled at each other as if we'd both witnessed the Second Coming, which we had. That evening, at the awards dinner, the big motorsailers won restoration trophies.

On Sunday morning Rob and I went to church. We toured the Mill, Mystic Seaport's repository for some four hundred small wooden boats. They sat, oarlock to oarlock, bow to stem, in an industrial brick building that's risen to become a cathedral. The Mill wasn't open to the public daily and had the air of an attic or barn that hadn't been scavenged by antique dealers. The boats, weathered, peeling, like dry corncobs in a crib, were at rest. Most of them would never see the water again but seemed satisfied with their lot, the last examples of their kind, content to wait till somebody took their lines and built a fleet of replicas. Here and there was an old marine engine, still coated with oil and grease: Rob bowed before each of these iron idols. We walked out into the sunshine and I thought, Here's some proper work, a job worthwhile, curating a lapstrake library, bringing boats together to teach men.

As much convincing as it took, as difficult as it was to arrive, once we were at the boat show, Yonder decided she'd do her best to stay. When it came time to leave, we backed out of our slip, waving good-bye to Rob, Beverly, and Cutter, and joined another parade of departing boats that seemed more like a flock of tame ducks fighting over a single piece of bread, which was the gut leaving the harbor. Somehow the slowest of us won and led the rest in another tour of the harbor but at half the speed of the previous day's parade. Once at sea we battled against an incoming tide that seemed almost as strong as the Piscataqua's. Spray drenched us. I raised the jib, and the halyard promptly parted, leaving the sail popping like a batting cage. Heather took the wheel and I crawled out and preached from the bow pulpit, an inebriated but wholly repentant evangelist. Finally, I saw it was impossible to rewind the halyard on the roller furling tackle, so I simply knocked the clevis pin out and tied the stay, sail, and sheets to the mast. I slid back to the cockpit, cold, wet, and nauseated, and took our first opportunity at refuge at Point Judith, Harbor of Refuge.

A V-shaped breakwater of boulders protected us from the rough seas, but all through the evening and night the wind blew so hard, the mast and stays turned into bass strings, emitting a consistent chord. To Heather it sounded like a group of monks performing a medieval liturgy on deck. We drank hot chocolate to this free concert, and after each swallow I'd stick my head up into the doghouse to see if the anchor was still holding.

In the morning, Rhode Island Sound had been chastened, the water beyond the breakwater as calm as that we anchored in. I rebent the jib, and we caught the outgoing current as if we were swinging onto a moving bus. The skies were clear; my wife was a coast of dunes, lying out on the raised deck before me. I sat under my patented awning thinking I could write a book about all this, with the boat show and this beautiful day as the triumphant closing chapter, and then the engine began to blow steam again. The temperature gauge needle was buffeting against its stop, so I quickly shut the motor down. Not again, not two seasons in a row.

Heather sat up. "What is it?"

"Engine's hot. I don't know."

We were at the entrance to Buzzards Bay, between Cuttyhunk and Gooseberry Neck. Off to port was the rusting hulk of a steel barge broken on the rocks. At least this time the sea was calm. I splintered the engine hatches with my fingers. The belt was intact, no antifreeze in the bilge, no split hoses. Either the freshwater or raw-water cooling pump was out. I took the exit hose off the raw-water pump and had Heather turn the engine over. Nothing. Something wrong there. I loosened the fan belt and pulled off the pulley and housing of the pump to inspect the rubber impeller. It was fine, no abrasion whatsoever, but when I tried to spin the impeller, the sheared shaft fell out into my hand.

"Great," Heather said. "Now what do we do?"

I looked up at her. A warm wave of overcoming swept through me and broke out of my rock-bound mouth in a frothy smile. "I have another one," I said.

"Really?"

"I bought it last summer when we were in Marblehead. It cost a fortune, and I thought I was a coward for buying it. A real mechanic would have been satisfied with a spare impeller."

"But just the impeller wouldn't have fixed this?"

"No. The shaft is broken. We'd be calling someone to tow us in right now."

I took the fittings from the broken pump and put them on the new, and bolted it to the block. We started the engine and she held at an even 180, her healthy body temperature.

"That's great, honey. You did it," Heather said as we motored along again. My wife has said these words to me on only two other occasions: when I installed the first toilet in our home, and when one of my novels sold to a big producer in Hollywood. I'd now accomplished the hat trick of husbandship.

We spent the night in Onset Harbor. I found it much simpler to enter in daylight. When I called my father, he was as excited as I'd ever heard him. Not about my conquering the raw-water pump, but about his new boat: he'd just purchased a Nauticat 44, a big Scandinavian motorsailer, an ocean crosser. It cost more than his house. I hung up the phone and thought, Well, now you've done it: you've gotten your father interested in boating. I walked and rowed back to my own boat, wondering why my parents couldn't just buy a motor home like everyone else their age. I never had doubts about their abilities, I just didn't want them in the same situations I'd been in during the past week. I was thirty-four years old now and still as selfish as I'd been with my bottle of milk.

This time I went through Cape Cod Canal with the current, and *Yonder* popped out into Cape Cod Bay like a cork. Off Manomet Point the weather fouled, the wind began to buffet my patent awning, and so we called it a day at Scituate. We spent a relaxing afternoon at the movie house and shopping along the waterfront.

I dreamed that night that I argued with a bitter seaman. I recognized it in the morning as another anxiety dream, similar to the ones I had in college where I showed up for a calculus test having skipped all my classes that semester. I told the seaman, "I don't think old wooden boats and electronic navigation are mutually exclusive."

He snickered.

I went on. "With my loran, my handheld global positioning system [This was a lie in my dream: I didn't own a GPS], and staying within eyesight of the coast, I think I stand a pretty good chance of getting there."

He snickered again. "And what if," he said, herring swimming out of his open mouth, "what if your boat loses electrical power, the batteries in your GPS go dead, and a sudden fog rolls in all at once? Won't you be sorry then?"

"You what-iffers are the same guys who single-hand around Cape Horn, race your boat to its limit, and try to ride out hurricanes in the harbor by putting out the spare anchor. Who's taking the bigger chance here?" And I harrumphed. Why I harrumphed I don't know, because I practice dead reckoning occasionally to make sure the charts are correct. Then I climbed up on *Yonder*'s doghouse to preach to a huge crowd in sailing dinghies. "As Thoreau might say," I said, "we should take as much preparation to live as we do to die. As Twain might say, if we took as much preparation to live as we do to die, we'd get the same result." They seemed to receive these statements with much interest. Sheets slackened in meditation and sails luffed. Someone raised their hand to ask a question, and realizing I was undone, I woke. We were socked in.

Fog turns the world into a stage, all the scenery close at hand. The sun shone as through a scrim. I always half expect some fantastic scenery drop or a mechanical prop to enter the play currently shrouded in mist.

We ate a leisurely bowl of cereal, used the dew to wipe the salt from the mahogany, and listened to the radio for weather reports. A sailboat motored to the mouth of the harbor, disappeared, then entered stage center and took up its mooring once again. An hour later a lobster boat came in, and I hailed him.

"What's it like outside?" I yelled.

He frowned and shook his head, which I took to mean no better than inside. I brought my log up-to-date. Heather read. We were somewhat frustrated because we thought this would be our last day at sea. Portsmouth was a long day's cruise away. At ten we performed the same rite the sailboat had earlier, motoring to the mouth of the harbor, becoming disoriented, and running back to our mooring with our rudder between our legs. At eleven there seemed to be some diffusion, as if the fog were confused. I'd put all our waypoints into the loran and memorized the compass headings. Heather went forward in her life jacket, hugged the mast with one arm, and blew a foghorn every thirty seconds. We'd be crossing Massachusetts Bay, and therefore the shipping channel into Boston Harbor. Just outside the breakwater the fog enveloped *Yonder,* and Heather used the foghorn to mimic her heartbeat. We passed in close proximity to two lobster boats working the shoals. But a half mile out the fog rose to a height of twenty feet above us, and we had a quarter mile of visibility. So it remained for the rest of the day, an eye-wearying haze above slack water. *Yonder* and I moved through it as if drugged. I tried to wake myself with the radio, but even it seemed muted, so groggy it needed to be doused with a pail of water.

And so the most memorable moment of our cruise arose in the torpor of its final day. In the midst of this dream someone opened a steam valve. Heather dropped her book, and I looked at my temperature gauge, sure that I'd blown a hose on the engine. And then, in both of our minds, a process awful and wonderful occurred: we remembered something we'd seen and heard on TV. The engine was at its proper temperature. We were alone on a wide sea, near the R2 buoy off Cape Ann. It happened again, a blast of pressure. Heather shrieked, held her loose bikini top to her heart, and both my hands came off the wheel to blunder about in midair. Just off to port, like the sudden memory of all I'd forgotten, a whale, black, sleek, longer

than *Yonder,* rose, blew a shaft of spray into the air, and sounded. I
turned the engine off so that the only sounds were of water, wind,
and whales. Another surfaced a bit beyond the first, then another,
something rough on its back. My heart luffed. The power of their
breathing made us hold ours, as if there weren't enough air for all of
us to breathe at once. The heavy grace of their sounding seemed to
be an effort beyond muscle and will, as if the whales became the
water, as if they were waves and current. Another whale surfaced so
far away it looked like a boat sinking. And then they were gone.

I began a cruise in a gripe of engine problems. What I yearned
for most in my life were things of which I could not dream. Water
caroled along the hull. *Yonder* lolled in the waves, while my wife and
I silently scanned the ocean, children looking across the backyard one
last time before letting Easter go.

31

~

I have walked much to the sea, not knowing what I seek.
Loren Eiseley,
The Star Thrower

NOT KNOWING WHAT I seek, but I always seem to end my search
there. The ocean casts up countless offerings. I find things I hadn't
known I'd lost. I came from the Pacific and the Gulf to the Atlantic.
Here at Hutton's Landing, I didn't turn away. Have I discovered the
ocean once or several times? My shoes at the end of the day: worn,
hollow, gaunt, completely undecided.

When Rob and Beverly moved from Connecticut to Maine,
Heather and I began to spend more and more time along the river's
edge in front of Nanny's home. The water here was as unapproachable, as dangerous, as any ocean, but its very constancy of character
led me to believe through familiarity that I could walk along its
boundary and venture into the foreshore as the tide receded without fear of death or contamination. Heather introduced me to the
archaeological evidence of almost four hundred years of historic
human contact with the river: sherds of pottery scattered among the
stones and periwinkle shells of the beach. She and her cousins had
collected them since childhood, prizing those pieces that still retained
color and pattern: a flow-blue child, a majolica strawberry, the cap-
ital Y of an ABC plate, Homer Laughlin's signature. Every winter the
ocean turns over the beach and every spring we walk this new
ground, filling our pockets with sherds and bits of kaolin pipestem,

an occasional glass button. I'm still looking for a broken arrowhead. What was once trash is now jewelry. Beverly has begun lately attaching pin backs and earring studs to our beachcombing efforts, and we now wear these Tidal Jewels like totems. She's even made Christmas ornaments of sherd, musselshell, periwinkle, and slate so that the foreshore has become part of our religion, textured witness of soil, weather, ancestry, and sacrifice.

I walk this ocean's edge, with the ebbing tide's permission, day after day, year after year. I'm faithful because I'm never disappointed. Lifting a clump of kelp from the rocks seems so much like taking a load of wet laundry from the washer that I'm amazed to see tiny crabs falling from pockets and cuffs. The diluvial line of wrack at the reach of the spring's highest tides is interweaved with silver branches and sticks that are inherently valuable. My boat, my very heart, are bits of flotsam such as these. There are stones that fit my closed hand so perfectly that before long they assume my body temperature and I no longer know I carry them. And still the tide falls away, revealing, enticing, offering: a board that we can use on the dock, a leather-brimmed cap that my grandmother will wear when she learns I found it in the sea grass, and yet another ravaged seagull. Farther out, but within the range of a walking stick: a lobster buoy cut free by a prop, a swollen and eyeless dogfish, a rectangular chunk of Styrofoam. The tides cut as the moon wanes. I can walk out farther onto the sea's floor. There's mud there, some vegetation; a fish head stumbles by in the shallows. This is where things end. I back away.

Not content with what the waves bring in any hour, I look under the surface. With a metal detector I scan patches of coarse sand and pockets of gravel. There's so much metal in the soil, the detector is almost useless, sounding off like a pinball machine. The beach is composed of as much man-made iron as it is broken-down rock. But when I dig these objects up they're unrecognizable lumps of rust. Setting the detector to eliminate ferrous materials, I find artifacts of brass, copper, and lead: a key, a grommet from a canvas sail, a twenty-year-old dog tag, the back of a clock dated Nov. 5, 1907 (the year my grandfather was born), a gold-plated pocket watch, a handful of bullets, a triangular fishing weight, and—in a scatter that makes me think someone, a hundred years earlier, dived into the water at high tide before emptying his pockets—a half dozen coins dating from 1844 to 1892. Someone had lost sixteen cents. The brass and copper are coated with verdigris; the lead is the color of death.

All time seems condensed here on the beach, everything preserved and available, everything rotten and lost. How does something as consistent as the tide remain also perpetually new? The answers are in the foreshore, at times underwater and at times above. I walk until the littoral begins to lose the light, till even the waves have shadows. Then I'm able to make it through another night.

Beverly brings a piece of flotsam to the airport when she picks us up. We've come for a funeral. A book has finally washed up on the beach at Hutton's Landing. Beverly dried it on the radiator. Splay-spined, its leaves are crammed with sand and broken shell. The pages are stiff and singular as stalks of dried sea grass. The content is a selection of four novels. I've never heard of them or their authors before.

32

~

Yonder **when she was** *Bay Queen*

MR. REYNOLDS'S SERENDIPITOUS discovery of his old boat at Mystic gave me the incentive to contact the family of *Yonder*'s original owners. The scrap of notebook paper listed Frederick Mason as deceased, but there was an additional note in red ink: the name Frederick Mason, Jr., and a partial address. It took little detective work to complete it.

Dear Mr. Mason,

Recently I bought a boat which I believe was first owned by your father: a 1934 motorsailer designed by John Alden and built by Harvey Gamage of South Bristol, Maine. I am an author (hopefully the enclosed book will prove I'm not a complete flake) and I'm currently writing a book about this boat (which I call *Yonder* but which I believe your father called *Bay Queen*). I would be very grateful for any help you might be able to offer me as to the history of the boat, how your father came to have her designed and built, anecdotes, old photos I might copy and perhaps include in the text. How long did he own *Bay Queen*? Who did he sell her to? Etc. At the WoodenBoat Show at Mystic Seaport, I met a Mr. Reynolds, who said he'd owned the boat for a short time in 1943. He remembered your father sailing in Buzzards Bay, towing two small sailboats for his children. Two heavy stern-posts still exist. Is the story true?

The boat is still in fine shape. It's true some of her ribs are sistered and a few planks have been replaced, but I think you'd find her much as she was in the thirties, a fine boat, well built. I've found a set of the original plans, still carried by Alden. At the WoodenBoat Show thousands of pictures were taken of her and she was once again queen of the bay.

Can you help me? Perhaps you and your family would like to come up for a day sail.

Sincerely,
Joe Coomer

Soon there was a reply. I ravaged the envelope. It was from Frederick Mason, Jr.'s, daughter, Laura. It began: "Dear Mr. Coomer, How pleased my father would have been . . ." I'd missed him by ten years. But Laura and her mother were able to offer some general background and what were to me dazzling details.

Frederick Mason, Sr., was a dedicated yachtsman of Narragansett Bay, Rhode Island. He once sailed from Newport to Lisbon with John Alden aboard *Malabar X,* the last and finest schooner of the famous, race-winning Malabar series. For some fifteen years he owned and raced *Dolphin,* a thirty-four-foot auxiliary yawl designed by Alden (#385) and built by N. Blaisdell and Sons of Woolwich, Maine, in 1929. As the story went, Mr. Mason purchased approximately a dozen Beetles, small catboats, with the intention of introducing this racing fleet to Narragansett Bay. His son John received sail #1 and Fred Junior, sail #2. (Laura, as a teenager, raced sail #185.) He sold the remaining boats to local sailors. *Yonder,* or rather *Bay Queen,* would tow the fleet to Buzzards Bay in search of races. Laura was only fourteen when her grandfather died in 1959, and remembers him as "a quiet, patient man who always beat me at checkers!" Her first letter concluded with a note saying they'd found some early sepia-toned photographs of *Bay Queen,* including one of her sitting on dry land after the Hurricane of '38.

Later, on the phone, Laura and I made plans to have the photos copied. She'd also come up with a story remembered by one of her father's friends that involved bathtub gin, anchoring *Bay Queen* on one side of Narragansett Bay, and waking up the next morning on the other side of the bay, an amazing feat of anchor-dragging.

When the photos arrived, five-by-seven black-and-whites enlarged from the smaller sepia-toned pictures, I stared at them for hours, unresponsive to all other sensory data the planet offered. Here was my boat, sixty years earlier, twenty-five years before I was born. She was virtually the same. The main differences were in the details. Her hull was white instead of green. There were double companionway doors instead of a single bi-fold. She originally had rat-lines, the rope-ladder rungs that climb shrouds. There were no life-lines, but there were two short handrails atop each side of the doghouse. The doghouse itself was shaped like home plate, as in Alden's plans. Currently the doghouse had six sides, the point squared off behind the mast. The engine hatch seemed to rise above the cockpit sole by six inches. There was the original step under the wheel, just like the one I'd had Paul Rollins add, and the original wheel and throttle control, which were still on the boat. There'd once been a short traveler for the main sheet block. Running lamps hung on the shrouds. The lockers that now provide seating in the cockpit were once plain benches with water or fuel tanks beneath them. Strangest of all, mounted on the cockpit bulkhead next to the companionway was what appeared to be a household 110-volt electrical outlet.

Photographs from the Hurricane of '38 showed *Bay Queen* heeled over just off Mathewson Road, not far from the police station in Barrington, Rhode Island. The hurricane surge had lifted her over a seawall and set her down softly, a cracked rudder and bent bobstay the

Hurricane of '38

only apparent damage beyond some scuffing. In the starboard photo notice the attitude of the house and mast beyond the boat. My favorite picture is the one of *Bay Queen* towing ten, count 'em, ten small boats:

eight Beetles, an Indian, and a dinghy. She was a mother ship. Mr. Mason himself looks assured and gratified in his felt fedora, a good friend at his back pouring a bit of cough syrup.

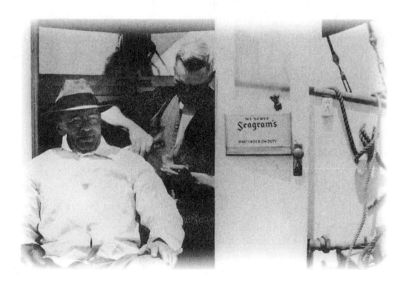

With the photos was another letter. Laura had found a contemporary of her father's, Dunc Colley, who confirmed that *Bay Queen* was "designed expressly for the purpose of towing fleets of small boats—Starboats, Beetles, and Indians primarily—to and from Marblehead, Buzzards Bay, all over Rhode Island and as far south as Great South Bay, Long Island." Dunc reminded Laura that her grandfather and father were both men fond of tall tales. Then said, "The story was that on the day they drove up to Maine to take delivery [of *Bay Queen*] the stock market (to which Mr. Mason was addicted) had such a strong run-up, the boat was paid for by the time they got there! Do you know how much that boat cost?" he asked Laura. "A thousand dollars—signed, sealed, and delivered. Not an inch of brightwork on her—all paint. Timbers so green we thought she would sprout leaves in the water!" After the Hurricane of '38, Dunc saw a light on in *Bay Queen*'s cabin as she lay listing on the road. He climbed into the cockpit, which should have been easily done. "As I entered the cabin, there was Mr. Mason, behind the door with a club, ready to repel looters!"

To this day I'm planning a trip down to Barrington and Mathewson Road. Laura says she can show me the very spot. I never knew Mr. Mason, but I somehow miss him. I miss all the hours and days and stories of the long cruise *Yonder*'s been on. I am only the current captain of this enterprise. My portion of *Yonder*'s story is such a small share, the last wave to fall on the beach. Perhaps in fifty years I'll go to a boat show, see my old boat there, restored as new. I'll shake that future captain's hand. He'll be just a boy. But *Yonder*'s age and the young captain's will only make me remember mine. Hey! I'll think, stunned, I made it to eighty-five, just like my grandpa. I'll walk away.

33

~

We have always placed a reasonable premium on returning alive.

Captain J. Y. Cousteau,
The Silent World

THAT WINTER, WITH the prospect of crewing on Dad's boat out of
West Palm Beach, my uncle Tommy and I took scuba diving lessons.
My brother was already certified, and I couldn't see myself watching him sink into the ocean alone. Our classes took place in a strip
shopping center and an eight-foot-deep pool at a private home,
structures so unlike the sea that we could concentrate on equipment
and dive tables. My dive buddy, Nola, was a striking mother of two,
my uncle's a pretty nurse, whom he required, he argued, because he
was so old. You share only two things with your dive buddy, your trust
and your mouthpiece. My uncle and I both counted ourselves lucky
that we'd signed up for class separately. The idea of sharing a mouthpiece with each other, even in an emergency, was, well, plainly taboo.

Sitting at the bottom of the pool with Nola, trying to pry up the
drain, practicing hand signals, looking at her big, distorted eyes, I suddenly realized I'd been underwater longer than any time since the
womb. I gazed at my own hand, at Nola's undulating hair, the Band-
Aid suspended in the water, and then listened to my own breathing
to see if any evolution had occurred in the previous four minutes. I
wanted more than anything to smile, but I couldn't without risking
drowning. At the end of twenty minutes, our hands full of pennies,

we gave each other the thumbs up and rose slowly, so as not to contract the bends, through the clear six feet of water to the surface.

Open-water certification took place at Lake Travis, outside Austin, Texas. Divers had trained at this scuba facility for so long, the instructor recommended we bring hot dogs to feed the tame bluegill, bass, and catfish. Mid-November, the lake temperature at sixty-eight degrees, visibility about ten feet: nothing like the crystal-clear water scuba magazines promised. Fish attacked the nubbins of turkey dogs in my hands. We found this somewhat unnerving, especially as the school followed us afterward through our procedures. At the end of the first dive, Tommy surfaced with bloody ears. A catfish had mistaken his lobes for Oscar Mayers. Nola and I swam through our requirements, exploring boats sunk for our exploration. When the instructor suddenly signaled that Nola was out of air, we calmly passed my mouthpiece back and forth for a couple of minutes and then rose to the surface, surrounded by a concerned school of fish. Down at thirty-five feet again, it was my turn to suddenly run out of air, and Nola, for an alarming moment, simply grinned. I could see her teeth on each side of the regulator. "Very funny," I mouthed, and reached for the knife strapped to my calf.

"It was strange to come eye to eye with a fish as flat and narrow as the space between my eyes. It was strange to look up at the sun through thirty-five feet of water and the air bubbles I'd just exhaled, but I didn't feel as much alien as prodigal: the fish and I both got to thirty-five feet with our own gifts. The fish didn't appear surprised to see me; he almost seemed to have been waiting. He acted as if I was late, that I was dumber than he'd thought."

These are lines from a character in one of my novels, but they're lifted from my dive journal almost verbatim. I never once reached out in fear for the bubbles of my breath that floated up and away from me. Why did I feel so comfortable in that cold, murky water, as if I were returning rather than arriving for the first time? Perhaps it was because I have a habit of quoting myself. I'd imagined the moment for so long, I felt a foglike, couch-induced sense of déjà vu.

I hugged Nola once we had our certification cards in hand, which was a reckless thing to do, the hugging, because her remorseless wit was as sharp as fish bones on the roof of your mouth. But we'd trespassed in water for the first time together, and I wanted her to know I thought we were brave.

DAD QUICKLY BECAME proficient with his boat. We ran into sandbars once or twice on the first journey from the marina to the open ocean, but once *Restless* made deep water she shook the Intracoastal grime from her rudder with a flourish. We were across the Gulf Stream and in a slip at West End, Grand Bahama, in about the same time it took *Yonder* to get to Wood Island Harbor.

I'd purchased a full set of dive gear: buoyancy compensator, wetsuit, regulator, tank, weights, and computer to go along with my classroom snorkel, fins, and mask. I hadn't owned this much personal equipment since I was a child and my mother outfitted me for the Fort Worth Fat Stock Show in a cowboy getup.

The first rule of diving is never do it alone. My uncle was along, but he'd come down with a sinus infection (he was without his nurse) and couldn't dive. There I was with all my new equipment, a warm clear ocean all before me. I felt like I'd been denied my first opportunity for sex because my date had a sniffle. And so, as with my first sexual experience, I decided to go it alone. Just off the breakwater entrance to the marina, a hundred feet from the edge of an abandoned Jack Tar Village, I slipped into the water, exchanged my snorkel for my regulator, and descended into the heretofore unapproachable ocean. Even though the water was relatively warm, I shuddered when the first trickle seeped down the back of my wetsuit, as if it were a liquid family of spiders. I was breathing so forcefully with anticipation and fear that the whistle and flap of the air through the regulator was deafening. I kicked along the sandy bottom with my dive computer in my hand: ten feet, fifteen, twenty, twenty-five feet of depth. I checked to see if I hadn't already used up all the air in my cylinder. There were clumps of sea grass potted in the sand. The first object I came upon wasn't a shell, a sponge or coral, or even a fish, but two feet of charred planking that contained a bronze thru-hull. Farther out, half embedded in the sand, was a coral-encrusted brass stern light. Treasure! Apparently a boat had burned and sunk here. Ominous portent.

Swimming across the sand, I suddenly noticed I had two shadows, one just beneath me and another ten feet away. I rolled over and looked up, hardly believing I had to squint, but the sun was still glaring through twenty-five feet of salt water. Above me, snorkeling on the surface, mirroring my every move, was my bald, infected uncle. I waved and he waved back, sick with envy. I worked toward what looked like a log from a distance, which turned out to be a square concrete pillar lying on its side. Marine life now made architectural use of the column, living beneath instead of beside it. Small, bright fish, like prostitutes' eyelids, squirted along the concrete in bursts of anxiety. Another ten feet out and I ran into the Gulf Stream. The current was solid, inhabiting a true channel. When I realized I couldn't win, I swam back over the stream's bank to still water and then ascended slowly to join my uncle.

"How was it?" Tommy asked, bobbing along beside me.

"Look what somebody left me," I answered, holding the charred plank and the stern light out of the water.

"You don't need to hold them in the air. I could see them just as well twenty feet under water. How was it?" he asked again, impatiently.

"It was just like Jacques Cousteau, except there was no couch and no TV and no French accent. It was great." I took a mouthful of seawater, gagged, and spat it out. "It was"—I searched for a word— "satisfying."

"I knew it would be," Tommy said.

On the south side of the island, among a dazzling array of life and life-born rock, I hung motionless, suspended in the sea. A flight of three stingrays, each three feet from wingtip to wingtip, had just altered its formation a bit to avoid me, then continued on their errandlike way. A spotted moray eel watched from a niche in the coral. Beneath him, a lionfish hid under a toadstool. Moving along then, a myriad of tiny, fluorescent creatures poked their heads out of crevices in the coral wall, a thousand cuckoos all set on different times. Conch shells littered the seafloor. Almost all of them were empty or inhabited by hermit crabs. Wary barracudas hung in the water, mobiles in a museum. Occasionally I'd glance over my shoulder. My father was in the dinghy, watching me with an inflated underwater viewer. "I'll be able to see every move you make," he'd consoled me. His face was warbled, oddly unfamiliar. At last I came to an open sandy area in the coral. I couldn't decide if it was for the actors or the audience: in the middle of the sand was a plastic chair covered with a mold of coral. I swam down, pivoted, had a seat, and waited. If I was the audience, I'd watch any show that came along; if I was the actor, I was already playing my part. What had I been worrying about all these years? But then I fidgeted, aware once again that I wasn't sure of my lines. I'd immersed myself in my fear, but still wanted a script to roll in my palms, a way to save myself.

THAT SUMMER I jumped off the float at Hutton's Landing. I knew the water would be cold: my thin wetsuit was designed for Florida temperatures. Still I wasn't expecting a bathtub full of ice cubes at an insane asylum, which is what fifty-four degrees in the Piscataqua felt like. My skull was being tested for hardness by a ball peen hammer; my arches cramped within the fins. I spat the snorkel out of my mouth and told Rob, who was standing on the float hugging himself, that it was impossible for water to reach this temperature without freezing.

"You'll get used to it," he said, grimacing.

Previously I'd hired a diver to check out *Yonder's* mooring, but I thought I'd save myself the expense this year. By the time I reached the mooring ball and beached myself, I was worn out with fighting the tidal current. It was twice as strong as the Gulf Stream. Next time, I thought, I'll row out. I clung to the big chain and cleared my ears as I descended. A colony of mussels, six inches in diameter and twenty-five feet long, lived on the links. I stripped them off as I dropped, which allowed the chain to swivel again. There was barely three feet of visibility, even at high slack water. Sediment and living nutrients made the water thick and pasty. I felt uneasy, as if I were following the thread that led to the Minotaur's lair. I was standing on the bottom before I saw it. It seemed a vast field of mud and jagged rocks, barren of life. As I pulled myself along the rusty chain toward the mooring stone, I was suddenly very near a big lobster, easily a three-pounder, even though I knew that objects can appear as much as thirty percent larger under water. (Which always made me wonder why masks aren't made with a thirty percent reducing lens.) The lobster stood his ground and waved his claws menacingly. I advanced. He turned, in what I thought was an attempt to escape. I'd forgotten that lobsters travel tail first. In an instant he'd shot toward me, spun around, and begun snipping at my air hoses. From my face mask, his eyes appeared as big as an antelope's. I let go of the chain and let the current sweep me back, snagging another link just before I was out of reach. Then, stupidly, I picked up a rock and carried it with me as if the lobster could be frightened off with a stone like a bird. Inching back along the chain, I found he'd moved away. I could see no other life on the bottom. The current swept everything away. But beside the mooring stone, a three-foot-by-three-foot chunk of granite that anchored the planet to the galaxy, I found a small white minnow. He looked as cold and frightened as I felt. I mumbled something about lobsters and he went and hid on the far side of the mooring block. He was to the world a drop of water that in the ocean sought another drop. An eyecup of water had found its way into my mask, and now my nose too was cold. I blew the water out but forgot to close my eyes. Salt spray and my own snot blinded me. I climbed back up the chain hand over hand to the surface, where I cleared my eyes and found Rob sitting in a dinghy.

"What are you doing out here?" I asked.

"I was watching your bubbles," he said.

"I'm so tired," I said.

"Here, take hold of the painter. I'll tow you in."

"The water won't let you rest," I explained. "You can't get away from it." And I allowed myself to be towed into shore, like the carcass of a whale, yet I was happy, because I was no longer alone. I felt sorry suddenly, as I lurched out of the water onto the float, remembering the lonely pale minnow, hiding behind the foundations of the world. It occurred to me then that God had created a world of vast diversity and intricacy so that He, rather than I, could find someplace to hide.

34

It is not only the oceans which respond tidally to the Sun
and the Moon; the Earth's surface does as well, rising and
falling twice a day. When the Moon is directly overhead
it is pulled up by half a meter.

James Hamilton-Paterson,
The Great Deep

THROUGH THE WINDOW before me channel markers blinked. Between each wink I forgot where they were. I didn't know whether
to believe in them or not. Perhaps I was being led astray. Who can
trust a full eclipse? The darkness between each flash swelled like a
drop of water at the tap. There they were again, the green buoys to
port, red to starboard. Red, right, returning. Then they were gone
once more, and the length of Long Reach from Boiling Rock to
Dover Point existed no longer.

There is no man more likely than me to accept the coming of God
or to refute His existence once He's gone. To be convinced is to admit
defeat. Take nothing for granted. Allow all possibilities. No one can
tell me I have to choose. Doubt is always reasonable. The worst insult I can receive is to be told I am a man of my convictions. I would
live my life in suspense.

The window I stood before was in our second home. Heather and
I had spent two months looking for a summer place with a water view
and were ready to give up, put off the search till the next year, when

Nanny greeted us one evening with the sentence "I've found your house." She had the local classifieds in her lap. We'd looked at the same paper for weeks and found nothing. Nanny wanted to discourage our recent search for a home in the Strawberry Banke neighborhood of Portsmouth. She wouldn't say why, but offered, "Well, you know . . ." and from this we'd understood it wasn't a neighborhood where nice people lived. Heather tried to explain to her that the last red light in the district had blinked out fifty years earlier, but Nanny wouldn't be convinced. "You want to be on this side of the river," she countered. She had ninety years of experience. We were weary from a long day of house shopping. All the water views in our price range were distant views over rooftops, through power lines. Water at that range looked like another slate roof. "I know just where it is," Nanny said, which meant she was serious enough to get in the car and show us the way to the home she'd chosen for us. Lately the view from her kitchen window had been all she required. I held her arm as we walked out to the car. She took each step as if the earth might drop out from beneath her. We made one or two false starts, but within five minutes were in a driveway at the end of a gravel road. The house was before us. It wasn't what we were looking for. Heather wanted something with some age, a Cape or saltbox. Here was a raised ranch. We certainly hadn't come to Maine from Texas, an entire state of ranch houses, to buy another. "Now, there's your home," Nanny said firmly. To appease her we made plans with a local real estate agent to view the house the next morning, a Saturday. By Monday we'd made an offer, and days later had an agreement. We closed near the end of the summer, a few weeks after returning from Mystic. Our house sat on a thirty-foot cliff at the dangerous narrows of the river known as Boiling Rock, that underwater obstruction blown up years earlier to facilitate navigation. The river itself, at ebb, seemed to flow into our living room. The length of Long Reach, three and a half miles of ocean in a valley, ran out before us all the way to Dover Point. It was somewhat disappointing that we could spend only three weeks in the house before we had to be in Texas, but we knew we'd be back for Christmas. Before the summer was gone we brought Nanny over and sat her in our only chair in front of the large window that looked out on the Piscataqua, the river she'd lived beside for nine decades. The window, six feet by eight, was filled with water and light. In midsummer the sun set at the head of the river and its reflection cascaded over the water and splashed into our home. Off to starboard we could see Nanny's home, Hutton's Landing, and out front, a pretty boat with a green hull and a narrow white waist at her mooring. "I knew it would be this way," Nanny said. "I'm so happy for you kids."

THE PREVIOUS YEAR I'd hired Independent Boat to haul *Yonder* from the river for the winter. I'd flown up to Maine in late October, lowered the mast, topped off the fuel tanks, and then met Independent at Badger's Island. Rick lowered an expensive trailer, bristling with hydraulic pistons, into the water on purpose. Then we pulled *Yonder,* a skittish horse, over the trailer, a rope at her nose and one around her rump. The hydraulic pistons raised supporting arms and pads and formed a custom cradle.

"How much does this boat weigh?" Rick asked.

"The surveyor said eighteen thousand pounds," I said.

He shook his head. "No way. Maybe nine thousand."

I shrugged. "I've got to stop believing and repeating things other people have told me."

The trailer, with *Yonder* aboard, was winched out of the water and connected to a semi. The boat slipped so easily out of the sea, she hardly dripped. *Yonder* looked like a tank making an amphibious assault on Badger's Island, her mast/gun jutting forward from her doghouse/turret. Tufts of seaweed, a gloss of black grime, and a hairy moss clung to the bottom paint. Rick knocked all of this off with 2500 psi of water pressure. There was a small nick in the prop, and a two-foot section of the bronze stem cap was missing. I thought this was light damage for my first season. Following *Yonder* along the highway at forty miles an hour, I felt an almost jubilant sense of relief that I hadn't sunk her. When we arrived, Rick jumped down from

his cab and said, "Fifteen thousand pounds, and not a pound more."

A rudder kicker, standing in Paul Rollins's yard, sidled up to me, winked, and said, "Crocker design, eh?"

At the end of our second season I decided to wet-store *Yonder* at Great Cove Marina in Eliot. Wet storing would be simpler, and according to all the experts, better for the boat. Her planks wouldn't have the opportunity to shrink and expand as they do when the hull is exposed to wind and sun. So when the time came at the end of our second season, Rob lowered the mast and took *Yonder* a mile downriver to a slip at the marina. The lowered mast and the boom are a perfect ridge row, supporting a tarp without the need for additional skeletal bracing. A little diesel bacteria inhibitor added to the fuel tanks, a shot of antifreeze for the head, draining the water tank, and *Yonder* was bedded down for the winter.

UNLIKE MY GRANDFATHER, Nanny was ill only for the last hour of her life. Instead of flying to Maine to put *Yonder* away for the winter, we flew up for Elinor Hutton's funeral. She was buried in the Eliot cemetery, beside her husband, who'd died twenty-five years earlier.

We'd lived in our home at Boiling Rock for three weeks before she left hers at Hutton's Landing. I knew Nanny for the last ten years of her ninety-year life, but this wasn't like reading the last chapter of a book or catching the final ten minutes of a movie, where there's always only a nebulous understanding of some indecipherable epiphany. Nanny's epiphany was ninety years long, and every day that I knew her she was experiencing it in its blooming brilliance: the flowers in her garden, the cards in a bridge hand, the light on the river. She was an inveterate reader, and we'd often walk into her living room to find her drugged by a novel. She'd offer Heather a cookie and then say to me, "Well, Joe, I wish you'd write a good mystery set on the river, because well, you know . . ." And I'd almost stumble into her lap, leaning forward, because I didn't know and wished she'd tell me. What was the mystery?

WE RETURNED TO Maine again at Christmas. Heather's brother, Tom, crossed the Pacific to join us, and her sister, Emily, crossed the Atlantic. I crossed two thousand miles of land to find *Yonder* twelve inches down in the bow. There was six inches of water above the sole from the head to the companionway. The upper four inches was a rotten scab of ice. I knew this was a recent event because Rob had been checking on her all through the fall. I scrambled aboard, knocked a chunk of ice off the electric bilge pump, and activated the float switch. Nothing. I checked the battery levels; they were up. A wire leading from the float switch to power had corroded. Since the electric bilge was clogged with ice, I manned the new Edson manual pump I'd installed over the summer. Even though I knew water wasn't entering the boat as fast as I pumped it out, I pumped that way, till I thought my heart would explode. After half an hour of pumping, clearing limbers, and pumping some more, *Yonder* was up to her waterline again. A riddled cake of ice remained. I broke this up into chunks and tossed it overboard, pausing from time to time to blow on my hands. I worked in a thick ache of panic and guilt. What kind of an idiot would let his boat sink at the dock? When the bilge was finally free of ice, I rewired the pump and rigged a hundred-watt bulb over it, which would burn till I returned in the spring. I knew *Yonder* had a leak but hadn't known it was so substantial. Rob promised to watch her carefully, but I knew it would be the boat's last winter afloat till she was in better condition. A dry hull was better than one ten feet underwater.

LOOKING OUT OUR window upriver, through falling snow, we could see Nanny's empty house. A flock of seagulls rode an ice floe downriver, took flight as they reached the turbulence that still exists at Boiling Rock, and flew upriver to light on another floe and begin their journey all over again. A pair of seals surfaced in the little cove below. At first, I thought they were blackened driftwood, sinuous branches, but then I realized they were looking somewhere, that they blinked.

In John P. Adams's *Drowned Valley*, a mouthful of oral history from Richard Pinkham, born in 1898 (five years before Nanny), is recorded: "In the narrows of the river was this Boiling Rock. There was a danger of these gundalows, these vessels, going night as well as day, of hitting that thing. Tides going so fast. They figured, when they got past Boiling Rock and to the old Portsmouth bridge that they were half way to Boston, no matter where they were going. That rock was a hazard, and they'd watch for it day or night to miss it. And when they passed it, if they had anything to drink everybody would have a drink aboard the ship that they'd safely passed the Boiling Rock."

Our house is embedded in Boiling Rock. Perhaps Nanny knew the safest way to avoid a hazard is to stand on it (this works for bullies too). For those of us enamored of the tides it's comforting to know the earth is affected by the moon and sun almost as much as the water is, that in our homes, and in our graves, we yet undulate with the rhythm of the sea. Every time we look out our window, we thank Nanny for the view. She was right: we needed to be on this side of the river. Her house was still the family home: Rob and Beverly would move in that spring. My wife and I celebrated our new home with a New Year's party. Heather and her cousin, Bobby, mooned the *Thomas Laighton* as she cruised by with her tourists. "Welcome to Maine!" they yelled. In that sudden white flash I recognized Nanny's smile. Then we drank a toast to our new home, and then another to the *Thomas Laighton,* and one to Nanny, to their safe passages.

35

Yonder and *Restless*

DAD CAME ALL THE WAY UP from Miami in *Restless* the next summer, shuttling crews. When *Yonder* and I met *Restless* off the Isles of
Shoals, my mother was aboard, as well as my brother and his family.
Phil and Cheryl's four children, all in life jackets at my father's orders, bounced around the boat as if it were a king-sized mattress. I
swung *Yonder* around in a wide arc and led *Restless* into my home port,
under the three bridges to a mooring at Hutton's Landing. From that
point on, poor *Yonder* spent most of the summer on her mooring in
the shadow of a bigger motorsailer and our new home. Heather and
I devoted most of our spare time to the house, building a new deck,
painting, furnishing.

The summer's long cruise was to be on *Restless*. Dad and Rob and I planned to make Nova Scotia, but Dad had made better time than he'd planned, and neither Rob nor I was ready to get under way. So in the meantime my mother and father took a shorter cruise downeast with my grandmother, Uncle Tommy, and his wife, Linda. I wasn't on this cruise but played a part in it. I've lately found a ninety-year-old chart of Richmond Island, and although this island holds a special place in my heart, I gave the chart to my father. This was where he had told me he was going to buy a boat on our first cruise together. And this is as far as *Restless* went on the cruise with my aunt and uncle and grandmother. At the close of their first day at sea, fog rolled in, completely obscuring all reference points. Dad knew the harbor from our stay there. He put Grandma on the foghorn and told her to blow it every few seconds. There was a radar on board, and working along slowly, Dad made a safe entrance, even though he could hear water breaking all around him. He anchored and then stood on the pulpit trying to peer through the fog to the shoreline. After a few minutes he realized that although he was safely anchored, the tenseness in his shoulders and neck hadn't abated. Grandma, as ordered, was still sounding the foghorn by the second hand on her watch.

"Quit that!" Dad yelled back to the helm.

Grandma yelled, "Well, you never said to stop."

"I'm saying it now." He laughed.

Then a foggy silence, three days long, shrouded the boat. Although they were only a couple hundred feet offshore, they didn't see it till they followed the rumors of waves in their dinghy. Dad called me at the end of the second day on a cellular phone. NOAA weather offered little hope. The fog was general along the coast. They'd continue to wait. The next day I drove up to Crescent Beach State Park, across the harbor from Richmond Island. I hadn't been able to reach them on the phone. Paying my two dollars and walking down to the beach, I hailed *Restless* on my portable VHF radio. Their radio, with great good fortune, was listening. My mother answered from somewhere out in the fog.

"This is *Restless*. Where are you?" Her tone implied that I'd better not be on a boat.

"I'm on the beach across the bay. Everything okay?"

"Yeah, we're just guarding the fog."

"Do you need anything?"

"No, we've got plenty of food. But let me ask Tommy if he——" Static interrupted, and then the haggard voice of a fisherman telling someone he'd found the mackerel.

"Joe Alan?"

"Right here."

"We're going to bring Tommy and Linda and Grandma to you. They're going to start home. We don't know how long this fog will last and they're on a schedule."

Dad took the mike. "Joe?" They were only a few hundred yards across the water, but I couldn't see thirty feet their way.

"Yeah, Dad," I said, "follow the breakwater till you get to the mainland and then come along the shore. I'll walk down and meet you. Don't cut across the bay, because there's rocks in the middle of it."

I jumped from rock to rock, working my way down the coast to the breakwater. In mid-leap I dropped my radio face first on a boulder. The LCD readout was shattered; a black blotch foamed behind the lens.

"Dad?" I called. Nothing. "Dad?" I heard the snicker of the bitter seaman.

"Joe, we're on our way."

The dinghy was the color of the fog, which was the color of the water. My first sign of them was a bleat from a compressed-air horn, and then they were there, my father, aunt, uncle, and grandmother, scooting through the thick atmosphere, seemingly seated on the wind. We moved back along the shore to the sandy margin of the beach. There Dad shut off the engine but couldn't raise it, so Tommy had to climb out in knee-deep water and carry Grandma in. I met him halfway and took Grandma in my arms so he could go back for Aunt Linda and the luggage. She was as light and fragile as a dry driftwood limb. "I knew you'd rescue me," she said. "I walked all the way around that island." She was in a good period. After Grandpa died she'd developed shingles of the neck and head, excruciatingly painful. She had beaten it for the most part and seemed to be recovering. I carried her up the beach a few yards and set her down the way you would a bird's nest. "Go get my rocks," she ordered. I waded back out and took a bag from Tommy. It must have weighed fifty pounds, full of wave-washed stones and brittle white sticks. Grandma had been collecting rocks on her vacations for seventy-five years. Her backyard, the drawers of her coffee table, her shelves, were crowded with pebbles and petrified wood. There were rocks in her house where you'd expect recipes and paper clips.

"Grandma," I said, "at this rate there won't be any islands left along the coast of Maine."

She grinned with this possibility, and gave me back a hat I'd loaned her for the trip. She ran her hands through her sparse white hair and then said, "I don't think it's any of these hats: I think it's my head."

36

Joe, I'm afraid you need to decide how much you love this boat.

Bernie Horne,
Patten's Yacht Yard

What fool hath added water to the sea?

William Shakespeare,
Titus Andronicus

IT HAD BEEN A HECTIC spring and early summer, but we were finally beginning our fourth season aboard *Yonder,* on our way to Christmas Cove to attend a wedding. Chip (Heather's cousin) and Jen chartered their boat, *Blitzen,* a 1939 fifty-five-foot Sparkman & Stephens sloop, out of the Cove and invited wedding guests to attend in their sailboats. We were looking for an early start, Heather and I, but spent the morning changing out the starter and solenoid, which had locked up with the dew (only explanation possible). I had a spare: the rebuilt starter that had locked up the day before the Mystic cruise two years earlier. And so one disaster resolved another. We took on fuel and water at the Portsmouth Yacht Club and peeled away from the dock using the current as a knife. Later in the day we discovered we'd inadvertently switched on the galley pump and drained all thirty gallons of fresh water into the sea as we blithely motored along. Blue skies, bordered with clouds like old cobwebs. A fifteen-knot breeze off the land allowed us to reach all day on a single heading. As we rounded Cape Elizabeth a stronger gust rolled off the point, but *Yonder* was too heavy, too obstinate to heel any more. The mainsail blew at the throat. We were the last to arrive at Cocktail Cove that evening and so took our anchorage at the rolling end of the harbor. The wind dropped away and flies took its place, fanning our food as best they could. That night someone's halyards tolled infinity against their mast, and it seemed that someone had left marbles in every compartment on our boat. They rolled back and forth with the waves, as stubborn as gravity. I dreamed that night that it would be possible to repair the torn sail with electrical tape. Cruising is a constant confrontation with minor emergencies, a gauntlet of ignored maintenance, great beauty interrupted by flies.

GRANDMA HAD BEEN ill again that spring. She went into the hospital with pneumonia and heart failure, and these were complicated by a resurgence of the shingles and a new medicine that made her hallucinate. She had always sat in the background, a dishrag over her shoulder, when her family gathered. But now she became verbose, commenting on the visible and the unseen. We sat around her in the hospital room, looking up at the ceiling when she did, looking out the fifth-story window when she pointed at a motorcycle cop whizzing by on the narrow window ledge. We'd never known her to lie, so it was hard not to believe her. Her overriding concern was her flooding room. It had rained so long that the ceiling tiles, waterlogged, were disintegrating, dropping pieces of plastic on her. Water ran down the walls. We sloshed through water when we came to her bedside. A drop of water would fall on her head, she'd clap her palm to her skull and look up, and we'd look up too.

"Can you see where that water's coming in, Joe Alan?" she asked.

"No, I can't, Grandma."

"Well, you're standing in two feet of the muddiest water I've ever seen."

I looked down at my feet. Grandma was as amazed as we were, incredulous that such a good hospital had such a bad roof. She asked us to look out the window to see if Montgomery Ward's was underwater again.

"When was it under water before?" I asked Tommy.

"Nineteen forty-nine," he said.

Grandma called her rice "beans and macaroni." Her iced tea bubbled. "Somebody must have made it with carbonated water." All the while she was perfectly coherent. She knew everyone, fed herself, made other comments that were correct in observation and tone. "That durn ceiling plastic. There's some more of it." She picked it off her tongue and dropped it over the side of the bed. "I wish it would stop raining." The water was closing in on her. "They told me stories. Your mother and Tommy and Melody and June," she said. "Said it wasn't raining. I told them I wouldn't say it anymore. But I knew I heard it raining. All the kids have gone up into the ceiling. You should have seen them kids coming out of the ceiling. They were flying. Waving their hands like an airplane. I'd be afraid to do that. They just hold their hands out this way and go around and around." She smiled.

My aunt June, Grandma's first child, walked up to her hospital bed and Grandma snapped, "June! Get a Kleenex and clean that snot off your nose. How can you stand that snot on your nose?"

June jumped for a tissue as if she were nine years old.

And to my mother, "Why did you walk in that knee-deep water to get here?"

"It doesn't bother me," Mom told her.

"It's better to stir sugar with a fork," Grandma said. "Today is today."

The hallucinations left when her medicine was changed, but a month later she lay dying in her living room. The family sat at her kitchen table writing names and places on the backs of old photographs. My aunt Melody said, "Aunt Effie believed she got arthritis because her mother didn't teach her to dry between her toes."

The day before, Grandma had decided not to take additional medication. "I won't have any more pills," she told Tommy. The hospital bed replaced the living room recliners. She slept when she wasn't groggy, when her children weren't hollering at her. There was food everywhere, but her house smelled like the inside of a medicine bottle, the dust of pills. My mother and her siblings, once again, became closer to one another than they were to their spouses. Grandma was dehydrating. Her muscles ached and she moaned, searched for a way to roll away from the pain, but she was too weak and finally subsided, gave in. It was so strange to see her grimace, hear her cry: she'd always kept her pain private, was modest and proud of her strength. Her breathing became shallower, shallow. She died at four A.M., when everyone was out of the room, just as Grandpa had. By 5:30 the funeral home had picked her up, and there was for the fifteen of us present suddenly nothing left to do but eat breakfast, clean the house a bit.

For the family there seemed to be some sense of a burden eased. Grandpa's death had prepared us for Grandma's, and her death released her from a two-year-long struggle.

For me, there's one less place in the world to hide. She was my last grandparent to go, watching over all of us as long as she could. It was poignant that she died three feet from her kitchen. She'd spent her life there, in personal and professional careers. It was always a great irony to us that such a good cook was married to a man who would eat anything, be it burnt, raw, mildewed, or frozen. She lingers in a doorway, in the present tense, a spoon and a dishtowel in her hands, watching us leave with mingled concern and anticipation. Work was her religion, and her family was life's meaning. I'm sure, as an artist, she never thought us quite finished.

I ARRIVED IN Maine three weeks after Grandma's funeral. "Joe, you need to decide how much you love this boat," Bernie advised. I'd asked him to look for the leak that had almost sunk *Yonder* a year earlier when her bilge pump failed. There were seven planks that needed to be replaced, and the garboard seams needed to be recaulked, but worst of all, the stem was rotten. I was at a stage in my life where it was hard to lie.

"I'm writing a book about this boat, Bernie. I can't get to the last chapter and say I scuttled her. I just need an estimate."

"Okay, Joe, I'll do the best I can."

I thought of all the beatings *Yonder* had taken, off Cape Ann and Cuttyhunk, her bow holding together only by long habit. *Yonder*'s hull, much like my family, was a mold, and I'd poured myself into it. It took seven thousand dollars and a month and a half of Dana Wise's careful craftsmanship to get *Yonder* on her way to a wedding at Christmas Cove. The day before the big event there was a sailboat race in which *Yonder* took part as committee boat. Off South Bristol, *Yonder*'s birthplace, we awarded victory to *Blitzen* and her engaged crew.

I THINK WE take on some of the characteristics and mannerisms of those close to us when they die. My grandmother always put emphasis on your name with an appalled sauce. I find myself doing this now, calling even my dog's name as if she were the only one on the planet I could love.

For all my love for my grandmother, she looked at last like something that had washed up on the beach, something lost or forgotten. She once told me she'd lived so long there were some things, important things, that she'd learned two and three times, having forgotten them, and years later discovered them anew. She couldn't decide if she was lucky or stupid.

AFTER THE WEDDING, Heather and I were stranded on *Yonder* in the fog, but we were safely moored in the Cove. Once I'd thought of the fog as a stray dog who wouldn't leave my porch, I felt better about it. Heather and I took turns rowing around the still harbor, feeding the dog. The next morning the skies were clear and we spent a long day across the Gulf of Maine, going home. Deep in *Yonder*'s hold, emotional ballast, were my grandmother's smooth stones she'd gathered on Richmond Island. I'll return them someday.

37

I LIKE TO READ BOOKS in which the characters, in the beginning, might be helped by something I could tell them, a way to alleviate their suffering; by the end of these books I've learned something from the characters, a way to alleviate my suffering. They make this progression without me or even themselves consciously recognizing it. I'm here now, having fetched water from a boiling rock. To the list of *Yonder*'s repairs I add "1995—new stem." I have plans to mount the old stem on a mahogany plank and attach an engraved brass plate: "60 Years of Service."

The last sail of the season was a short reach out to the Isles of Shoals. My brother and I anchored off White Island and fished half-heartedly for a couple of hours with no luck. Perhaps this was because we dropped our lines overboard, then napped in the sun till it was time to go. On the return we passed what seemed to be a wounded gull, struggling to stay afloat. It reminded me of a duck on our farm pond, fighting to get away from a turtle that had bitten into his foot. We made another pass and saw the gull had a large plastic fishing lure caught in his beak and the webbing of one foot. On the third attempt, Phil brought him aboard with the net. He was a young gull, big but still feathered in brown. Phil held his beak while I snipped the barbs of the treble hooks. The hook in the bird's foot had slashed into the veined webbing, which bled profusely; the other had passed all the way through the nostril in the upper beak. Once the bird was cut free, I gathered his wings from the net while Phil held the beak closed. Then, on three, we lifted him up into the air. I wish I could have that moment of setting him free, I wish I could have it over and over. On three. On three. We wiped our hands of the salt water and blood, watching his wing beats become entangled in those of a thousand other gulls over the islands. Once again, *Yonder* paid for herself in a single moment, an hour out of the harbor. I saw that my happiest life was not where I came from, or where I was bound, but that life on the way. It seems that whatever it is we seek, water might take us there.

There's a famous photo in our family, hanging in places of honor in three homes, which was snapped aboard *Yonder* during our third season. My father, Rob, and Heather's uncle Charles are lounging on *Yonder*'s port cockpit locker with erect Cuban cigars protruding from their jaws. These three men in their late fifties are at once captains of industry, patriarchs of their clans, magnanimous with their love and perilously tipsy. In the blackness of night beyond them cigar smoke and evaporating scotch mingle with the pungent detritus of fireworks. We celebrated the Fourth of July that year on *Yonder*, milling about Portsmouth Harbor with a hundred other boats, watching bombs explode above the city. Like a blessing ordered down from the Founding Fathers, slack high tide coincided with the fireworks schedule, and all that was required of me as captain was an occasional tap on the throttle to hold the boat in place. Uncle Charles, perhaps confused about country or holiday, or perhaps in the spirit of fraternity rivalry, led an off-key chorus of "O Canada." Horns barked, bells broke like windows, cannons raped the air, my wife whooped till her neck and head looked like those of an ostrich, and all of this over freedom. I counted heads, counted life jackets, counted heads. Back at the dock, for the first time ever or since, I saw Rob stumble while getting off a boat. In the morning he and Dad and I would leave for Nova Scotia aboard *Restless*.

But *Restless* and her crew never made it to Nova Scotia that summer. Fog delayed us at Northeast Harbor and we decided to run up the coast to Quoddy Head rather than across the Gulf to Yarmouth. "It's not that important to me anymore," my father told me. "I was always afraid of that water up there. I'd look down on that awful water from my plane. I thought if I went up there and sailed those seas, I'd feel better about it. But I'm not afraid anymore. It was silly to feel that way all these years."

He was speaking of a time thirty-five years earlier. In the Air Force, stationed in Newfoundland, he worked aboard a KC-97 as inflight refueler and electrician. His plane was forced to ditch in the North Atlantic. The crew inflated a life raft and climbed aboard, but Dad went back inside the sinking plane for another raft in case they should need it. When he stepped back out on the wing the rest of the crew was a hundred yards away in the rough seas. Dad inflated a single-man raft and tried to catch up with them but couldn't. They were rescued later that day. Dad floated by himself in the freezing water for two more days, and all he remembers of his own rescue is opening his eyes and seeing the helicopter above him.

After my first season aboard *Yonder,* my parents gave me a four-man Plastimo life raft for Christmas, still trying to save me from drowning in my milk.

I've been on the water for a year now, four summer seasons of three months each. I wanted to be as confident as water finding its way to the bottom of a bowl. But I feel as if I've forgotten something I once knew. It can't be helped. The only alternative to growing old is death.

Many boats have been built from books, but few books are built from boats. I've written this log, aptly named, on thin boards of paper, and so have constructed a wooden book to compliment my old boat. To know the mystery of this river, I must hold the sheets in my hands. The only thing I've ever discovered with my boat is myself, but since I was the only explorer in the world capable of making this find, I count myself fortunate. No sailor has ever come so far in making such a small circle. I don't yet know where I came from, but happily don't have any memory of having been afraid when I was there. My Texas grandparents are buried, side by side, in the life-born rock of a long-ago sea. A boat, like my empty skull, like my mind, displaces less water than it will hold. So we float. For my sake, Grandpa, why weren't you afraid to die? I don't expect an answer. Instead, I hold out my hands and whisper, "On three."

Fall is here. *Yonder* is under a blue tarp in Rob and Beverly's backyard. I have aspirations to round up stray leaves, throw my wife and dog into the pile and then dive in after them. I'm for fur, fire, corduroy, tears in my eyes. I'm for the bare branches of a tree, being able to follow a bird's flight through a copse. I'm for smoke and evaporation, rot and ruin, sleep and fog. I'm for the sun going sooner and the moon staying longer, a day so dense it seems drugged with night. The fall makes me feel privy to rhythm and part of the pendulum's arc: that point where it decides, in a moment of shivering instinct, to return to a life it's known and loved.

My little brother has just bought his first cruising sailboat, a twenty-two-foot Catalina that we sail on Eagle Mountain Lake. I worry about him as I teach him the names of lines. But this brown water seems so accepting, so familiar.

I have been in love with the familiar: my family, my dog, my sweater, an old wooden boat, and now I have become so familiar with the unpredictability of the ensuing moment that I'm in love with it too, and am forced to admit at last that I'm simply in love. My past has caught up with the present. I'm sustained by the very same spoonful of water that would drown me. I've come to the end of another book alive. At times like this I'm always at a loss for words.

~